Children's
Voices

Children's Voices

Children Talk About Literacy

Edited by

Sally Hudson-Ross
Linda Miller Cleary
Mara Casey

HEINEMANN
Portsmouth, NH

HEINEMANN EDUCATIONAL BOOKS
361 Hanover Street   Portsmouth, NH 03801
Offices and agents throughout the world

Library of Congress Cataloging-in-Publication Data
Children's voices : children talk about literacy / edited by Sally
 Hudson-Ross, Linda Miller Cleary, Mara Casey.
      p.   cm.
    Includes bibliographical references and index.
    ISBN 0-435-08737-1
    1. Language arts (Elementary)—United States.   2. Reading
(Elementary)—United States.   3. Children—United States—
Interviews.   4. Children—United States—Attitudes.   I. Hudson
-Ross, Sally.   II. Cleary, Linda Miller.   III. Casey, Mara.
LB1575.8.C47   1993
372.6′0973–dc20   92-33307
                                                        CIP

Cover design by Jenny Jensen Greenleaf
Printed in the United States of America
93 94 95 96 9 8 7 6 5 4 3 2 1

CONTENTS

INTRODUCTION

In the year 2010, the children featured in this book will be between 26 and 35 years old. They will experience and participate in a world we have not yet imagined. Yet in most of their roles—as workers, professionals, consumers, parents, citizens, friends, lovers, sports fans—they will find reasons to read and to write. This book captures the voices of their childhoods just as their definitions of literacy and attitudes toward the written word are being shaped, just as they are discovering what reading and writing can do for them.

As you meet them here, the children are in kindergarten through eighth grade. They are involved—by joy, need, or demand—in worlds full of reading and writing. They gain insights daily into how literacy might fit into their lives, through going to school, playing with friends and alone, observing adults, and experimenting and getting feedback on their attempts. In this book, they share their present wisdom.

The book is unusual in that we hear the actual voices of children rather than those of adults. Although we are often adult participants in children's literacy events, we rarely hear extended versions of their perceptions of literacy, either because we do not ask or because, in our busy lives, we cannot find the time to listen. When we do—as in this book—we may be enriched, excited, disconcerted, saddened, or reassured by their honest insights and perspectives. Hearing a child's continuous monologue can be an emotional experience: each fresh voice forces us to confront our own actions, to understand the impact of our smallest words, to realize how we—as parents, teachers, neighbors, and friends—help children construct outlooks toward literacy that will last a lifetime. We cannot help but realize that we do make a difference. If we listen now, we may yet be able to alter or enhance the experiences that will define literacy for this and future generations.

FORMAT OF THE SELECTIONS

The profiles in this book are built from children's actual words. Like Studs Terkel's unique brand of interviews with Americans on various themes (*Working,* 1972; *The Good War,* 1984; *Division Street: America,* 1967), these profiles present children speaking in monologue, directly to readers.

Each profile was constructed from one or more interviews, usually between the same adult and child. (One example of an exception is Mary Elizabeth who talked to both her mother and her aunt, as well as tape recorded her own answers to printed questions which appear in the appendix to this book.) In many cases, the children were talking to people they knew well—mothers, aunts, neighbors, family friends, teachers—who were collecting data as formal researchers or simply out of their own sincere curiosity. In almost every case, the adult worked with the child closely over an extended period of time both to forge trust, when necessary, as well as to collect more detailed information. In several situations, children actually read, revised, or helped construct the profile.

Settings for interviews were varied: children's homes, their classrooms, car pools and parks. Some interviews were conducted as part of previously established research projects while others were collected specifically for this book. Descriptions of individual research settings and profile development appear in the Contributors' Notes on page 243.

Adults speak little in these pages. The contributors introduce the children in an introduction to each piece, then they step back and let the children speak. When adults are essential to uphold their end of a conversation, we allowed them to stay in the text. Thus, the kindergartners interact with an aunt, a scribe, a teacher, or each other in structured classroom settings, and their words are presented as dialogue, edited for ease of reading from actual transcripts.

Otherwise, the selections in this book are presentations of reconstructed data, children's words which have been selected and shaped, not to support findings, but to present the children themselves as they discuss reading, writing, schooling, and literacy. Although overt adult commentary is avoided, the contributors have, nonetheless, constructed and interpreted the data in other ways. Because contributors selected particular children, spoke with them at particular times and places, and asked them particular questions, certain voices emerged. Other choices—of children, of settings, of questions—may have led to other voices.

Contributors also edited transcripts and notes to delete interviewers' questions and mold the interview material into coherent, readable forms, a process presented in the Appendix at the back of this book, and discussed by Seidman (1991) and others. In the shaping of the interview data, however, contributors strived to maintain the integrity and dignity of the children's voices, their authenticity and specialness, by asking: "Does this sound like her?" or "Can I hear him talking to me?" Contributors also tried to be fair to the larger context of the interview material, being sure that artificially juxtaposed segments left readers with the same impressions they would have if they read the actual transcripts.

The voices of children tend to be obvious when they are bored or less than honest. In Cleary's book based on interviews with high school students who have struggled with writing (1991), she talks of an "outer voice" that arises when students are trying to figure out what an interviewer wants. But as students sense an interviewer's interest in their experiences and perceptions, they fall into an "inner voice," one that is:

> a thinking voice: thinking to remember, thinking to get what happened into words, thinking to understand it and fit it together with present experience. . . . The inner voice would come on as the students became interested in rendering the past. It moved in as they came to trust me and out as they suddenly wondered what I was thinking of what they were saying (Cleary, 1991).

Readers will hear many inner voices here—sincere, concerned, wanting very much to share their experience with someone else. In many cases, the children themselves fervently wanted to send these messages out to teachers, parents, and other children who might listen. As a result, many chose to use their own names rather than pseudonyms.

This chorus of young voices also repeatedly supports research findings in literacy and education, while providing new angles and new issues for our consideration. In interesting and innumerable ways, readers will hear children reiterate advice gleaned from decades of formal research and theory. Here, however, informants speak for themselves. Happily, when children's words match the research findings, it validates our research; however, when the children invite other interpretations and expose contradictions to what we "know," we should be challenged to ask questions and to explore our data both more deeply and in new ways.

Finally, and perhaps most importantly, these profiles resonate, for each reader, of other children's voices. They evoke each reader's own stories, experiences, and insights, and force us to recognize and confront our own intuitions about reading, writing, literacy, and schooling. They encourage us to make explicit the connections we perceive among these voices and others, and to find meaning beyond the singular experience.

SELECTION OF THE CHILDREN

Although the editors made no systematic effort to include profiles of children representative of American society, we have attempted to include a diverse range of girls and boys from a variety of American ethnic groups, socio-economic groups, geographic regions, and backgrounds in reading, writing, and schooling. These children come from across the entire country: Alabama, California, Georgia, Illinois, Indiana, Maine, Massachusetts, Michigan, Minnesota, New Mexico, Ohio, Pennsylvania, and Texas. They include eleven African-American, two Japanese-American, four Mexican-American, and thirty-three white, American children. In fact, there is more diversity than their voices or our descriptions of them reveal, for we have not "labeled" children in the profiles by race or geographic area, unless such information is relevant to the stories they tell.

Their stories are beautiful both for their uniqueness and their universality. For example, six-year-old Lacey, crayon in hand, speculates about what first grade just might be like next year. Martin, Jeralynn, and Mark work with a scribe, while two sets of writing partners, Scooter and Chanell, and then Justin and Dylan, collaborate with each other to construct amazing stories—real and imagined. With their teacher, kindergartners Kareem, Tony, and Amanda collaboratively learn how language works. Shannon tells of being held back twice and of whole language classrooms that begin to make sense for her. Emily, Nicole, Regina, and Chandra share the worlds of young writers who write everywhere for their own heartfelt reasons. Reggie, whose world few of us know, tells of a mother who defies stereotypes of readers and ghettos. Rosa, Paul, and Lisa explain the power of writing for their own social purposes. Then there is Adam whose Tourette's Syndrome complicates but does not stifle his writing; Katherine, Hobbes, and Becky who reflect on the split curriculum of resource room children; and Asuka, José, Robert, and Joey who understand language and literacy within two cultures, both of which are components of America's diversifying society.

Ashley, Nathan, Matthew, and Kristin along with Nicki, Andy, Abigail, and Paul sing the praises of whole language classrooms, while Ben, Mary Elizabeth, and Owen find ways to fit their dreams and giftedness into more traditional school walls as they explore worlds beyond. Butch, Bobby, and Jane share why they read, Mario builds stories from everything around him, and Matika overpowers us with her transformation as a young black woman empowered by books about her own people. Matt and Kristy speak from their world, an island off the coast of Maine, while Noriko and Kirsten, best buddies in Chicago, discuss their eighth-grade world views. Dave and Page, who we get to know in grades 3, 6, and then 8, conclude by touching chords across the years and thus across all of these voices. Because of their stories—both unique and universal—each of these children has been invited to speak.

RECURRING THEMES

As editors, we cannot help but notice recurring themes in reading these profiles. The following list may guide readers, although by doing so we do not want to limit direct experience of the children themselves. For that reason, the profiles are presented not in thematic groups, but in simple, chronological order, from youngest to oldest. This allows for a sweep across the elementary and middle school years, but it also allows us to avoid cubbyholing profiles as representative of one or another "meanings." We encourage readers to use the index to locate discussion of various topics across children. We strongly feel that each profile has much to say on several of these issues; many will also bring out issues for some readers that we may not have even considered. That is where their richness lies.

Across these profiles, you will often hear children discussing the following:

SCHOOL IS OFTEN A MATTER OF GRADES, OF GIVING THE TEACHER WHAT SHE WANTS.

From kindergarten through grade 8, children talk about the limitations of schooling. Many see learning in school as learning the ropes for success, learning to "give her what she wants" in order to "get a grade." Even children labeled as gifted in science, math, or reading and writing find school to be a place to do what they are told, no matter how silly. Of course, no teacher intends this lesson, but in many small and seemingly insignificant ways, our actions, requirements, and expectations daily portray school as a place for getting assignments done, rather than for learning.

SCHOOL IS SOMETIMES A BAFFLING PLACE WHERE PURPOSE IS DIFFICULT TO FIND.

Many children, especially those buffeted about by life and school, are never invited to learn the basic lessons of how to succeed in school. Children who function in resource rooms (where curriculum is sometimes contradictory to that of the regular classroom) must search for meaning among conflicting demands, assignments, and attitudes. Often these approaches leave direct reading and writing at the door. Or, while more successful peers have "free time" for independent reading and writing, some students must do extra "work" in order to get extra help. As a result, school activities for many children provide little intrinsic motivation, the subtle messages conveyed by assignments remain unexamined, and those who most need to understand "why" reading and writing matter rarely get to do either.

TEACHERS, OTHER ADULTS, AND PEERS ALL SUPPORT LANGUAGE-LEARNING IN IMPORTANT WAYS.

Children in the early years of school may enjoy the help of an adult to support or scaffold their initial steps into literacy. Vygotsky (1978) talks of the "zone of proximal development," that area of learning where children are ready to grow but need a social, interactive opportunity to try things out before they are ready to stand on their own. Children sometimes use older scribes or teachers to help them write or focus attention on strategies for learning. But just as often, and as early as kindergarten, children can work together to make these important leaps.

Unfortunately, collaboration in reading, writing, or learning is often not supported in American schools. Luckily, the whole langauge and collaborative learning movements seem to encourage the continuation of this important building block for learning. Literacy need not, and probably should not be learned alone. As Nancie Atwell (1987) has suggested, it is the comradery of the "dining room" table and the reward of an honest, caring audience that make us want to continue reading and writing.

REAL READING AND WRITING INSPIRE SELF-DISCOVERY.

In this collection, two young black women, among others, highlight the liberating power that comes with real reading and writing. Matika, from rural Georgia, recognizes her heritage for the first time through an interactive book club outside of school. Chandra, bussed from inner-city Boston to Brookline, Massachusetts, finds both fulfillment and social entry through her writing and its power. Many other children also express the joy of reading and writing for reasons of their own: in school, or out of school if necessary.

WRITING AND READING AT HOME— AND INDEPENDENTLY AT SCHOOL— PROVIDE SEED BEDS FOR LATER EXPRESSION.

Most children are writers and readers to some extent before schooling. Many continue habits of drawing, writing, reading, and experimenting long after school begins. Gradually, social demands, activities, and life in general take them beyond this usually solitary entertainment, but for those who begin at home, writing and reading usually continue to be important. Children in this collection talk happily of parents who provide books and writing materials, initiate library trips, exhibit their own curiosity about the world, travel and learn with their children, save writing in big boxes and share it on the refrigerator. Such support encourages children to find literacy of use in their own world, today and in the future. (Hudson-Ross, in press.)

CHILDREN NEGOTIATE SEVERAL WORLDS AT ONCE.

Whether in Hispanic, Asian, or mainstream American cultures; ghetto, rural, or suburban public school settings; or social or cultural situations more shaded and less obvious, many children today live in communities that differ from those experienced in classrooms or portrayed in textbooks and on television. School is only a part of daily experiences, and learning outside school walls may be more rich, varied, and current than the lessons learned inside. The children in this book explain, as no textbook can, what it is like to speak, read, and write in more than one language, to understand the diversity of present-day American culture, or to see American schools and society as outsiders looking in. As anthropologists try to do, they help us "make the familiar strange" so that we may examine our own systems through new eyes.

FREEDOM TO READ AND TO WRITE IN SCHOOL INVITES CHILDREN TO JOIN THE "LITERACY CLUB."

Frank Smith (1988) initiated the term "literacy club," and the children in this volume could be lined up pretty clearly on a scale of who is in and who is not. Here we see that inclusion is based as much on self-perception as on external criteria. In other words, if Rosa believes in herself as a reader, she will read. Whole language curricula seem to encourage that attitude among children who have experienced it. This of course goes back to the issues listed above: once the clouds of schooling are dismissed and children are invited to participate in sensible ways in their own learning, children find that they not only can, but they also want, to become literate. It's fun; it's rewarding; they can do it.

CHILDREN OFTEN USE METAPHOR TO REVEAL EMERGING UNDERSTANDINGS OF DIFFICULT LEARNING PROCESSES.

In delightful ways, these children frequently use metaphor to explain what reading and writing are like for them. You'll see why writing is like a trance, a central chip on a computer, tooth decay, Nintendo, combing your hair, drawing, relaxing and subdreams, or why reading can be like playing a VCR backwards. In these metaphors children share their perceptions and experiences of a world they sometimes sense but cannot yet articulate in abstract terms. They are, however, metacognitively aware of their experiences, and metaphor provides the link between their understanding and that of their adult listeners who, we must admit, struggle just as much when trying to explain the complex processes of reading and writing.

SOME ADVICE EMERGES REPEATEDLY AND STRONGLY.

So much so that we think teachers, in particular, will want to listen. These children, as a group, support the following. We'll let them speak in their own voices . . .

- *Choice:* After we feel safe with you and in this setting, give us a wide range of choice in what we read and what we write about. At the same time, don't force us out there on the edge, into a new world of free choice, until that trust is firmly established.
- *Collaboration and independence:* We need both if we are to explore our potential fully. There are times when we don't want to feel vulnerable and other times when we want to go our own ways . . . and we don't all have to be going in the same direction at once.
- *Time:* We simply must have at school the kinds of time we have to read and write at home. We need large chunks of time, the freedom to choose when we read and write, and both quiet time when we're left alone as well as social time when we can share.
- *Reading and writing go together:* We know these things make sense together. We like to read books about our interests and write about them too. We love to play with themes or forms from literature in our own explorations of the written word. Don't force us to do these things separately.
- *Real reading and writing versus basal "short stories" or "writing-writing":* School is often senseless to us, and it would be to you, too, if you saw it as we do. Those "short stories" (our way of saying "constructed") in the reading book aren't half as much fun as chapter books, even if we have to work harder at those. And in writing, when you control it too much, it becomes "writing-writing," not at all the same thing we can do when we're allowed to be writers. We're ready; let us do the real thing, and let us amaze you.
- *Each of us is different:* And that's the most important thing of all. What Mario likes would drive José crazy. What Lacey needs, Becky figured out years ago. And what I need today differs from what I will need tomorrow. Listen to each of us daily; listen to us as individuals; and support our unique needs and strengths.

HOW YOU MIGHT USE THIS BOOK

Rosenblatt (1978) and others emphasize that any text—heard or read—is created by the listener or reader who infuses his or her own experience, knowledge, and interest into the reading. As a result, something different emerges with each rereading and for each reader. The voices presented here should invite shared and open interpretations. As anthropologist Clifford suggests (1986), "Any story has a propensity to generate another story in the mind of its reader (or hearer), to repeat and displace some prior story" (100). As a result, he suggests that realistic portraits, to the extent that they are "convincing" or "rich," are like extended metaphors or patterns of associations that point to additional meanings. We think you will find your own meanings in this book.

We see the book, unique as it is, being used for a wide variety of purposes by a wide variety of people. Those who are serious about listening to children or who wish to conduct interviews or develop similar profiles will find the appendix to this book useful. In general, in using this book:

- *Parents* may want advice from children about ways to support their own children's literacy growth. They might interview their own children, as have some of our contributors, to learn in depth how their children perceive literacy and schooling.
- *Children* enjoy hearing these profiles and reflecting on how they agree or disagree with other children about reading and writing. Through reading profiles of other students, students can discuss the issues raised and become more conscious of the processes they use in reading and writing. Children might even interview each other to develop class books describing their literate community or profiles of authors as introductions to student-written books.
- *Teachers* may use these voices to reflect on their own teaching and experiences as learners. Current reforms suggest no better way to educate than by building communities of learners where children and teachers learn together. At the simplest level, this means that listening becomes a two-way street. As these profiles reveal, children offer critical insights into reading, writing, and schooling. By interviewing their own or each others' students, teachers can see how children are interpreting or misinterpreting learning experiences in their own classrooms (Casey, 1986). Teacher-developed profiles also provide rich data for long-term portfolio assessments and parent discussions.
- *Teacher educators* may use these profiles to supplement texts and readings in order to bring real classrooms and children into discussions. Reading these profiles in conjunction with research studies can support current research in accessible and credible ways as well as suggest avenues for future classroom research. As action research projects, preservice and inservice teachers can construct their own profiles of local students to gain and share further knowledge about children in their own geographic region, grade level, or areas of specialization. (For further suggestions, see Cleary and Seidman, 1990.)
- *Researchers* may explore these children's voices as complements to other qualitative and quantitative data to discover ways in which children themselves support current research findings, to provide alternative perspectives on existing questions, as well as to suggest further directions for research and theory building. We are beginning to accept the importance of children's perceptions in classroom and literacy research, but richly and fully developed voices of participants can enhance or make more accessible data presented to interested consumers, especially in the public sector.
- *Policy makers, administrators, members of school boards* may want to see local school settings as their number one constituents—the children—do. For years school leaders have included a student

on an important panel, polled the student body, or asked student councils for their opinions in decision-making, but usually such attempts are feeble. Current calls for school-based governance demand further and more genuine input from students, as well as from faculty and members of the community. Inviting older students or teacher education students or parents in to interview children (and other community members) and present their findings as profiles can bring findings up close and personal. Unlike faceless numbers or quiet faces, profiled voices demand to be heard.

Throughout this book, individual children speak for themselves in ways they have rarely been allowed to before: uninterrupted, at full natural volume, and on their own terms. They invite us into that special world of the child which we pass daily but usually see only from the outside looking in. The children in this book are unique in that they were *asked* to reflect on literacy in their lives. Throughout the research process, they felt valued and important as readers and writers and co-researchers. But every child can feel equally valued, equally important, equally knowledgeable—if parents, teachers, counselors, friends learn to ask . . . and to listen. Who knows how much such attention to reading and writing, to the nature of schooling and literacy might influence the emerging voices of the literate community of the twenty-first century. We invite you to listen.

Sally Hudson-Ross, University of Georgia
Linda Miller Cleary, University of Minnesota, Duluth
Mara Casey, University of California, Riverside
January 1992

1

Lacey

"OH, NO! I FORGOT THE RAINBOW!"

(Just After Kindergarten)

Contributed by Sally Hudson-Ross

In the summer after her kindergarten year, six year old Lacey wasn't reading yet, but she spent a couple of afternoons coloring and writing with me, her Aunt Sally, on her grandmother's bedroom floor in Ohio, a good trip from her Pennsylvania home. Downstairs, family members—including grandma "Mimi" and my husband Rex—visited, went out for shopping and play, and left us alone for an hour or so at a time. Lacey knew I was working on a book about children and writing, so she was happy to help. We had often colored and played together, but today she tried more than usual to explain to me how she did this thing called writing. We spread out with lined and plain paper, magic markers and pencils, and a little red stamp of a smiling apple that she had found in my purse.

In the following three vignettes, each surrounding a very different product, Lacey shares her insights. In the first vignette, which I've called "The Apple Trees," her talk extends her text far beyond what an admirer might see on paper; the story, it seems, is in the talk. In the second piece, "Sally, Rex and the Swimming Pool," however, Lacey intuitively explores the possibilities of drawing and adding print, some of which carries back into "The Apple Trees" which she had finished just a short time earlier. The words she chooses to write or dictate, simple nouns and verbs, parallel the types of words young children use in early oral language and point out the similarities in speech and writing development in young children. Finally, in producing the final product, her ABCs which she decided to show me,

FIGURE 1–1 *"The Apple Trees"*

she shares her emerging sense of the meaning of school, of what first grade might be like from her vantage point as one just beginning to figure out schooling and its traditions.

To highlight Lacey, I have edited out my comments unless they were relevant to her talk; in those cases, my words appear within the chronological flow of our conversation.

LACEY: Oh, I forgot. I planting a tree. That's you. We're playing out in the rain. Blue rain and green rain. . . . A baby, but it has pants. The Applebees in a dumb suit. Because his suit, it's just all green, and yours is green and blue. Okay, now I put a rainbow. Ooh, I forgot some flowers. Grass, *definitely* grass. And I know where you're, I know where I'm putting you. And then you're. . . . Okay? Apples, you're getting a gray one.

Do you know how to make, umm, a tree? Can you make me one?

SALLY: Sure, where do you want it?

LACEY: Right here. Oops, brown brown brown! You gotta make that leaf. The trunk and leaves. Now, it's an apple tree. [She uses the red apple stamp to put smiling apples all over the tree.] There. I should of made a strawberry tree. Okay, let's see you make it. I can't make trees very . . .

SALLY: It's just a little bush like this, I think.

LACEY: That's alright. Yeah, that's good. I know how to make strawberries.

SALLY: Green ones?

LACEY: Na. How about red ones? Strawberries *are* red. . . .

Now I know what I'm doing. Now I'll make the flowers. Want to see? A daisy. Now, I know what I'm doin'—look what I'm doin'—with my yellow, looks like black, but it's really yellow. Now, with this leaf. Now. This one's [the strawberry bush] starting to grow. Now I'm gonna make, can you make another one of those, another one of those trees?

SALLY: Where does it go?

LACEY: It's gonna go right here. I'm gonna maybe put a worm or something on it. [I draw a tree, and Lacey stamps apples.] Now, what I'm gonna do, is that green?

SALLY: Um, kind of browny-green.

LACEY: Is that one? Now, we're gonna be in the apples. You're not gonna eat it; of course you're not. If there's worms in these, that's a poisoned apple. If they're not in these, they're not a poisoned apple. So I put an apple in my hand. Not poisoned. Okay, now I need the paint. Um, [screams] I forgot the rainbow! I forgot to make houses too! What's your house gonna be? Green or blue? I like blue. House is kinda big. Here's the window. Here's another window. Another window. Got a *lot* of windows. A door. A little window. This is me and you sleeping, and Rex is sleeping right here. I think I messed up. [laughs] I put this [a line] across here. This is the door. But that's all right; it can be anything.

Now, want to see who this is? Johnny Appleseed, but *he* is poisoned. But he's not really all the way dead. These apples, if you take one of these, they'll save these.

I know I put two worms there, but how about I put a butterfly right there? Okay. What color? Blue. They can be any color. [She draws an X then fills in sides.]

SALLY: How did you know how to make it?

LACEY: Learned. See when I messed, when we were doing this stuff, I messed up, and I went like this [makes an X], so then I knew how to make a butterfly. I made two straight lines, and then I made an X. And I messed up.

SALLY: Show me what you mean.

LACEY: I mean like this. When I was working, with my kindergarten teacher a long time ago, we were making these [draws an *X*], and I went like this [closes in two ends]. And then when we were making little pictures I went like that and then went [makes butterfly], and I just knew [it was a butterfly].

Um, I'm putting *Sally* and *Rex*. [spelling] *S A L L Y*. Rex: *R E X*.

SALLY: That's right. How did you learn how to do that?

LACEY: Mimi teached me.

Now, how 'bout. . . . I gotta put more, now it's sunny. It's orange. [Draws sun, top left.] [The sun is] wearing sunglasses. Okay. I've got to put more apples. Falling apples. Because see, some apples fall. [Hums along as she stamps more apples.] These are the different worms. These are worms. This thing is really not . . . [ink is running out on stamp]. That's the last. Now, I gotta put worms.

SALLY: How do you know there are gonna be worms in that side?

LACEY: Well, I don't know. I just put worms.

SALLY: Now, is there a story that goes with this?

LACEY: Yeah. Um, um [thinking], you were walking down the woods. And then you picked one of these apples, and then you ate it, and then you died, and then you ate one of these, and you came back alive, and then you came to your house, and there was a butterfly on your house.

SALLY: Does everything you make have a story to it?

LACEY: MM hmm. But some of 'em don't. Well, I make pictures all the time. Sometimes I don't, and sometimes I do. And sometimes, like if I doesn't have something, don't have nothing to do, I just call Keisha, and then she'll come over and play with me. But sometimes she doesn't. We play hopscotch. We play jumprope. We play Barbies—she got a lot of Barbies. And we play house, and we play school, and we play Mom and sister, and we play . . . that's all we play.

SALLY: Do you ever write anything or draw anything for any of those things you play?

LACEY: Uh huh. That's boring.

LACEY: This is you and Rex. There's your hair. Now I'll put a dress on you. A shirt. Doesn't that look like arms? But it's really a shirt. I would use a shirt. Now *he*'s wearing pants, green pants. He's going swimming. So I'm gonna make a swimming pool. Got a long shirt. It's cold outside, so you got a skirt on, but a long, really long skirt. You got a bow in your hair. And a ring on your hand. How 'bout blue, red . . . I think red. Earrings. First we got to make ears. What color? What color? Blue. Look good? Color this one in. There. Okay, now . . . Oh, I forgot a necklace! Dear me. What color? How about, not black. How 'bout, brown with little diamond. I think you shouldn't use black because I can't see it. Okay.

Now what? Oh, I forgot his hair! Dear me. There, is that good? Okay. Boys can wear one earring. Okay. Now what?

FIGURE 1–2   *"Sally, Rex, and the Swimming Pool"*

Oh, I've got to make the swimming pool. Too little, but I'm gonna make it bigger; I'll need bigger. There, now I'm done.

Oh, I forgot to put Sally and Rex. *Sally:* [spelling] *S A L L E . . . E.* And *Rex.* Okay, *going:* g, g, g, g [sounds out *G* sound]. You got to help me with these.

SALLY: Okay, you tell me what you want, and I'll help.

LACEY: *Going.* And I think *going* to this one. Can you write it, 'cause I can't.

SALLY: Why don't you try?

LACEY: *G* [Lacey adds *A* and *Y* on top of her *O*.]

SALLY: Okay. *G O A Y.* That's close.

LACEY: *Walk.* How do you spell *walk?*

SALLY: *W A.* [Lacey writes *walk* and later *forest* on Figure 1.]

LACEY: Lower case or capital?

SALLY: Lower case. Then *L.*

LACEY: Lower case or capital?

SALLY: Lower. Then *K*

LACEY: Lower case or Capital? I hope it's a capital.

SALLY: Okay, make it capital. You can do it any way you want to, 'cause this is just for us. Good. That's *walk.*

LACEY: Now, how do you spell *forest? F.*

SALLY: Mm hmm. Then what?

LACEY: I don't know.

SALLY: *O R E S,* and it ends with (sounds out) *T. T.* How do you know when to go to the next line?

LACEY: It just gets to here [the left edge of the right tree in Figure 1–1, and when I see this touching, I just go to the next line.

[Lacey decides to make her ABC's.]

LACEY: *B C E* right? I mean *D.* [sings] *ABCD....* [writes *D,* then sings] *ABCDE. E* [writes *E*]. *F... G.* [makes sound] *ch. I...J... K...L...N..*[longer pause]. *O...P...Q* [sounds out *K, K*]... *R.* [sings] *ABCDEFGHIJKLMN....* [giggles, then sings again] *ABCDEFGHIJKLMNOPQR.* Yep, it's *R...S...T. T's* like this

FIGURE 1–3 *Making "About 80 C's"*

[draws vertical line] and straight line. [sings again] *ABCDEFGHI-JKLMNOPQRSTUVW*.... That's a *W*. Wait, no, after this is a *U* ...*V*...*W*...*X*...*Y*...*Z* [sings the *Z* on a high note of finality]! Now um, *A*, block *A*, block *A*, *AAA*. Lower case now?

SALLY: What's the difference between upper case and lower case?

LACEY: I don't know, but it's *very* hard! Very, very hard. Okay, I've gotta trace over these now.

SALLY: Which ones are hard?

LACEY: *P, L*, L's easy. Um, *Q, R*, R's easy 'cause you only gotta go ee uh uh [makes three lines of an *R* in the air.]

SALLY: Are any of the upper case ones hard?

LACEY: No. Only *P*.

SALLY: But the lower case ones are a lot harder?

LACEY: Mm hmm. 'cept *f* ... 'cept *f*; *f* is easy. You only gotta write Mm mm mm [makes lines of an *f* in the air]. *F*. A *g* is hard [thinking]; lower case *k* is hard. *o* ... *p*.

SALLY: How do you remember all of these?

LACEY: *q* ... like *e* is simple because I always don't forget.

SALLY: Why do you have to learn all of these?

LACEY: I don't know why, but so we can learn to read.

SALLY: Why are you gonna learn to read?

LACEY: I don't know how to read, that's why. Yeah, I don't know *how*, but [pause] I use, like I do good stuff, and I learn a lot. That's what I do. Like we had little tests, little thingies, and we did like stuff all during school.

SALLY: Show me.

LACEY: This is what you do [very sure now, as if this request is easier than the last]. If I get something back, then you give me a check, if I have—this is first grade—if you give me a check, it's bad. And this one is the *X*, and the *X* means bad. This one means *A* +, and this one means really good. 'Kay. "Here Teacher." [Wants to role play.]

SALLY: Okay. I'm Teacher. Thank you.

LACEY: Now you've got to put something on it, like . . .

SALLY: What do you think it should get?

LACEY: You got to put it on, you can't tell me.

SALLY: I have to decide?

LACEY: Yeah.

SALLY: Okay, I'm gonna give it that and that [an A+ and an apple stamp written on Figure 3–1. So I'm the teacher right? And I say, "Here's your paper back, Lacey." What are you gonna say?

LACEY: Thank you.

SALLY: What do you think?

LACEY: Good.

SALLY: Do you think it was an *A* + paper?

LACEY: Yeah.

SALLY: What would an *F* paper look like?

LACEY: An *F* paper would look bad too.

SALLY: Why would I give a child one of those?

LACEY:' Cause if you give, if I do something wrong and I mess up, you got to give me a *F* or a check. This is the *F* or either a check. Like small things, but I didn't mess up on this. Oh, you forgot to put something on these [Figures 1–1 and 1–2]. Wait, you can't let me see. Turn around. This is a *F*. This is a *F*.

SALLY: Okay. Well what would you say if I put an *F* on one of 'em?

LACEY: Um, if you put a *F* on one that means it's bad, really bad-bad. It would make me feel really mad and sad.

SALLY: Do any of the children in your class get bad grades?

LACEY: Some of 'em. I know that. Kelley got a check one time. He colored wrong, and he scribble-scrabbled. We have to stand by it and do it like it's 'posed to be. I got a star one time. A happy face means *very very* good.

SALLY: When you do your letters, what makes them good?

LACEY: Um, I learn about 80 *C*'s, and I write 'em good, and then I'll give them to my teacher, and then she keeps them, and hangs them on the wall. That's good.

2

Martin, Jeralynn, and Mark

"NOW DON'T WRITE THAT DOWN"

(Kindergarten)

Contributed by Beverly E. Cox & Leah Jones

Mark, Martin, and Jeralynn were three of the sixteen preschool and kindergarten children that Leah Jones, a graduate student, and I met through a study at a preschool in Indiana. All three came from strong literacy backgrounds in which literacy materials and events (e.g., storybook reading) were common. However, none had received any formal reading or writing instruction and none was reading independently.

We asked the children, all five years old, to dictate to a scribe an oral monologue as a story for others. Their comments to themselves or to the scribe suggest they had important insights: (a) the writing process takes time and though writing is permanent, at the composing stage it can be edited, (b) a text is meant to be meaningful, and (c) a text should be monitored by the author for accuracy, appropriateness of content, and comprehensibility for a hypothetical reader.

Martin was very mature and articulate for his years, and full of stories to share. In conversation, he spoke rapidly, initiating new topics of conversation, and asking to tell more stories. His story is a retelling of a complex, space adventure story about Transformers and The Great War.

Jeralynn was a very energetic and fun-loving child who bubbled with ideas and questions. Her self-confidence, sense of command and audience appropriateness, and lively ownership of her text are clear in her story of Two Christmases.

Finally, Mark was a very serious, precocious child, a contemplative author who planned and pondered the content of his text and its effect on his audience. He carefully plans, constructs, and monitors his story of a visit to his grandparents' house for "the other kids."

MARTIN: THE TRANSFORMERS

MARTIN: Well, do you know when The Great War was?

SCRIBE: Um hmm.

MARTIN: That was————. Well, I wanna tell you something. "Well, it all began during The Great War." (to scribe) I'll tell you this one slowly. "In the Great War, Megatron had gotten Optimus Prime. And Optimus Prime gave the matrix to Ultra Magness and Ultra Magness led the Autobots. One day when the Deceptakons were chasing the Autobots, they blew up their ship and Straffi escaped. But, and all the Autobots went into the resting place they had built for the Autobots that had been lost in The Great War. Then the Deceptakons came in. And the Autobots went in to look at Optimus Prime's coffin and it was empty. The Deceptakons came, and they were fighting when Prime blasted Gelvatron. That's the end of the story." (to scribe) And Gelvatron's really Megatron—get that straight?

SCRIBE: I think so.

MARTIN: Cause I've seen the movie. And there's one more thing. "During The Great War, Unikron had turned Megatron into Gelvatron. And Unikron devoured all the planets in his path and got rid of Gelvatron when he transformed to his robot form."

SCRIBE: (Re-reads dictation aloud to allow edits) "Well, it all began during The Great War. In The Great War, Megatron got Optimus Prime and Optimus Prime gave the matrix to Ultra Magness and Ultra Magness led the Autobots. One day when the Deceptakrons—"

MARTIN: *kons.*

SCRIBE: Oh, the Deceptatons?

MARTIN: (with emphasis) *kons!*

SCRIBE: Not *trons,* but *tons.*

MARTIN: (with some irritation) *kons.* with a *k* in there.

SCRIBE: Oh, Deceptakons.

MARTIN: Yeah, Deceptakons.

SCRIBE: Oh, I beg your pardon.

MARTIN: I always watch Transformers.

SCRIBE: Deceptakons, alright. Thank you for correcting that. See, I never watch Transformers, so I wouldn't have known the difference.

MARTIN: I watch it Saturday and Sunday. I mean, I watch it Sunday. It's on Sunday.

SCRIBE: (continues re-reading text) "One day when the Deceptakr—"

MARTIN: *kons.*

SCRIBE: "kons were chasing the Autobots, they blew up their ship and Straffi escaped. But, and all the Autobots went into the resting

place that they had built for the Autobots that had been lost in The
Great War. And then the Deceptakr- *kons* came in they checked
and then the Auto-, and then the Deceptakr—"

MARTIN: *kons.*

SCRIBE: "*kons* (embarassed laugh) came in and the Autobots went in
to look at Optimus Prime's coffin and it was empty. And the
Deceptakons came and then they were fighting when Optimus
Prime blasted Gelvatron. That's the end of the story." Is there
anything you want to change?

MARTIN: Yes, there's something missing. "During The Great War,
Unikron had turned Megatron into Gelvatron so Gelvatron's really
Megatron." And that's all.

JERALYNN: MY TWO CHRISTMASES

JERALYNN: "I had two Christmases. Well—" Don't write that down.

SCRIBE: Don't write down "well?"

JERALYNN: No. "I rided on an airplane by myself to Memphis, Tennessee." Oh, that doesn't look like in cursive [meaning handwriting].
Now, don't write what I just said down, "That doesn't look like
cursive." That would be a silly thing to write down, wouldn't it?
"And I had Christmas here and Christmas at Memphis. Christmas
at Memphis was the real one when Santa came on Christmas eve,
but the one here was not. The one here was—"

SCRIBE: Wait, I can't keep up. Here's where I am, "The Christmas at
Memphis was the one—"

JERALYNN: (with emphasis) "the real one—"

SCRIBE: The real one, um hmm.

JERALYNN: "—on Christmas Eve. I saw Santa playing on the plane
with the dishes. I wasn't sleepy and he started playing with the
dishes." Why do you have two pencils?

SCRIBE: In case one breaks.

JERALYNN: Why do you have a pen? Where are we at?

SCRIBE: (re-reads) "and I was sitting on a plane with the dishes."

JERALYNN: Sitting on the plane with the dishes! I don't mean that. I
said, "Santa was playing on the plane with the dishes!"

SCRIBE: "Santa was playing on the plane with the dishes?"

JERALYNN: Yeah, and on Christmas Eve (laughs).

SCRIBE: Oh, *Santa* was playing with the dishes. (Jeralynn laughs
again.) "And on Christmas day—"

JERALYNN: "Then on Christmas day, I got a Sweet Secret and it had
make-up in it." (whispers in sing-song to herself while scribe
writes.) Make-up in it, make-up in it. "and, and, I got a bed, a bed
for my babies at Memphis. That's all I remember. That's all I
remember that I got from Memphis." (noting scribe is writing at the
bottom of the page) No more room?

SCRIBE: Oh no, I have lots of room.

JERALYNN: I'm gonna do it at Indiana now, ok? "I got this Rock 'n Roll
star, Popple. And I got this football player, Popple." (to herself)

Thinking, thinking, thinking. (to scribe) Oooo where, where are we at? You're writing so much.

SCRIBE: Um hmm. (re-reads) "I got this Rock 'n Roll star, Popple. And I got this football player, Popple."

JERALYNN: "I got this Sweet Secret. It was a pencil. It has ah, and when you open the seat, pa- the pad of it, the thing, um. There's a, um, there's this bed for him. And a-, um, there's these two, a bunny and a bear, for him to sleep with. There's a bed—"

SCRIBE: Wait a minute. I can't keep up. Here's where I am, "I got this Sweet Secret. It was a pencil. And when you open the pad of the thing—"

JERALYNN: "There is a bed with a bunny and a bear and a lamp on it. There was this little table that has the lamp on it" (long pause, waiting for scribe to write) "And my mom's boyfriend—" (pause) Where does it say "mom"? "—gave me, this, this um ducky, from Land Before Time Ducky. And um, Ducky and Sarah." Sarah's the one that is mean to Little Foot. "And they had, they had a bottle and they had a bib to it." Sarah's a girl and Ducky's a girl. "And he, also, my mom's boyfriend, also gave me, gave me this, these magnets. One was a Mickey and one was a Pluto and they keep breaking and fall off, they fall off the, um, frigerator and breaking." I guess that's their favorite thing to do———to fall off the 'frigerator and break. (laughs) "That's all I got. That's all I can remember. Well, I got two LiteBrites, one at Memphis and one here. That's all I can remember that I got here. (pause)

Can I tell you about Easter, what I got for Easter? I got some things for Easter, and what I got from Valentines?

SCRIBE: Well, let's finish the story about Christmas in Memphis.

JERALYNN: That's all I can remember that I did. What does that say?

SCRIBE: I'm still writing the things you told me before.

JERALYNN: Why do you keep saying "I can't keep up with you?" I'm not saying it very fast.

SCRIBE: (Re-reads dictation to allow edits) "I rided on an airplane by myself to Memphis, Tennessee, and I had Christmas here and Christmas at Memphis. The Christmas at Memphis was the real one on Christmas Eve. And Santa was playing with the dishes on Christmas Eve."

JERALYNN: Playing with the dishes?

SCRIBE: (pause) "And on Christmas day, I got a Sweet Secret and it had a make-up in it. And I got a bed for my babies at Memphis. That's all I remember that I got from Memphis. I'm gonna do it at Indiana—"

JERALYNN: I didn't want you to say, "That's all I remember." I didn't want you to say "That's all I remember from Memphis." Take it out. (Scribe draws line through appropriate part of text.)

SCRIBE: (continues re-reading text) "I'm gonna do it at Indiana now. I got this Rock 'n Roll star Popple and I got this football player Popple. I got this Sweet Secret. It was a pencil and when you open the pad of the thing there was a bed with a bunny—"

JERALYNN: (interrupting) Pad with a thing?

SCRIBE: Did you want to change that or is that ok?

JERALYNN: "Pad with a thing" sounds silly, so I don't want to put that on there.

SCRIBE: Oh, ok. So, "when you open the pad of the thing there was a bed with a bunny—"

JERALYNN: (interrupting) Get that "thing" off. I don't like that part.

SCRIBE: Ok, so just say, "when you open the pad?"

JERALYNN: (thoughtfully) Yeah.

SCRIBE: "—there is a bed with a bunny and a bear and a lamp on it. There was this little table that has the lamp on it. And my Mom's boyfriend gave me this Ducky and Sarah. Sarah's the one that's mean to Little Foot. Sarah's a girl and Ducky's a girl—"

JERALYNN: (interrupting) Can I, ok, can I tell you that, like Ducky, no, "Sarah's a Triceratops and Ducky's a—," I don't know what kind Ducky is. "And they're all dinosaurs. And Little Foot's a Long Neck, so he's a Brontosaurus." I know what kind Ducky is. I think Ducky's a Crown Head. He can't be a Crown Head. No, he's not a Crown Head. Don't put that in there, ok? Just say the only thing that's on there [in the text] is "Ducky."

SCRIBE: (re-reads edited text) Ok, so say, "He gave me this Ducky and Sarah. Sarah's a Triceratops and Ducky's a . . . dinosaur, too?"

JERALYNN: Yeah, and put Ducky, and say Ducky, ah, nevermind.

SCRIBE: "And they're all dinosaurs."

JERALYNN: Yeah. See I don't know what kind Ducky is.

SCRIBE: "Sarah's the one that's mean to Little Foot. Sarah's a girl and Ducky's a girl."

JERALYNN: Did you put Little Foot is a, um, Brontosaurus?

SCRIBE: Oh, no I didn't. Should I put that, too?

JERALYNN: Next to "Sarah's mean to Little Foot." (sings to self as scribe writes)

SCRIBE: (pronouncing as she writes) "Little Foot is a Bron-ta-"

JERALYNN: —*to*saurus. Not a Bron-*ta*-saurus, a Brontosaurus.

SCRIBE: (continues re-reading text) "Sarah's a girl and Ducky's a girl. He also, my Mom's boyfriend, also gave me these two magnets. One was a Mickey and one was a Pluto."

JERALYNN: "There's a planet of Pluto and there's a, there's a dog in Disney; it's named Pluto and that's Mickey's dog." And that, that's the part you just put on. (as scribe makes the edit) Don't write, don't write "That's the part you just put on." Don't put that on.

SCRIBE: Don't put all the stuff you just told me on there?

JERALYNN: Not the part I just said.

SCRIBE: Ok. (continues re-reading text) "They keep breaking, they fall off the fridge and keep breaking. I guess that's their favorite thing to do."

JERALYNN: (laughs) Um, I like that part.

SCRIBE: That's a funny part of the story, isn't it?

JERALYNN: And now what's now [meaning what is next in the text]?

SCRIBE: "And I got two LiteBrites." Now, did you want to add anything else?

JERALYNN: Well, maybe one's, um, a G. I. Joe one, maybe. I don't know. I haven't opened the one here. But the one at Memphis is not a G. I. Joe. I haven't opened the one here. Might do that when I get home tonight. I might if my Mom has a light bulb to put in it. I like the snowman best. (referring to the scribe's writing) What does *G I* mean?

SCRIBE: That's where I said "G. I. Joe." (re-reads text) "Maybe one's a G. I. Joe one. I haven't opened the one here, but the one at Memphis is not a G. I. Joe one. I might open the one here when I get home—"

JERALYNN: (interrupting) I don't want that part, it's silly.

SCRIBE: Oh, that's not going to be part of the story? Ok. Anything else you want to add about your Christmas in Memphis?

JERALYNN: Um-um, that's all I want to, to tell you about, about my Christmas in Memphis.

MARK: A VISIT TO GRANDMA'S AND GRANDPA'S

MARK: "We drove to their house." (to himself) Think what you say before you say it. That's what my dad always tells me. Think before you say things. (to scribe) I didn't want you to write that part down. "I had a good time. It was fun making up a new game. I had a good time." (to scribe) Did I already say that?

SCRIBE: Yes, take it out?

MARK: Nah. Did I already say that it was fun being at their house?

SCRIBE: No, want to?

MARK: No. Well, are you gonna tell it to other kids? No, I don't want you to write that though.

SCRIBE: Ok. Tell me what you did.

MARK: "I like playing with the kitty cat toy." Oopsie! Don't say, don't write that down, please.

SCRIBE: Ok.

MARK: "It was fun being at their house, I liked playing with Tiger Doggy, and I also had fun playing with the toy dog. The End."

SCRIBE: Re-reads the text and asks, "Want to add anything?"

MARK: Erase "The End." There is something I want to add. "When we went to their house on the second school day, I told them I hunted for Easter eggs." (noticing the scribe is writing at the very bottom of the page) Take two pages to do that please! Don't write some things that I say down. "Made by Mark. The End." Well, this time I'm sure that I did do everything I wanted to.

Mark, quite satisfied with his tale, made no further edits.

3

Scooter and Chanell

"WHAT CAN I MAKE IN A BOOK?"

(Kindergarten)

Contributed by Janet B. Taylor &
N. Amanda Branscombe

April, 1990

Scooter: "Stories are fun work. You gotta make 'em up outta your head. You can't make 'em up off TV. You gotta write 'em and draw 'em and put 'em together. I know. I'm a bookmaker. People like my stories because they never hear 'em before."

Chanell: "Bambi makes a good story. Bambi has so many friends in the forest, and he play with them. One day I might get me a brother. I don't have no friends where I just moved."

Five-year-old Scooter entered the schoolroom door on his first day of kindergarten, not looking like a writer, but rather like a miniature football hero. In his number 23 Miami Dolphin aqua and orange jersey he greeted his classmates by saying, "I'm a Dolphin. I play football. My name is Scooter. What's yours?" Scooter developed his fascination for literacy behind this macho facade. Because he wanted his voice heard and valued, he spent many of his center times engaged in book making, drawing, writing, or reading his stories to classmates. By April, he defined himself as a bookmaker.

Chanell, a black child new to the neighborhood and the school, viewed stories and their origins in a decidedly different way from Scooter. Chanell's daycare experience had trained her to "do school" and please the teacher. When she entered kindergarten some considered her the model student. However, unlike Scooter, five-year-old

Chanell did not view herself as a story maker, but rather as a responder to stories written by others.

The following text is a spontaneous, unsolicited dialogue that we recorded during center time as Chanell and Scooter worked together across four days to make a book. Only the talk extraneous to the task has been deleted so that you can see how the book evolves through the talk in a nonlinear fashion across all six pages. As we listen to children in the process of making a book, we come to know the whole story rather than the bits and pieces they are able to encode in pictures and words.

May 10, 1990:

CHANELL: What can I make in a book?
SCOOTER: Make a ice cream one like mine. An ice cream and spaghetti book.
CHANELL: What else can I make, Scooter?
SCOOTER: Ummmm, you can make a farm book.
CHANELL: What else?
SCOOTER: Um, an animal book?
CHANELL: What else, Scooter?
SCOOTER: A space book . . . a rocket book.
CHANELL: What about a airplane book?
SCOOTER: That's a good one!
CHANELL: How do you make a book? (begins to write book) *B o o* [?]
SCOOTER: (Waits) *K*

FIGURE 3–1 *"My Very First Chanell Book" by Scooter and Chanell:* Title Page

CHANELL: What do you want me to make [a book] about, Scooter?
SCOOTER: Airplane book.
CHANELL: I don't know if I can make a airplane.
SCOOTER: I think I can.

May 11, 1990:

CHANELL: (Talks and looks at Figure 3–1 Page 1 as she writes) "I like planes dat fly up in the air." (Writes) *L* . . . . *N* . . . . plane.
SCOOTER: (Numbers the page) Number 1 . . . we're gonna . . . Number 1. We're on our letters now, okay?
CHANELL: Fly
SCOOTER: Fly
CHANELL: *F* . . . . .Wait, I got my letters too little. *L* . . . . I mean *F*.
SCOOTER: (Drawing planes) That's only one of them. That one is going faster than that one. We're telling about airplanes.
CHANELL: We're making a book about airplanes.
SCOOTER: Airplanes.
CHANELL: "Airplanes were flying up in the air."
SCOOTER: We are gonna need a little white [crayon].
CHANELL: "Airplanes flied up in the air."

FIGURE 3–1 (cont.) *"My Very First Chanell Book" by Scooter and Chanell:* Page 1

SCOOTER: (Hums) Dum - dum- to-dum- dum . . . Air-o-planes. "Airplanes go up in the air." (both begin to color)

CHANELL: We gonna leave that one. We not gonna color that one. "I like airplanes that fly up in the air."

SCOOTER: Hurry up! (regarding Chanell and her coloring) "Go up in the air."

CHANELL: *N* in

SCOOTER: *N* (making letter)

CHANELL: *N*. Scooter! You got you *N* backwards.

SCOOTER: Right! Okay, now we are gonna read it.

CHANELL: Scooter colored that 4 [numeral for page number] fast. We got the last one. (looks at book) I made that. The end.

SCOOTER: Is that good? It's real good, cause they can see it. Because it was fun making it.

May 14, 1990 (The next Monday)

SCOOTER: (Looking at title page, Figure 3–1) Now, I wrote Chanell's name too. I copied it off the top. (Page 1) It's gonna say, we want it to say, "I like airplanes."

CHANELL: I got something else. "Airplanes fly up in the air." (as she writes) Ooops. I made a *P*. I meant to make an *F*.

SCOOTER: I'm gonna do the next page. (writes and says) *U . . . p..*

FIGURE 3–1 (*cont.*)   *"My Very First Chanell Book" by Scooter and Chanell:* Page 2

CHANELL: Scooter. After you do yours, I'm gonna do the other one.

SCOOTER: No, no, *In* . . . not *N i.*

CHANELL: Air.

SCOOTER: *A*

CHANELL: *I*

SCOOTER: *R.* That's crooked.

CHANELL: Me'll write it right.

SCOOTER: You want me to write it.

CHANELL: Yeh! You erase and me write.

SCOOTER: Me and you are gonna read it to the class.

CHANELL: I got it now. "I like airplanes."

SCOOTER: *i* . . . *i*

CHANELL: Another *i?*

SCOOTER: Now write airplanes.

CHANELL: Put an *a.*

SCOOTER: Does that say airplanes?

CHANELL: (Looking at Figure 3–1 Page 1) Scooter, you did a good job on this. Gonna make a number *1?*

SCOOTER: Write it big on this page.

CHANELL: What's that? That's not no *1.* Yeh, that is a *1.*

SCOOTER: Now turn the page.

FIGURE 3–1 (*cont.*)   *"My Very First Chanell Book"* by Scooter and Chanell: Page 3

CHANELL: You can write it big on that one. My mama taught me and now I can remember. I wanna look back at the *1*.

SCOOTER: We're gonna go on and do the numbers.

CHANELL: You do the numbers, and I'll do the words.

SCOOTER: No, we'll both do the words! Okay?

CHANELL: (Looking at Figure 3–1, Page 4) Okay. *4* . . . You put "The End."

SCOOTER: (Looking at The End, Figure 3–1) Does that say "The End?" No, it needs an *nd*.

CHANELL: Do you wanna make another airplane?

SCOOTER: No, that's all the planes. We'll take it [the book] home. We'll take turns taking it home.

CHANELL: You didn't put no *N*.

SCOOTER: Put . . . uhh . . . *N* . . . write it. Somebody told me wrong. They said *in* was *i n*. (looking at Figure 3–1, Page 2) Page 2. Now. (pauses and thinks) Hey, I gotta see what it looks like inside here. (attempts to look into the airplane they have drawn)

CHANELL: A door . . . it's where the stairs come. The door . . . make the stairs come out. When me and my mama took Miss Tellie to the airport we saw it.

SCOOTER: I saw my daddy at the airport . . . a 1000 times. He went to China.

FIGURE 3–1 (*cont.*)   *"My Very First Chanell Book"* by Scooter and Chanell: Page 4

CHANELL: I never got to ride a airplane.

SCOOTER: I gotta airplane badge. It's got eagle wings, and it's grey. There's the back of the airplane.

CHANELL: You gotta make the stairs.

SCOOTER: No, it's up in the air.

CHANELL: You making the clouds, Scooter?

SCOOTER: This is a airplane. (points to Figure 3–1, Page 3) This is a jet. (points to Figure 3–1, Page 1) These are the bombs. (Both children work in silence for a while.)

SCOOTER: I like to ride in airplanes . . . I . . . (talks as writes, Figure 3–1, Page 3)

CHANELL: I got a red. Be real careful or you'll . . . if you don't you'll go outta the lines.

SCOOTER: You just scribbled!

CHANELL: Not um!

SCOOTER: Yes you did!

CHANELL: Just play scribbled . . . play scribbled . . . got outta lines. Scooter, we gonna coior something else?

SCOOTER: (Makes sounds of planes taking off and bombs dropping) That's how it goes.

CHANELL: Color here. (looking at Figure 3–1, Page 2)

SCOOTER: Go get one [crayon]. Get the black.

FIGURE 3–1 (*cont.*)   *"My Very First Chanell Book" by Scooter and Chanell:* The End

CHANELL: I'm gonna color this one gray. I don't see no gray. I'll have to get me another color and color something else. I'll color this little bit.

SCOOTER: They'll say we colored this airplane real good.

CHANELL: When I took my picture I done, my grandmama and granddaddy looked at it and say, "Who is this little girl?"

SCOOTER: Yeh. (looking at Figure 3–1, Page 1)

CHANELL: I colored that right there. Scooter, you write that *I* like *a?*

SCOOTER: Not um.

CHANELL: Yes you did! What else does it say?

SCOOTER: "I like airplanes. . . . airplanes . . . airplanes" . . . *a* . . *r* . . now what? . . . *p.*

CHANELL: Where did the airplane land, Scooter? Oh, I know. England! That's what I said. Color this . . .

SCOOTER: You're messing the plane up, cause you're covering the door and stuff. (referring to Figure 3–1, Page 2)

CHANELL: Door back! I made the door back, Scooter. Leave that part white. I left that part white. How you like our airplane?

SCOOTER: Gotta be careful with that color.

CHANELL: I looked at yours fore I do mine.

SCOOTER: Gotta erase.

CHANELL: What?

SCOOTER: With the pencil . . . that black! . . . Oh, I need the yellow.

CHANELL: Okay.

SCOOTER: (Talking about how the airplane in his picture works) It turns around. It turrrns . . . it goes whirrrr . . . yeh . . . and then it spins and then this part goes up and ummmmmm.

CHANELL: He have some little bombs. He have some big bombs.

SCOOTER: Pretend like . . . pretend like . . .

CHANELL: Say Scooter, make some little bombs and some big bombs.

SCOOTER: This part goes up like this. And then the bad guy behind them. Here's a bad guy, and then the bombs drop out on the bad guy.

CHANELL: I'll make 'em big.

SCOOTER: Yeh!

CHANELL: We got to make the bad guy behind . . .

SCOOTER: Yeh! Yeh. What's this? What's this?

CHANELL: I just try to make another bomb . . . two bombs . . . big bombs.

SCOOTER: Erase that. That's not a bomb.

CHANELL: I'm going to make the bad guy.

SCOOTER: No, no, no, no! He gots to be back here where you can't see him.

CHANELL: There's another bomb . . . another big bomb.

SCOOTER: Red . . . again?

CHANELL: No, the bad guy was on this page! We didn't have enough room to get the wings on. You colored on the table, Scooter! Now, how we gonna make the bad guy?

SCOOTER: We don't cause you can't see 'em. Now, see the bombs went emmmmmm. Then they shot the bad guy. He fell over and fall down.

CHANELL: No, the bombs went boom, boom, boom, boom.

SCOOTER: You can't see 'em.

CHANELL: Wowwww I need gray!

SCOOTER: We already do 'em. You can't see 'em. Put some right there. Then stop!

CHANELL: Scooter, I have to color this one. (looking at Figure 3–1, Page 3)

SCOOTER: Yeh, but you are not gonna color this, this, and this.

CHANELL: I'm not gonna color those. I just colored the edges.

SCOOTER: Okay.

CHANELL: Cause . . . I got mines out of a book.

SCOOTER: So . . . it's not gonna be looking like a book. I'm gonna make the bad guy. He's gonna crash.

CHANELL: You . . . you gotta make the blood. Scooter, are you gonna make the blood?

SCOOTER: Now, there's the blood. These are the . . .

CHANELL: (Looking at Figure 3–1, Page 2) Number 2 . . . Let's make little ones and big ones. Scooter, do a bomb drop outta this one?

SCOOTER: No, we gotta make a bomb dropper. Make it big enough.

CHANELL: You making the bomb dropper? I'm coloring . . .

SCOOTER: Think this is big enough for the bombs?

CHANELL: That's better cause it's big now. I'm going to color this [part] this color. Okay? Not gonna get outta lines. (Scooter begins to hum. Chanell joins him. The two create a humming race to see who out hums the other. Scooter ends the game.)

SCOOTER: Now, remember he is the bad guy.

CHANELL: When I hurt my finger I licked my blood, and it had no taste. (laughs)

SCOOTER: Well, my sister tasted her blood one time. It tasted, it tasted, it tasted like ice cream. Well, does it?

CHANELL: I didn't. . . . Well, when I sucked my blood at home, it didn't have no taste to it.

SCOOTER: Like this. (makes gesture)

CHANELL: Yeh.

SCOOTER: (Points to Chanell's red fingernail polish) Like really blood?

CHANELL: No, that's fingernail. Like this was blood, and I have a little bit.

SCOOTER: Oh ummmmm.

CHANELL: For real! I licked that blood. It [their book] be looking pretty.

SCOOTER: (Looking at Figure 3–1, Page 2) "I like. . . . I like when airplanes take off."

CHANELL: We got to color it Scooter.

SCOOTER: Not yet. You better not color. . . . You can color this.

CHANELL: No I don't!

SCOOTER: Wait!

CHANELL: Red. I do need brown. Get red. Oooooo red! What can I color Scooter?

SCOOTER: Wait! You got to . . .

CHANELL: Oooooo! This the same green, but this is light, and this is dark.

SCOOTER: Okay, now color . . . color right there.

CHANELL: Move your arm where I can . . .

SCOOTER: No, no, no! Red! Should be red!

CHANELL: Scooter, we got white tissue. Scooter, you went out on the green.

SCOOTER: Yea! Green. I think red, white, and blue.

CHANELL: Red, white, and blue.

SCOOTER: White like . . . when airplanes take off.

BOTH: (Hum) Do-de-do-do-de-do-diddy-do . . . (laughter)

SCOOTER: Not the kind that comes out. The kind that's alright to say. You know.

CHANELL: The doodle-de-do . . . (laughter)

SCOOTER: Not the bad words. That's not a bad word, right? Do-de-dodo.

CHANELL: I'm just gonna color this part.

SCOOTER: Whenever we get tired let's tell her [the teacher].

CHANELL: We got to leave all of that one white. I wanta color the *2*.

SCOOTER: We might not color it.

SCOOTER: . . . you have to work hard to make it.

CHANELL: Pretty. Then they [classmates] all . . .

SCOOTER: [Sing song fashion] Making a hard old book! Are you glad you making a airplane book?

CHANELL: Umhum!

May 15, 1990

SCOOTER: It was easy whenever we made this one. Next is a hard one! So we gotta get ready for the hard one.

CHANELL: We need a black. (hums)

SCOOTER: Okay! Black! Then a black and green one.

CHANELL: I wanta color the two. We gotta leave this one white.

SCOOTER: "I like when . . . when airplanes take off." (looking at Figure 3–1, Page 2 and talking as he colors) Whewwwww!

CHANELL: Hurry up cause I'm gonna color another one.

SCOOTER: "I like when . . . when . . ."

CHANELL: Look! Do you like that coloring?

SCOOTER: *W* . . . *e* . . . *i* . . . put *e* . . . air. How do you spell air!?

CHANELL: (Hums)

SCOOTER: *A* . . . *r*, . . *a* . . . *r* . . . *r* . . .

CHANELL: Airplanes.

SCOOTER: Airplanes.

CHANELL: Scooter, can I color this all?

SCOOTER: Let me tell you what colors . . . okay? Ha! See, told you it was the hard one next. It's the army one. We are not going to write nothing but just color on that airplane.

CHANELL: Wait Scooter! I wanna color this right quick. *It's our book!*

SCOOTER: (Looking at Figure 3–1, Page 2) "Airplanes take off" . . . rumummmm. "Look at the airplane". . . . *t* . . . *a* . . . *a* . . . *a* . . .

CHANELL: Army . . .

SCOOTER: What's that say?

CHANELL: Take off.

SCOOTER: Oh boy! I did it! I did it! Don't color until I tell you to! Now color this all the way to here . . . all the way to there . . . Okay?

CHANELL: Okay. Scooter, why did you make that mark? Color the top of it Scooter?

SCOOTER: Oh . . . all the way to there okay?

CHANELL: Okay.

SCOOTER: Then I'm gonna use this color.

CHANELL: Don't break it. (hums) I colored the wings. Okay! I'm through.

SCOOTER: Put that one back. Don't put it back in there. I gotta use it again.

CHANELL: I did the *2* all by myself. We gonna leave the jet white. Aren't we, Scooter? We gonna color the next airplane. Aren't we Scooter? Like the one that's not colored.

SCOOTER: (Looking at Figure 3–1, Page 3) There now . . . that's a Army thing. There! You like it!?

CHANELL: Umhum. Drop some bombs?

SCOOTER: Not um!

CHANELL: The army helicopters do drop bombs. They shoot.

SCOOTER: But this is an airplane. Hey look! Know how it does it? Look at it. It goes boom! Boom!

CHANELL: No. There's suppose to be a good guy.

SCOOTER: They can go like this. They can go rummmmm boooom.

CHANELL: Scooter! Let's make a good guy.

SCOOTER: This is a good guy.

CHANELL: No! That's a good airplane.

SCOOTER: Not ummm! That's a good guy. This is what a good guy is. He's right there, and then goes in the door. Now, on this one we gonna say, "I do not like to blow up."

CHANELL: Throw up?

SCOOTER: Blow up!

CHANELL: I do not like to blow up. . . . Throw up! (laughter)

SCOOTER: No, I said blow up. You could get sick by a bomb. Some bombs are bad. They make you sick. Right?

CHANELL: Umhum . . .

SCOOTER: They could really . . . They could make you really sick!

CHANELL: But that's what come out of. . . . people come out of airplanes too!

SCOOTER: They do! They are right here. He (points to cockpit) inside there. He inside there. He inside there. Somebody messed up that *r*. It was supposed to be right over here. Now, this is where the man goes. Right in that hole. He jumps up there and goes over there and jumps in there. Or he could go the shortcut way. Hummm to the back, and, see how the back is? That's the shortcut back. No other way back. Then you get in front where you drive. Then you jump right in that hole. And then all the way down into the airplane desk controls.

CHANELL: Oh well! I know what I can write! I got a suggestion. It says, it can say, "I like airplanes that go up in the air." That's one of my suggestions.

SCOOTER: "I do not like to blow up."

CHANELL: Mine gonna be . . . It's gonna be, "I like airplanes that fly up in the sky." (looking at Figure 3–1, Page 3) How do you like that Scooter?

SCOOTER: Ummm. Why don't you write, "I like airplanes to go up in the air. I see them go up in the air."

CHANELL: Wait! I'm gonna write . . . "I like airplanes cause they go up in the air cause we see 'em sometimes."

SCOOTER: That's too much! Too much cause! Too much because . . . because you said because two times and we only need it one time. Like "I like airplanes because they go up in the air!"

CHANELL: "I . . . " (Looking at Figure 3–1, Page 4)

SCOOTER: That was one time.

CHANELL: "Like . . ."

SCOOTER: "Like that?"

CHANELL: "Like . . . air . . . air . . . air . . . air . . ."

SCOOTER: Hey! "I like airplanes." That's okay. We messed up on the "Air . . . *p* . . . I like airplanes."

CHANELL: "I like airplanes. I like airplanes that fly up in the air."

SCOOTER: "I . . . we . . . I . . ." Can't do that. That's not the right word.

CHANELL: How you make the *ar* sound?

SCOOTER: Air . . . *r*. . . . I think . . . *e*. Not like that! "I like . . . I do not like to blow up."

CHANELL: Hey! Maybe we could write our own words!

SCOOTER: We're gonna figure them out by sounding them out.

CHANELL: I'll write, "I like airplanes that fly up in the air."

SCOOTER: (Reading last page, Figure 3–1) THE END!

4

Kareem, Tony, and Amanda

"NOW I JUST THINK IT. I THINK ABOUT WHAT I WRITE"

(Transition Grade 1)

Contributed by Heidi Mills

Kareem, Tony, and Amanda all live and learn together in a transition-first-grade classroom in South Carolina. They have been identified as "at risk" by district criteria although their teacher, Mr. O'Keefe, holds a very different view of them. Because he is a whole language teacher, he sees their potential and builds on their strengths when making curricular decisions. I, too, have become a member of this community of learners by spending one day per week for the past three years as a collaborative teacher-researcher in this classroom. This contextualized vignette represents the actual conversations of several six-year-old children reflecting on reading and writing during the course of classroom events one day in April, 1990. As their young voices come through, we catch glimpses of the things they have come to appreciate about their own growth as language users.

FIRST CLASS GATHERING OF THE DAY: STRATEGY SHARING

MR. O'KEEFE: I would like to share a strategy I noticed Kareem use yesterday during writing time. Kareem wrote me a message. He wrote, "How are you today? I hope you feel fine." (Mr. O'Keefe writes the message on the board.) Of course I wrote him a message back. I wrote, "I like your sweater. It has a *V* on it." (Mr. O'Keefe writes his message under Kareem's.) When Kareem first read it, he came to a word he didn't know. Kareem, tell what you did.

27

KAREEM: I didn't know *sweater* so I skipped it, and when I got to the part that says it has a *V* on it, I knew it was sweater.

MR. O'KEEFE: That was a good strategy. When you come to a word you don't know, sometimes it helps to skip it like Kareem did, to try to make sense by looking at the rest of the sentence, and then just go back.

WRITING WORKSHOP

Tony is writing the daily entry on the class calendar. He decides to write about something on which he is currently working.

TONY: I'm making a book. [I'm macking a book.] (He reads this to Mr. O'Keefe who is also working at this table.)

MR. O'KEEFE: How did you know to write *I'm* like that?

TONY: I just learned that you [Mr. O'Keefe] had an apostrophe in your name, and I already knew how to write *I'm,* and I remembered it started with a capital and then a lower case because it was the beginning of the sentence. I memorized how to write *I'm* from my brother's math book.

MR. O'KEEFE: How did you know how to write *making* [macking]?

TONY: I've seen you put *ck* on the end of words. Then I just wrote the *m* and the *a* and *ing*.

MR. O'KEEFE: How did you know the *ing*?

TONY: You taught me that they go together.

(Another child at the table, Paul, interrupts to read his text to his teacher. As Paul begins reading, Tony glances at his text and comments.)

TONY: Some kids use one letter for a word. See there are some words in there where he [Paul] just put single letters by themselves; I bet a lot of kids write like that when they start writing, even me. (Looking at his teacher) I bet you did too.

AMANDA: Yea, even Kareem.

TONY: No, I don't think Kareem or Stephen did.

MR. O'KEEFE: Do you think they started with whole words?

EVERYONE: (In harmony) Na!

MR. O'KEEFE: How do you think they got started?

TONY: I only know Kareem sounds his words out.

AMANDA: By his brain.

MR. O'KEEFE: What do you mean?

TONY: That's what I sometimes hear Kareem do when he is reading. I can hear him sounding out the letters sometimes when he is reading.

MR. O'KEEFE: There are other things he does too—like that strategy he shared this morning. He just figured out what it meant. He had it make sense.

TONY: Yea, he does that too. When there is a word he doesn't know he goes to a page that it is on. He finds the page, looks for the word and then reads until he sees it in context. (Tony leaves the group to get a book to use as an example.)

REFLECTING ON HOW THE CHILDREN HAVE GROWN AS WRITERS: SMALL GROUP DISCUSSION

Tony and Amanda gather their journals and recently published books to reflect upon how they have changed as writers this year.

TONY: Well, at the beginning of the year, I didn't know how to spell *cat.* I spelled it the best way I could. (He points to an updated version that is spelled conventionally.)

RESEARCHER: How did you know how to spell it like that?

TONY: Because *A* if it's with another vowel says its own name. If there's a vowel at the very back or if two vowels are walking together. I just took one vowel to make it say cat. (looking through his journal, Tony continues) That's a true story. (he reads) "Me and Mr. O'Keefe went into . . ." I can't read my own writing then.

JUSTIN: Read the one about the lion.

(Tony looks through his journal. He doesn't read his lion text but does comment on it.)

TONY: See, I did not know how to spell *lion* until we were going to the zoo, and I heard the word, and I read it the first time on a piece of paper. I kept putting *S's,* and then I remembered that was just for lots of them, so I erased the *S* and that's how I learned to spell lion.

RESEARCHER: Tony, read the piece you are currently working on.

TONY: "One day a squirrel came out. He did not have a mom. And he played with a rabbit but the squirrel jumped and scratched the lion. And the lion left the rabbit and said, 'Do you want any carrots? I will get you some nuts.' The lion busted into the food place the rabbit split the carrots and the rabbit hopped away." (Tony looks up.) I'm still working on the rest of the story.

RESEARCHER: When did you start writing [publishing] stories like that?

TONY: Well, Mr. O'Keefe's the one who started it. We were just writing in our journals. One time we were having gathering [reading Dr. Seuss books] and he said, 'You know we could make our own books like Dr. Seuss did.' That's the way I write now [publish my books].

AMANDA: I have two books [that I am working on] now, and I have one more that I need to publish, it's in a group [co-authored text].

RESEARCHER: Amanda, tell me how you have changed as a writer.

AMANDA: I made lists of names. And another way, I used to write my ABC's, draw pictures and phone numbers. (She looks through her first journal.) When I was in kindergarten and then I came in first grade, I made lots of *L's.* I wasn't trying to figure it out. Now I think it. I just think about what I write. If I don't know what to write, I'll do a survey to think about what I'm gonna write in my journal.

TONY: This is how I used to write *look* [LOK].

AMANDA: I got one question, he needs one more *O.* (Tony inserts another *O.*)

AMANDA: Everyone is working on stories about Teenage Mutant Ninja Turtles now.

FIGURE 4–1   *"Teenage Mutant Ninja Turtles"*

FIGURE 4–2

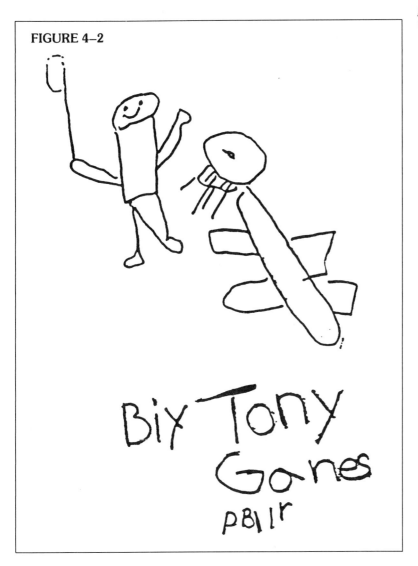

TONY: (His eyes light up as he pulls out a recent Ninja Turtles publication, Figure 4–1. He begins reading.) "Teenage Mutant Ninja (Ninga) Turtles by Tony." Oh see, this is where I messed up. (Pointing to an early published book, Figure 4–2) You can tell the difference in *By*. I used to spell it *BIY,* and now I spell it *By*. I thought it said *B-I!* (He returns to his text [exact replica]).
"Michael Angelo said, 'Shred Head.' Leornarrdo bet up BeeBop.
And Rock Steady got one turtle.
Donatello kicked Rock Steady. He was out!
And Shredder was in the tedrom.
The turtles got in the tedrom and beat up Shredder.
Michael Angelo left to see April.
Then they went back to the sewer.
The end."

(Tony turns the page and reads what his mother wrote about his book on the last page:) "I could read all of his writing. I was proud of Tony's book. He did a great job! Mom's not prejudiced! He drew good pictures. I wish I could have been there as a little mouse to watch him create his book. To see his smiles and listen to what he said."

5

Justin and Dylan

"WE'RE ONE WHEN
WE WORK TOGETHER"

(Grades 1 and 3)

Contributed by Ronald D. Kieffer

Justin and Dylan picked each other to work together at the beginning of the 1989–90 academic school year. They were part of a first and third grade "buddy system" in a literature-based computer magnet school in an Ohio suburb. The primary purpose of this learning arrangement was to explore how to use the computer. As the year progressed, the buddies, both white males from middle class families, not only became quite competent and productive computer users, but moved far beyond a peer tutoring relationship as their growing friendship supported and extended their literacy learning.

Dylan, an eight year old, was a very strong student and used his expertise to challenge Justin's thinking. At the beginning of the school year, Justin, a six year old, was able to read and write. Through a language arts program that emphasized the sharing of an abundance of literature, reading and writing for genuine purposes, and using literature across the curriculum, Justin grew steadily in his experiences with print. In fact, the students in the first grade class as a whole were reading and writing so well that by March, the third and first grade teachers decided that the buddies were ready for greater challenges.

The groups were asked to write together on a topic of their own choosing. Justin and Dylan began to prepare for this project by talking about their interests, jotting down ideas in their own journals, and then generating a topic. Their story, encompassing six meetings in a two-month period from March twelfth to May eleventh, is presented here as a profile of each boy from responses to interview

33

questions, their videotaped dialogue while formulating the story, and the boys' actual texts. The texts are parallel in that they both write the same story simultaneously.

Justin and Dylan's completed story results from a willingness, by both students, to build ideas together. Their face-to-face interactions, sometimes sitting across from each other at one desk and other times sitting side by side on the floor, reveal that children can learn from each other, that writing seems more enjoyable when the burden is shared with others, and that writing develops as an interactive social process involving the exploration of both oral and written language. Justin and Dylan begin their unfolding story by sharing how they came to be partners and how their work evolved. We then pick up their talk after their collaborative story is in progress.

JUSTIN (AGE 6)

We just picked people for friends, and I just saw Dylan. I'm like, "Isn't that the kid from soccer and baseball?" and then I'm like, "Yeah it is" so I go over, and I go, "Hey Dylan you want to be my partner?" and then he goes, "Ok Justin." So that's how we became partners.

We made a list and so we said, "Find out what we agree on—soccer, hockey, indoor soccer, football, go to New Jersey's beach, and Nintendo." But I was gonna make just a regular book and then Dylan said, "Why don't we just make a book about a guy that wants a Lamborghini and then we have to get a get-rich-quick scheme somehow?" He thought up the book. So I just agreed.

He'll go down to the library with me, and I depend on him finding things. First we found Plettenberg [the setting for their story in

---

FIGURE 5–1

Justin   3/12/90   Dylan   3/12/90

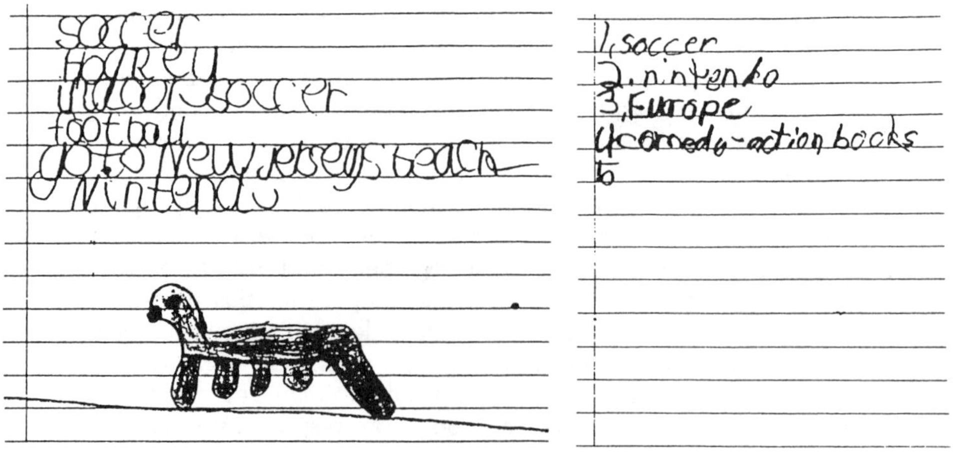

Germany] and then we just had to find a place around it for the rich guy to live. So then we went all around the map. It took us a long time, and then we found Hagen. That's about thirty-five miles—thirty-five minutes away from Plettenberg.

When we write, we both do the same things because he'll just write something down, and whenever he's writing without talking, I'll sort of peek over and look at his paper and see what he's writing down. He does most of the thinking, and I'll just peek over to see what he has down, and then I'll just write it down. I have to write it quick because I'll usually have to erase cause then he'll think of another thing.

He usually thinks of the ideas and then he'll tell me what to write. He's good at the thinking up ideas and then putting the words together. When I write, I think of ideas. Then he'll just tell me or I'll tell him and then almost every single time we agree. It worked good cause we're friends.

He was absent a couple days so I just wrote down in his book. It was a lot harder doing it because I just had to think of something instead of me and Dylan. You get more by two than one and a lot quicker cause two people know things just instead of one. He usually comes up with things, like I wouldn't go down and get an atlas to look up just some cities, so it's a lot more interesting than just one person.

DYLAN (AGE 8)

Well, his big brother and my big brother are on the same select soccer team, and we knew of each other from there. They were also on the same baseball team so we've known each other for a long time.

We had to sit down and think of ideas for what we are going to write about and then write it. We made these lists. I like soccer and Nintendo, I'd like to visit Europe, and I like comedy action books. It's just things we like to write about and talk about. We just talked to each other about it, then we started our writing and coming up with more ideas and writing with each other. It's better working with a partner. It's sort of boring working alone I think. It's really not as exciting because you only have your own ideas instead of other people's. You get more ideas cause you have two people working instead of just one.

Justin thinks of some ideas then I give it the words, then he adds the words too. I think of some ideas to write, then he adds on and then we both write. He's good at getting more ideas adding on to mine. And he gives me the ideas so then I can make them into written form. I put it into words. Like one time about putting the money in [our character's] pocket, I said "stuck it" and he changed it to "stuffed it." So it sounds a little neater when he makes it sound more realistic. We just thought up our ideas together and put it into words. It's like we're one when we work together because his weakness I'm good at and my weakness he's good at so we're like better that way.

Justin needs to use more words than he uses. To instead of just say words over and over, find new words to use. He needs to not goof off as much cause he goofed off sometimes. He started playing with his erasers and stuff like that.

If I was working with somebody else, I wouldn't know them as well as Justin, but since me and Justin are friends for a long time now, we know each other and then it's easier to work together. I just like working with a partner because then you get more ideas. You get better ideas. You get more interest.

We'll have to publish this book first then it'll probably be the end of school by the time we do. We're going to publish. We're going to type it up, go up to the publishing room, pick out some wallpaper for the cover like this, and put one of these spiral things or the rings in it to hold it together, and then once we're done with that we'll work on the illustrations. Each one does their own book, so then we wouldn't have someone take home the book and the other person doesn't.

Dialogue	Justin's Text (age 6)	Dylan's Text (age 8)
5/4/90		
DYLAN: He bought a grappling hook, a pair of		and pair of
JUSTIN: grappling	graflin hook	
DYLAN: black gloves I think. Yeah black gloves. He bought a grappling hook, a pair—		
JUSTIN: and	and	
DYLAN: and pair of black gloves. . . . gloves. . . . and a ski mask . . . . Ok from there, there, there	a pair of black

gloves and a ski mask. | black gloves and a ski mask. From there |
JUSTIN: From there there?	From their	
DYLAN: From there, he went		he went
JUSTIN: went	he went	
DYLAN: went to the . . . mansion. . . . . in	to the manchin	to the mansion in
JUSTIN: Hagen		
DYLAN: mansion in Hagen		Hagen.
JUSTIN: Hagen.	in Hagen.	
DYLAN: Ok here we go. . . . . Um, what else, um.		
JUSTIN: He went to the back where the—		
DYLAN: When he got to the mansion—		

FIGURE 5–2

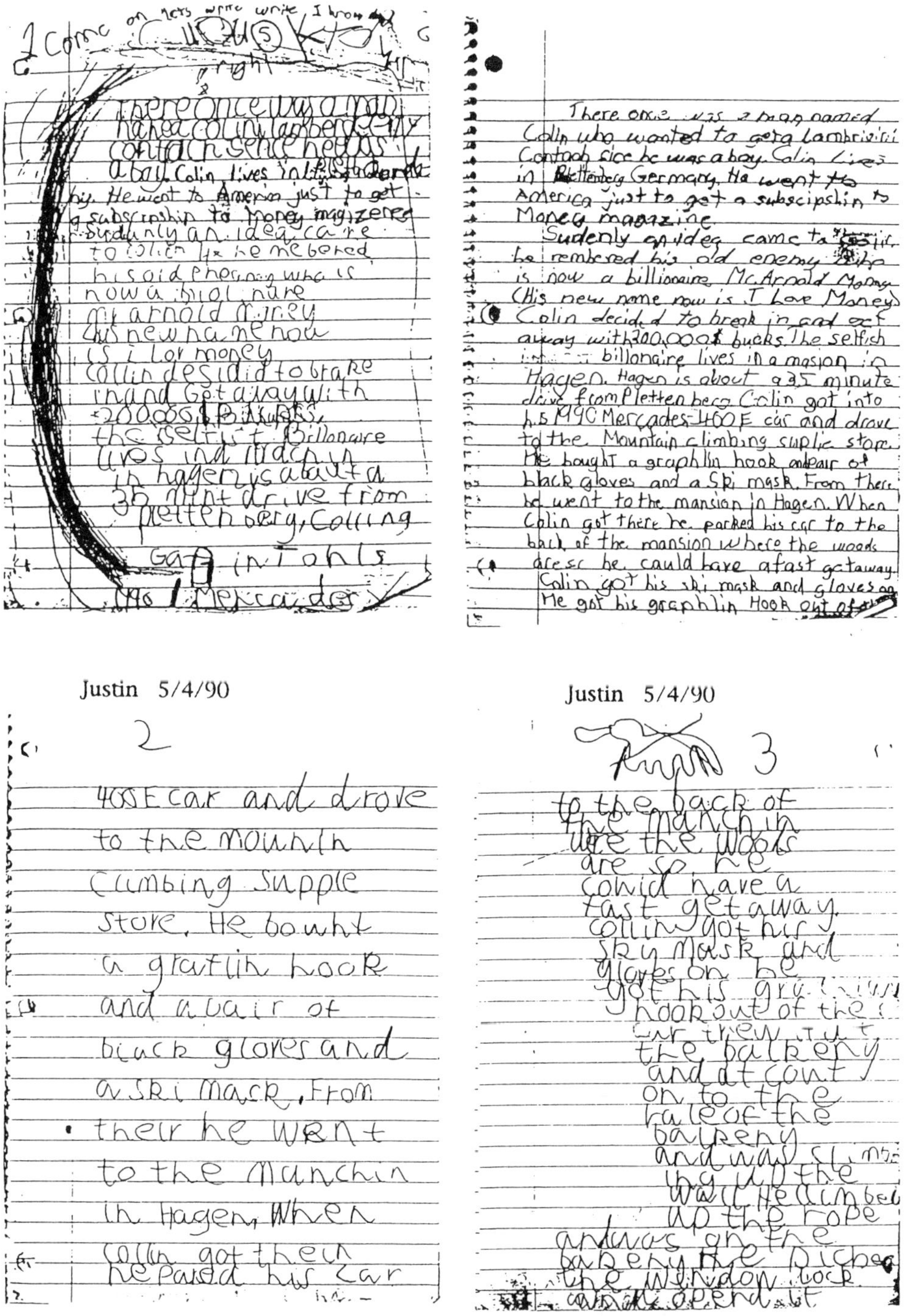

Justin 5/4/90

1 Come on lets write write I know
right

There once was a man named Colin lamberkenny contach sence he was a boy. Colin lives in Plettenberg Germany. He went to America just to get a subscripshin to money magizene. Sudenly an idea came to Colin. He remebered his old enemy who is now a billionaire Mr arnold money. His new name now is I Lov money. Collin desidid to brake in and get away with 200000 bucks. the selfish Billonare lives in a manchin in hagen. hagen is about a 35 minit drive from plettenberg. Colling got into his 1990 Mercades

Dylan 5/4/90

There once was a man named Colin who wanted to get a Lamborghini Contach sice he was a boy. Colin lives in Plettenberg Germany. He went to America just to get a subscipshin to Money magazine.

Sudenly an idea came to Colin. he rembered his old enemy who is now a billionaire Mr Arnold Money (His new name now is I Love Money) Colin decided to break in and get away with 300,000 bucks. The selfish billonaire lives in a masion in Hagen. Hagen is about a 35 minute drive from Plettenberg. Colin got into his 1990 Mercades 400E car and drove to the Mountain climbing suplie store. He bought a graphlin hook and pair of black gloves and a Ski mask. From there he went to the mansion in Hagen. When Colin got there he parked his car to the back of the mansion where the woods are so he could have a fast getaway. Colin got his ski mask and gloves on. He got his graphlin Hook out of the

Justin 5/4/90

2

400E car and drove to the mountin climbing supple store. He bouht a graflin hook and a pair of black gloves and a ski mask. From their he went to the manchin in Hagen. When Collin got their he parked his car

Justin 5/4/90

3

to the back of the manchin were the wools are so he could have a fast getaway. Collin got his sky mask and gloves on. he got his grapling hook out of the car threw it to the balkeny and it cont on to the rale of the balkeny and was climbing up the wall. He climbed up the rope and was on the balkeny. He picked the window lock and opend it

Dialogue	Justin's Text (age 6)	Dylan's Text (age 8)
JUSTIN: He shut off the alarm or something like that.		
DYLAN: he parked to the back where the woods were so he could have a fast get away.		
JUSTIN: What?		
DYLAN: OK when . . . Collin. . . . when Collin got there . . . when Collin got there, he parked	When Collin	When Collin got there he parked
JUSTIN: When Collin got there, he parked	got	
DYLAN: . . . . .his car. . . .	their	his car
JUSTIN: Wait! What do you have?		
DYLAN: When Collin got there he parked his car . . . to the back of the house.	he parked his car	to the back of
JUSTIN: Now what?		
DYLAN: car to the back of the mansion.		the mansion
JUSTIN: to the	to the	
DYLAN: back of the mansion . . . . . . I think where the woods are.		where the woods are
JUSTIN: back . . . of . . . the . . . mansion . . . What did you write of the mansion?	back of the manchin	
DYLAN: When Collin got there, he parked his car to the back of the mansion where the woods are so		
JUSTIN: where	were	
DYLAN: so		so
JUSTIN: the	the	
DYLAN: so he could get a fast get-away.		he could
JUSTIN: woods	woods	
DYLAN: have a fast get-away.		have a
JUSTIN: are . . . so he . . could . . have	are so he	
DYLAN: so he could have fast get-away.	could have a	fast getaway.
JUSTIN: fast	fast get away.	

Dialogue	Justin's Text (age 6)	Dylan's Text (age 8)
DYLAN: OK so he could have a fast get-away. You got with me?		
JUSTIN: Uh huh.		
DYLAN: Collin . . got . .		Colin got
JUSTIN: Collin	Collin	
DYLAN: his		his
JUSTIN: got . . his . . his what?	got his	
DYLAN: ski mask and gloves on		ski mask and
JUSTIN: ski . . mask . . . . black gloves on?	sky mask	
DYLAN: Yeah or just gloves . . on.		gloves on.
JUSTIN: and . . . . . . on . . . . . . What's that say?	and gloves on	
DYLAN: Collin got his ski mask and gloves on. He got his grappling . . . hook . . . out of the car	he got	He got his graphlin Hook out of the car

---

FIGURE 5–3

Justin 5/4/90

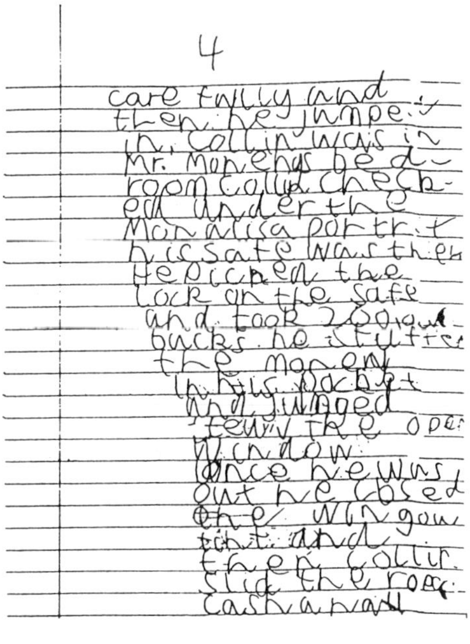

Dylan 5/4/90

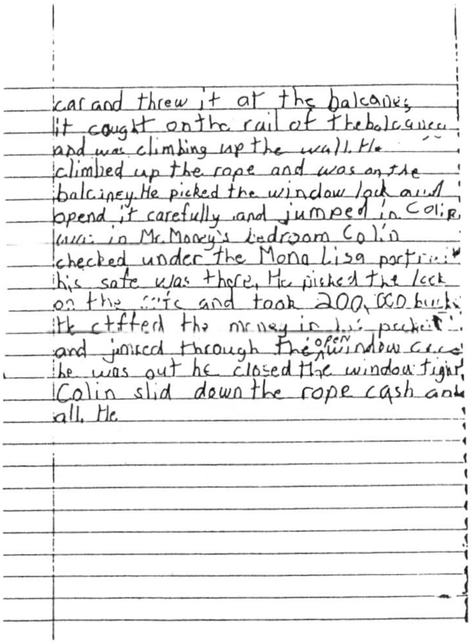

Dialogue	Justin's Text (age 6)	Dylan's Text (age 8)
JUSTIN: his	his grathlan hook	
DYLAN: out of the car		
JUSTIN: out . . of . . the . . car	out of the car	
DYLAN: and threw it . . .		and
JUSTIN: What?		
DYLAN: threw . . it . . . at the balcony.	trew it	threw it at the bal-caney
JUSTIN: the. . . . bal . . . co . . . ny. . . . next?	at the balkeny	
DYLAN: threw it at the balcony . . . . . It caught on and he was climbing up the wall. . . . it caught on to the wall		it caught
JUSTIN: caught on to the balcony?		
DYLAN: caught on to the rail I guess	and it cout	on the rail
JUSTIN: on . . to	on to	
DYLAN: on the rail	the rale	
JUSTIN: on to . . rail		
DYLAN: when he threw it at the balcony, it caught on the rail of the balcony		
JUSTIN: it caught on the rail		
DYLAN: of the bal-cony	of the balkeny	of the balcaney
JUSTIN: period		
DYLAN: and was climbing up the wall and then period	and was	and was climbing up the wall.
JUSTIN: climbing . . up . . the . . wall.	climbing up the wall.	
DYLAN: He was climbing up the wall, he was climbing up the wall		
JUSTIN: Now what? He..he climbed up the rope and got on the roof—		
DYLAN: got on the bal-cony		
JUSTIN: yeah and he got on the balcony and—		
DYLAN: picked the lock		

Dialogue	Justin's Text (age 6)	Dylan's Text (age 8)
JUSTIN: and like picked the lock on the window.		
DYLAN: and jumped in.		
JUSTIN: and jumped in and stole the money and like the safe and jumped out and slid down the rope.		
DYLAN: No he had to open the safe, he has to open the safe first. (Justin is drawing an animal on the top of his page.) on . . balcony. What are you drawing?		He climbed up the rope and was on the balcaney.
JUSTIN: What do you think it could be?		
DYLAN: Half dog half person		
JUSTIN: Half dog half person (laughs)		
DYLAN: Come on we got to write. (Dylan draws a line through his picture. Justin stops him by grabbing his arm. They continue.)		
DYLAN: He	He	
JUSTIN: climbed	climbed	
DYLAN: climbed . . up . . the . . rope	up the rope	
JUSTIN: We already put that.		
DYLAN: climbed up the rope . . . all it does, it said he was climbing up the rope, climbed up the rope and he was on the balcony.		
JUSTIN: and . . was . . on	and was on the	
DYLAN: the balcony		
JUSTIN: Now what and he was on the—		
DYLAN: on the balcony . . . . . on the balcony	bakeny	
JUSTIN: Now what?		He picked
DYLAN: He picked. . . .		
JUSTIN: picked. . . .	He picked	

Dialogue	Justin's Text (age 6)	Dylan's Text (age 8)
DYLAN: picked the, he picked the lock		
JUSTIN: He picked the window lock		
DYLAN: Yeah the window lock. . . .		the window lock
JUSTIN: the . . win . . dow . . lock	the window lock	
DYLAN: He picked the window lock . . . . and jumped in		
JUSTIN: and jumped in?		
DYLAN: No he's got to open it first (both laugh)		
JUSTIN: He can pick the lock		
DYLAN: He picked the lock and opened it carefully . . . it . . carefully . . . and opened it carefully and then he jumped in (laughs) he . . jumped in	and opend it	and opend it carefully and jumped in.
JUSTIN: care . . fully . . then	carefully and then	
DYLAN: he jumped in.		
JUSTIN: he . . jumped	he jumped	
DYLAN: jumped in. He opened it carefully and jumped in		
JUSTIN: in	in.	
DYLAN: and jumped in. Ok, he opened it carefully and jumped in . . . he was in Mr. Money's bedroom.		
JUSTIN: He was in Mr. Monday—		
DYLAN: Money's		
JUSTIN: Mr. Money's bedroom		
DYLAN: Collin was in. . . .		Colin
JUSTIN: was	Collin was	
DYLAN: Collin was		
JUSTIN: in		
DYLAN: was . . in		was in
JUSTIN: was in Mr.	in Mr.	
DYLAN: Mr . . . Mr. Money's		Mr Money's

Dialogue	Justin's Text (age 6)	Dylan's Text (age 8)
JUSTIN: Money's	Monenys	
DYLAN: Collin was in Mr. Money's bedroom		
JUSTIN: bedroom		
DYLAN: bedroom . . .		bedroom
JUSTIN: bed . . room	bedroom	
DYLAN: in his bedroom. Want to have him having the picture of Mona Lisa cause that's the most expensive picture in the world?		
JUSTIN: Ok		
DYLAN: and the safe was under it . . . Collin . . . checked. . . . Collin checked		Collin checked
JUSTIN: checked	Collin checked	
DYLAN: under . . . the Mona Lisa. I'll tell you how to spell that "M.O.N.A.L.I.S.A" Mona Lisa portrait, Mona Lisa portriat, his safe was there. . . . was there	under the Mona Lisa portrit his safe was thier.	under the Mona Lisa portruit his safe was there
JUSTIN: was. . . . there		
DYLAN: He opened–		
JUSTIN: He picked the lock on the safe and		
DYLAN: It took about an hour.		
JUSTIN: He'd catch him in an hour.		
DYLAN: Ok the safe was there period.		He picked the lock
JUSTIN: Now what?		on the safe
DYLAN: He picked the lock of the safe.	He picked the lock on the safe	
JUSTIN: the . . . lock . . on . . . . . the . . safe . . .		
DYLAN: and took		and took
JUSTIN: about 45 minutes		
DYLAN: no he picked the lock, the lock on the safe and took—		
JUSTIN: 20 minutes		
DYLAN: No let's just say and took 200,000 dollars.		200,000 bucks.

Dialogue	Justin's Text (age 6)	Dylan's Text (age 8)
JUSTIN: Wait, stop. How much did he plan to take?		
DYLAN: 200,000 I think (turns back some pages) yeah 200,000	and took 200,000 bucks.	
JUSTIN: bucks. . . . Want to put that was all of it?		
DYLAN: No that was just some of it. He's got like a billion more. OK . . . He jumped through the window and landed on his butt (laughs). . . . . . OK . . . he stuck the cash		He
JUSTIN: What?		
DYLAN: He stuck the cash . .		
JUSTIN: in his pocket		
DYLAN: yeah . . he stuck—		
JUSTIN: Want to put he stuffed?		
DYLAN: Yeah, stuffed, that's better. . . . that sounds better . . He stuffed . . the money	he stuffed the money	stuffed the money
JUSTIN: the . . money . . stuffed the money		
DYLAN: in his pocket?		
JUSTIN: Uh huh. He stuffed the money in . . his	in his pocket	in his pocket
DYLAN: and jumped		and jumped
JUSTIN: and	and	
DYLAN: jumped . . . through		through
JUSTIN: jumped	jumped	
DYLAN: and jumped through the window and closed it tightly		the window
JUSTIN: through . . the	tew the	
DYLAN: through the window. . . . .Once he was out . . . out		once he was out
JUSTIN: Wait threw, shouldn't it be and		

Dialogue	Justin's Text (age 6)	Dylan's Text (age 8)
jumped out the window?		
DYLAN: and jumped through the window		
JUSTIN: through it. It sounds like he jumped through the glass		
DYLAN: Fine through the . . . open		(adds "open")
JUSTIN: the open	open	
DYLAN: Once he was out		
JUSTIN: wind . . ow . . Now what did you put?	window	
DYLAN: Once he was out he closed the window. . . . closed . . the window		he closed the window
JUSTIN: Once . . was . . out he closed the window tight	Once he was out he	
DYLAN: tight . . tightly or tight . .		tight
JUSTIN: tight closed . . . the. . . . . wind . . ow . . tight	closed the wingow tiht	
DYLAN: Collin slid down . . . slid . . down the rope		Colin slid down the rope
JUSTIN: and slid down the rope.		
DYLAN: No just put a period put a period and then Collin slid down..the rope cash and all . . . slid down the rope	(adds a period ".")	
JUSTIN: Collin . . .	Collin	
DYLAN: cash		cash and all.
JUSTIN: slid	slid	
DYLAN: He slid, Collin slid down the rope cash and all		
JUSTIN: the . . . rope	the rope	
DYLAN: cash and all		
JUSTIN: and . . . all. Are we done? . . and he went out to buy a Lamborghini.	cash an all	

FIGURE 5–4

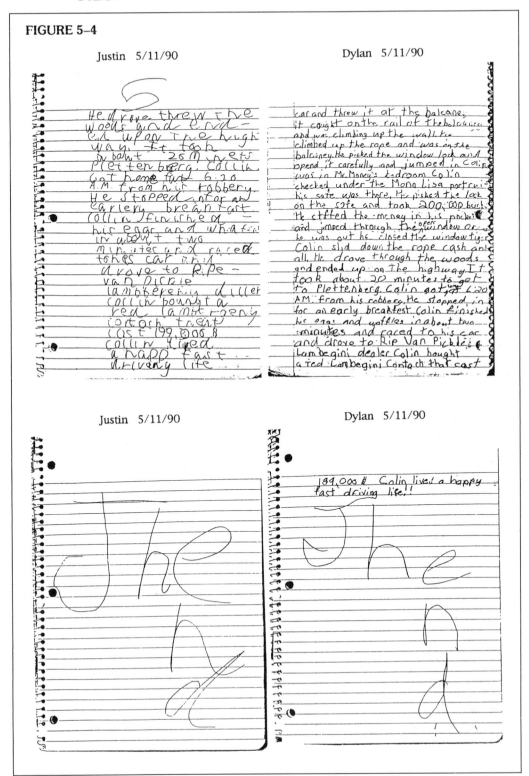

Dialogue	Justin's Text (age 6)	Dylan's Text (age 8)
DYLAN: No . . . . . . Um. He's got to jump. He jumped in (The teacher asks the first graders to line up)		He

5/11/90

Dialogue	Justin's Text (age 6)	Dylan's Text (age 8)
DYLAN: Ok he what?		
JUSTIN: He		
DYLAN: He drove . . He . . drove . . through the woods . . . through the woods . . . Oops I put wads (laughs). . . . through the woods and ended up . . ended . . up . . . and ended up on the high-way.	He drove threw the woods and ended	drove through the wads (erases and writes "woods") and ended up on the highway.
JUSTIN: ended . . up . . on . . the . . high . . way.	up on the high-way.	
DYLAN: highway . . . . . . and ended up on the highway.		
JUSTIN: Now what?		
DYLAN: It took about 25 minutes to get back to Plettenberg. It took about 20 minutes. . . . . about 20	It took about 20 minets	It took about 20 minutes to get to
JUSTIN: What are you doing?		
DYLAN: Thinking how to spell Plettenberg, to get to Pletten-berg. Now we've got to talk about how he gets his Lamborghini.	Plettenburg.	Plettenberg.
JUSTIN: Did I spell this right?		
DYLAN: Yeah, no that's an "e" not a "u". . . . Now what can we talk about? How he gets his Lamborghini. Then when we're fin-ished, we can work on publishing.	(writes an "e" over the "u" in Plettenburg making it Plettenberg)	

Dialogue	Justin's Text (age 6)	Dylan's Text (age 8)
JUSTIN: Then he went out about 26 miles to go get a Lamborghini.		
DYLAN: What could the dealer be called? (laughs) Ok Collin got back to his house at—		Colin got at
JUSTIN: 6:20		
DYLAN: Yeah 6:20 . . . 6:20 A.M. . . . . from his robbery.		6:20 A.M. from his robbery.
JUSTIN: You have "Collin to Plettenberg" Colin got at—	Collin	
DYLAN: Collin got, Collin got home at. I'll put a little arrow up there.		(adds "home")
JUSTIN: got . . home	Got	
DYLAN: at 6:20 A.M. his robbery.		
JUSTIN: Collin . . got . . home	home	
DYLAN: at 6:20 A.M.		
JUSTIN: at	at	
DYLAN: 6:20 A.M. . . . . from his robbery from his robbery. He stopped in for an early breakfast . . for . . an	6:20 A.M. from his robbery. He stopped in for an	He stopped in for an
JUSTIN: "an" or "a".?	an	
DYLAN: an early . . How do you spell early? "ea" or "er"?		
JUSTIN: "ea"		
DYLAN: e . . a . . r . . l . . y . . . for an early breakfast . . . . . . for an early breakfast period. Collin finished his eggs and a waffle in about 2 seconds (laughs)	earlery breakfast.	early breakfast.
JUSTIN: Like Collin finished—		
DYLAN: Collin . .		Colin
JUSTIN: his	Collin	
DYLAN: finished . . his eggs and waffles	finished	finished
JUSTIN: his	his	
DYLAN: his . . eggs		his eggs
JUSTIN: eggs	egg	

Dialogue	Justin's Text (age 6)	Dylan's Text (age 8)
DYLAN: and . . waf-fles. . . . . in . . about . . 2 seconds	and	and waffles in about two seconds
JUSTIN: Don't put 2 seconds	whaffal	
DYLAN: I'll put minutes. . . . In about 2 minutes and		(erases "seconds" and puts "minutes")
JUSTIN: in about	in about	
DYLAN: raced		and raced to
JUSTIN: two minutes	two minutes	
DYLAN: raced to his car . . . car. . . . .and drove . . to . . somebody Lamborghini dealer. Get a funny name.		his car and drove to
JUSTIN: Richard . . Dick		
DYLAN: Yeah Dick Van (both laugh)		
JUSTIN: Yeah		
DYLAN: Rip Van Dinkle (both laugh)		
JUSTIN: Yeah		
DYLAN: Rip Van Dinkle. . . .		
JUSTIN: Dick.		
DYLAN: Rip (laughs)		
JUSTIN: Dick.		
DYLAN: No (laughs) Rip . . Van (a boy seated near Justin and Dylan says "pickle") pickle. Rip Van Pickle (laughs)		Rip Van
JUSTIN: pickle?		Pickle
DYLAN: Pickle		
JUSTIN: Rip Van		
DYLAN: Van		
JUSTIN: Hickle		
DYLAN: No Pickle (laughs) . . . Lamborghini dealer. Come on. Will you write that down? Come on.		
JUSTIN: I don't know what—		
DYLAN: Raced to his car and drove to Rip Van Pickle Lamborghini dealer		
JUSTIN: to . . his . . car	raced to hes car	

Dialogue	Justin's Text (age 6)	Dylan's Text (age 8)
DYLAN: and raced	(puts an "i" over the	
JUSTIN: What? . . I already put that. Now what?	"e" to make "his")	
DYLAN: and drove, raced to his car and drove to		
JUSTIN: and . . drove . . to	and drove to	
DYLAN: to Rip Van Pickles (both laughs)		
JUSTIN: Rip. . . . Van	Ripe van	
DYLAN: Lamborghini dealer		
JUSTIN: pickles		
DYLAN: No just Pickle		
JUSTIN: pick . . .	pickle	
DYLAN: Pickle..drove to Rip Van Pickle Lamborghini dealer . . . Lam . . . bor . . . ghini dealer		Lambegini dealer
JUSTIN: Lam . . bor . . ghini	Lambbereny	
DYLAN: Collin . . bought		Colin bought
JUSTIN: dealer . . . Collin	diller Collin	
DYLAN: a . . red . .		a red
JUSTIN: bought	bouhgt	
DYLAN: Collin bought a red Lamborghini Lamborghini Contach		Lambegini Contach
JUSTIN: Lam . . bor . . ghini	a red Lambergeny	
DYLAN: Contach car that cost . . that cost . . Contach is spelled C . . o . . t . . a . . c . . h . .	contosh	that cost
JUSTIN: Contach		
DYLAN: Contach that cost 100,000.		
JUSTIN: Yeah!		
DYLAN: No! More than. . . . 199,000.		
JUSTIN: Yeah yeah!		
DYLAN: Oops! One thous . . one hundred not . . one nine nine comma zero zero zero and that's all	theat cost	199,000 $.
JUSTIN: One nine nine zero zero.	199,000	

Dialogue	Justin's Text (age 6)	Dylan's Text (age 8)
DYLAN: Zero zero three zeros . . That's 199,000 dollars and put the dollar sign.		
JUSTIN: bucks	$	
DYLAN: Collin lived a happy		
JUSTIN: life		
DYLAN: fast drawing, fast driving life.		
JUSTIN: Yeah "The end".		
DYLAN: But you don't..		
JUSTIN: Collin	Collin	Colin
DYLAN: lived a . . . fast		lived
JUSTIN: lived . . a . . a what?	lived a	
DYLAN: no a happy . . .		a happy
JUSTIN: happy	happy	
DYLAN: fast driving life (laughs)		fast driving
JUSTIN: fast . . driving . . life.	fast driveng (puts an	
DYLAN: life	"i" over the "e")	life!!
JUSTIN: life. . . . . I've got five pages and you've got three	life	

6

Shannon

"IF YOU WANT TO BE
A WRITER, YOU GOT TO READ"

(Grades 1 and 3)

Contributed by Betty Shockley & JoBeth Allen

When we first met Shannon, she was entering Betty's first grade, having repeated both kindergarten and now first grade. Her neediness was her most striking feature. She had a soft, high-pitched, pleading, younger-than-her-eight-years kind of voice: "Do I look good, Ms. Shockley? Tell me I look good. I don't look good. I do look good?" Helping Shannon believe in herself was a constant struggle, but nobody worked harder at learning than she did.

Betty's daily reading and writing workshops provided a new and natural base for learning that kept Shannon's interest high and offered her a chance to rehearse old and new strategies, with friends who helped her and without ridicule or a basal label. In interviews with JoBeth, a university researcher working in the school, she said that "real" practice was what she needed, and really practice is what she did. She wrote "almost all the time at home" and at school. Her own writing was her favorite thing to read and re-read. But each word was a struggle for her. Words caused her to "stagger," as a reader and as a writer.

At the end of the year, Shannon was promoted to third grade. During each third-grade interview with JoBeth, Shannon reflected back to the things she had done in first grade with Betty, whose significance as a model for literacy increased as the stability of Shannon's new situation decreased. First, her third grade teacher, Ms. Willis, became ill, and Shannon suffered the instability of having ten substitute teachers, each with different structures for reading and writing instruction. She also began receiving services for a learning disability and was often out of the room when the class wrote. Opportunities for the vital writing/reading connection became less dependable, and by the end of the year Shannon rarely wrote.

What follows is Shannon's talk, in response to quarterly literacy interviews, as we conversed through first grade and the following year in third grade.

FIRST GRADE: SEPTEMBER

I'm learning how to read and draw good, and how to draw hearts, and get better doing work, and about Mondays. Ms. Shockley, she get a book and sometimes she read them. And we learning to take care of Hunan [a new student in the class]. I like this class better than last year's class. I like writing really. That's my best. And doing work, but not that hard.

I might want to learn about being a police, and a singer, and a body builder, but I might change my mind about being a body builder. Ms. Shockley, she help me, and other kids help. I help other kids spell. I help Summer with her words. I help her see it and spell it.

When I grow up, I'll need a tablet. I'll save some paper—and pencils—and read about the caterpillar, and the gingerbread man, and Curious George. I'll have to read the Driver's License book—my mama did.

I'm learning how to spell hard words like "flower." I already know "help." Want me to spell it? *H*—*e*—right?—*l*—I learned it—oh,—*p* that's the last one! Ms. Shockley teach me. She a good teacher. Sometimes I look on her paper, how she spell things. I know "to"—*t o*. Want me to spell all the words I know? *a n d, a, i s, h e l p, e m*—oh, "me"—*me*. I'd like to spell the biggest word. I'd like to do a program, *The Fox Went Out On A Chilly Night*. I want to learn to spell surprise—*s e r i*—two *i*'s? I'm learning better from Ms. Shockley. I know how to spell "bat" and "sat" and I put them in my backpack to take home. See. I'm learning a lot from Ms. Shockley. Wallace, he know a lot of words. I forgot some words and he say, "You can get that!" He know how to spell some big words and my mom know how to spell "surprise party" and I put it in my backpack and look it up and read it over. I'll need to write in cursive when I be grown up but I don't know, and when I be happy . . . I wish we never get old so we can have a long, long time.

FIRST GRADE: DECEMBER

In reading, I'm learning how to spell "dinosaur" and "Christmas." It's fun and sometimes I don't know the words, but I try to spell. I'm doing good in reading, but I don't do no bad words. Ms. Shockley, Ms. Elder [teaching aid], and Jeremiah, and Brenda help me. Me and Ms. Elder read almost a whole story in one day. Sometimes I be staggering over the words, and Ms. Elder let me tell her and she say it for me and tell me to read. We read a story about a apple: "No I won't turn red if I eat the apple!" You know Ms. Shockley Teacher Of The Year? I hope all the teachers in here get Teacher Of The Year!

I want to learn how to spell "surprise." It's *s u r p r i u e s,* or something like that. Next I'm gonna learn—you know that purple book? [*Trumpets,* 3rd basal preprimer] I learned "Go To Bed Jed" in that book. You learn if you just read what you know and ask Ms. Shockley the new words, and sometimes I figure them out, like in *Parades* [1st primer]. I want to read *Parades* when I grow up.

I'm trying to learn to spell "Ms. Shockley." I looked how she spelled it. Delia and Ms. Shockley and Gavin and Jeremiah and Missy and Colin helps me. At my table, Missy and Karen helps. Next I'll learn "surprise," that's a long word. When I grow up, I write: "I be a police." And I'll write everything I'm doing.

FIRST GRADE: APRIL

I'm learning to put question words and periods, and new words. And the words I don't know Ms. Shockley helps, and we might sound it out. I learn from Ms. Shockley and friends and books. Some of the words I already know. Sometimes we skip on or sometimes we sound them out or Ms. Shockley helps us. Ms. Elder [aide] and Ms. McCrobie [student teacher] and Jeremiah, Brenda, and Gavin and sometimes Trisha help.

I want to read big books like Ms. Shockley be reading, that you go and borrow, that she reading to herself, and *The Night of the Twister* [chapter book Betty read to the class]. I'll learn if I pay attention, listen to Ms. Shockley and Ms. Elder or Brenda or Jeremiah. I ask words; Trisha sometimes don't know. When I grow up like I read my own books and other folks' books, my friends' books, and some Ms. Shockley has.

In writing, I'm learning songs and how to write poems because Gavin write one and I keep on asking him to help. I found "rain," and he helped me write "rainbows." He said, "It's just a little story," when I asked him how to write a poem. I still need to learn where to put question marks and how to write big words. I don't know how to spell "dinosaur." When I grow up, I'll need all of my books [the ones she wrote], poems and stories and songs, because I want them to come out with good illustrators, and I'm gonna publish them in New York!

FIRST GRADE: JUNE

I'm learning to read new words and read *The Doorbell Rang.* I learned it last night because Ms. Shockley gave me the book to keep, and I read to my sister with no help while she was in bed. But when I first didn't know, my sister and my mother helped. I want to read long words and how to spell them. I'll learn if I listen to the teacher when she be spelling some words on the board and on paper. When I grow up, I read monkey books [her chosen research topic]. I can be president of the whole wide world! I'll read monkey books and a president book!

I'm learning to write gooder. You should look in my writing journal. I been practicing. I write almost all the time at home. I want to write in cursive. I can learn by a teacher if she help me. I'm gonna write monkey stories or stories like a president.

THIRD GRADE: OCTOBER (PROMOTED DIRECTLY FROM FIRST TO THIRD)

I read big words. Ms. Willis [her third grade teacher, who resigns in early February, due to illness] and Ms. Shockley reading books and I read and they tell it when I don't know a word. I like to learn to read more gooder, read more words. I'll learn if I read—*read*. Ms. Shockley and Ms. Willis and my sister, my eleven-year-old or my older sister, will help.

When I grow up I want to read my own stories, ones I write when I was a kid, and some new ones. My job will be to read stories and write your own. If you want to be a writer, you got to read stories and poems.

I want to write in cursive, a cursive *s* and *d* and *h* and *t*. Ms. Willis give us a tracing sheet. I want to write little and not leave out words and capital letters, and I like to write in cursive more gooder. You got to listen, and if you get more work, you learn more.

I want to learn how to be rich when I grow up. I'll be rich and get shoes everyday. I'll work, make a song, maybe a lot of songs.

THIRD GRADE: JANUARY

I'm learning to read good because I read. Ms. Shockley teach me. At home I read a bear story, and a girl and a fox, and *The Doorbell Rang;* that was my favorite story, but I lost the book. I want to learn to read in cursive next. I'll learn if I try to read in cursive—I can read that! (reads interview sentence JoBeth has written) When I grow up, I'll read everything.

I can't say it, but in writing I'm learning to put periods at the end of the sentence or question marks and punctu—exclamation marks. If you're asking a question, you put a question mark; if you're asking a punctuation—I don't know what you put. I'm learning it by my teacher. I don't know how. My mama, she told me, I was just trying to get it right, and I said, "When you asking a question you put a question mark, and when you ain't asking a questions you put a period?" And she said, "Right."

I want to learn to write in cursive. I don't know how I'll learn it—yea—my teacher. She give us a cursive handsheet, but that won't do it because you'll forget. Practice is a better way.

THIRD GRADE: JUNE

I'm learning to read more books like this one. (picks up book she just read) I don't know how I'm learning it. Ms. Shockley helped me. Words I don't know she'll tell me, like at the end she'll tell me to go back to a page, like *The Doorbell Rang,* and I got used to it. I want to learn to read in cursive. I don't know how I'll learn it. When I grow up, I'll read my books and be a police, and a teacher, and a singer, and the President of the United States. I'll help the poor, and the Africans, and I'll bring them to America and buy anything they want.

I don't know about writing. I hardly write any. I'd like to write in cursive but I don't know how to learn it. I like to write now at home some.

7

Emily

"THERE'S NOTHING I LIKE BETTER THAN WRITING"

(Grade 2)

Contributed by Bonnie Cramond

My daughter Emily was a verbal child from the start. As a new-born she watched a speaker's lips intently and moved her own. Speech came early, so it seemed like a natural extension when she began to write. Like most children, her first stories were pictures on pages with oral explanations. Sometimes there were scratch marks for words. My husband and I began to record the stories that she told on the pages with the pictures in order to keep them. By the time she was three, she began to enlist the aid of any adult that she could to take dictation as she paced back and forth composing her stories. Parents, babysitters, teachers, aids, grandparents, and even an older cousin helped document the flood of stories Emily created. An avid consumer of books on tape, her stories often contained vocabulary and other elements from the many books she had "read."

Interviewed in second grade, Emily has long since escaped the bounds of books on tape and dictated stories. She is now an independent reader and prolific writer. A tall seven-year-old, with short straight brown hair and large dark eyes, Emily was in turn quite animated and reflective when we taped this series of interviews at home. Perhaps because we had set aside times when our conversations were not to be disturbed, or because the tape recorder and my demeanor as an interviewer set the tone, Emily told me things about her writing process and motivation that I might never have known through our normal daily interactions.

There's nothing I like better than writing! I like it because it's nice to do, and I just like it. I like plays and doing them—acting and writing the plays.

Making up your own story is like making a movie, and you get to decide exactly how it's done. I like making the pictures a lot, too. Some stories have pictures, but some I leave plain so it will look like a chapter book. The chapter books I've written had different stories in them. One was ABC's, another was about a cat, and all that stuff. My favorite story is the one that I'm working on right now—*Family Tales*. It has all these different stories that children, and grown-ups, and the whole family will like.

I also like to write letters, thank you notes, and happy birthday notes, and stuff like that. I write jokes, songs, maps, games, and phone numbers. I like to write homework. I write poems, and I'm working on a play now. It's in my *Family Tales* book. It's called "The Starling." This starling is called a starling because it's a baby star. I wrote a report about Martin Luther King, Jr., but I needed a book to read about him first. I just did that because I wanted to do it, not for school.

When I have an idea, I don't decide to do a song or play or story or something. It just turns out that way. I wrote a song about Martin Luther King because I can't find a poem about him. It always turns out to be a song. I don't really know, it just happens. It pops out that way. A poem is sort of like a song, cause usually poems rhyme and so do songs. And it puts it all together to make a song. I wrote the Martin Luther King song on Post-it notes so that the verses would stick together, and so I could change the order.

I'd like to keep the song to myself because I think it's not good. I like it myself, but I don't think other people would like it, because . . . I don't know . . . I just think so . . . because, lots of kids in my classroom always tease me about what I do, and I don't think they would like it or anybody else.

I like to write about my life and what happens and about my own characters I make up, like Marshy, a marshmallow. I like to write about animals the most. I think animals are cute and interesting. The things they do are, well, fascinating! Some can jump real far, others can jump real high. I like how they do things. I like them all. I like horses and deers the most. I like the ones that are tall because they kind of do more action sometimes. Sometimes I write about them like real animals; sometimes I write about them like people.

When I don't have anything else to write about, I look around and see what's happening, but if I do have things in my mind that I'd like to write about, then I write about them. Sometimes I can't think of ideas to write about, but usually if we have a problem, my teacher puts some ideas on the board. Or if I'm at home and I don't have anything to do, I try to see what would be kind of interesting, like what's happening around me. I look around and see.

FIGURE 7–1 *"The Buger Eater"*

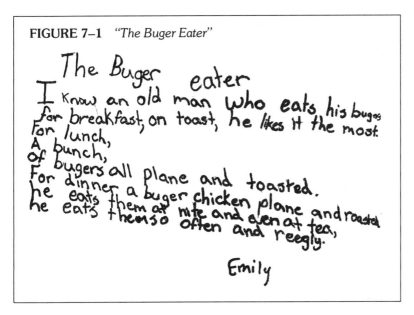

The Buger eater

I know an old man who eats his bugers
for breakfast, on toast, he likes it the most.
For lunch,
A bunch,
of bugers all plane and toasted.
For dinner a buger chicken plane and roasted.
he eats them at nite and even at tea,
he eats them so often and reegly.

Emily

I wrote the poem "The Buger Eater" because my brother Adam was picking his nose and eating his boogers and Dad said, "Adam stop eating your boogers!" (See Figure 1.) It would be more interesting in the poem to be an old man and not a little kid because it's unusual to be an old man, but it's not unusual to be a little four-year-old booger eater. It sounds weird doesn't it? I can't help that, it's just a poem. I don't worry about what people think at all. I don't care what other people say.

Lots of time I'm thinking of things to write, but only when I feel in the mood to do it. When people are talking about my writing it gets me in the mood to write. Like now, talking about it makes me want to write.

I daydream a lot. I think about what's been happening around me and how that feels to me. I write about those things.

I'm a very sensitive person, and I get my feelings hurt easily. It helps me with some sad poems and helps me make stories that have sad endings. If I'm sad I write. I'm going to write a poem about sadness, and I call it "Thunder Dreams." Thunder sounds gloomy, and when it happens, it's very gloomy. That's why I call it "Thunder Dreams."

I don't know how I started writing. I can't remember not writing. Sometimes people help me—my mom, and my teacher, and my dad. But, if my mom and dad didn't help with writing, I would try to keep on writing. It's not that they're encouraging me; it's just that I want to write. If my teacher didn't give me time in school to write, I would just finish up my work and start doing my writing.

When I finish my work at school, I get a book and read or get a paper and write a story. Usually I don't get finished my work. One reason is because I go to two reading books, and another reason is

I'm off in a daze. Besides, we get to write sometimes. Everybody gets to write to somebody, a pen pal. We have a writing folder so we get to write a story for every month. We have writing classes once a month. Each month we have a special writing sheet that we have to write a story, and then copy it, and then put it in there for that month. When I want to write other stories I do, the teacher has paper for us. Every day we have some writing on the board and on Tuesdays or Wednesdays we write journals.

My teachers have helped me write. My first-grade teacher got us to think about what we were writing and to really know what to write and stuff. That makes her interesting. She started out with reading us a story, "If you give a mouse a cookie . . ." Then we kind of made a little summarizing, but in different ways, like I did, "If you give a seal a steak . . ." That was just an example. We did other things. She helped us have confidence in ourselves like helping us know that it's okay if you don't spell words right, but it's just going to be fine, 'cause you're not writing to someone, or anything like that. Just for writing, that's all.

But in kindergarten I didn't really have the time to. All the time we were working on things like art, and stuff like that. I don't know. The kindergarten teacher only one time let us write. I forgot what we wrote. Maybe he thought that we were a little bit too young for writing a lot, so he only let us write our name. I don't really know why. I mean, I'm not the teacher.

If I was the teacher, I would write a lot and let them write as well. And maybe write every day. Maybe like writing letters to other people. My teacher gave us pen pals from Elm Street School, and we write to them every week, but our names would be on the board if she found out that we were sending letters to other people in our class. But I think that what she should do is tell everyone that they can write a letter to someone in the class that they would like to write a letter to.

I write at home more than at school because I have more time. I write the same kinds of things at home, but I write more of it—longer stories and more stories. At school I can't make a thick book. It's only one sheet I can write.

If I didn't have homework, I could have more time to write. If we didn't have to work in school, I'd write stuff. Sometimes I would read, sometimes I would write. Art would be the only work we'd do. I wouldn't do math, no way! Do writers need to know math?

My favorite way to write stories is on a computer because you don't have to go back and make sure that you have capital letters and stuff. Well, sometimes you do, but the computer helps you find out. If I don't like it on the computer I can always change it, but if I write it down, it would take a long time to change. Besides you don't have to go like this [makes writing movement with hand], you just have to go like that [makes single finger movement like punching a key], and then it's finished. So that helps me a lot when I'm making big letters. Sometimes I have problems. I was writing the stories for my book, and I couldn't find out how to make it go to another page. So I quit.

I don't use a computer to write stories at school because we don't have one. I don't think the computer is the reason I write more at home, though. It's just that I have more time. I like to write in the afternoons or at night. I don't write when my tummy hurts, but that doesn't happen much.

I keep my stories in a special folder at school or at home. I read them a lot. When I feel comfortable that I did a good thing, I like people to read it. I do it, and then I read what I did, and see if that makes sense and make sure that people might like it. If I don't like it, I change it or I just say to myself not to save it.

The most important thing is that I like it, but sometimes when I don't like it I think other people won't like it. You have to know what you're going to write about, and you've got to be proud of your writing. Try to make it like you would like it to be, not like other people would say it's to be. If everyone said bad things about something I wrote, I would feel bad. But I would keep it! Because I think it's good and I don't care if other people laugh at it. I would keep it to myself and not tell it to anybody else except for the people I really trust not to laugh.

Sometimes other people show me the things they've written. And they all ask, "Is it good?" I tell them what I really think. I just tell them what they're missing in the story or in their picture, and they could do it. I wouldn't say anything bad about it. I tell them how to make it better and not erase anything.

I don't really know if I write more than other children. I haven't seen other children write. Other children in my class usually go to centers and play with something when they finish their work. I prefer to write. Susie likes to write notes to people. Felicia writes poems, but she doesn't do it in place of going to centers.

Felicia's poems are good, but you know it's hard for her. She doesn't have very good English. Like she says "this were good," and stuff like that. And that doesn't make sense. I don't know if her poems are good . . . sometimes they're good, sometimes they aren't. I think she's a very good drawer, and I like the way Felicia does her handwriting; it's interesting. She would do writing an inch away or an inch and a half away from the next one. That's what's interesting about it; she puts it far away.

Some people don't like to write! Maybe they think it's too boring. I know my friends don't like to write. They just say they don't like to write. When I'm writing stories at my house, they go home because they don't like to write. I got out my stationery to write letters one time when Kathy came, and I started writing and she said, "I might as well go home." I offered to let her write, too, but she didn't want to.

My mom and dad write notes. Sometimes they write stories, but not a lot. My brother likes to do writing homework. He's four. He says he's going to be a chef, a bridge builder, and all that stuff. I think he doesn't have enough time to be a writer.

My teacher usually writes things like notes. It's really funny how the teachers bring messages to each other, they don't come in the class.

They make notes and ask for somebody to send them. Some might be jokes. Like Ms. Nelson might send a joke, and my teacher might say to a kid in our class, "Bring this to Ms. Nelson. Tell her it was so funny I forgot to laugh." They keep it to themselves, and we don't really get to know what it says. Usually they don't do jokes; they do notes like about something she forgot to do or plans they like to do. I like to write a lot of that stuff, too. I wrote two secret admirer notes, one to Judy and one to Susie.

I want to be a writer and a movie star when I grow up. I'd also like to be a singer. Well, a movie star's kind of like a singer, so that will be kind of like the same thing. I don't know what a writer's life is like. Some people are happy, some people don't know what to write . . . like they don't know what they think about things. Sometimes it's hard, because sometimes I feel that way.

Children who want to be writers should look back at their stories and read them and see if they're okay. Moms and Dads should get their children into writing. They should tell them to write, cause it's fun . . . and it is!

8

Nicole

"AT HOME I DON'T REALLY DO 'WRITING-WRITING' "

(Grade 2)

Contributed by Sally Hudson-Ross

Nicole was in second grade when her teachers pointed her out to me. An only child, she had been actively reading and writing since long before school and her extremely mature vocabulary revealed that breadth of experience. Her home was filled with books which she had written on her own, and her parents were proud, supportive, and even somewhat awed by their precocious child's interest in writing. In school, she had been writing in journals and experiencing a writing process classroom all along. My interest in unique young writers led me to adopt Nicole as a confidant and friend. She agreed to save her writing—from home, school, and community settings—and we met three times at school over a period of four months. At each informal interview, we spread her recent writing out on a table and together explored the nature of a child writer's world.

Nicole's world, like that of Harriet the Spy, is full of rich and exciting places to be, things to see and hear, roles to play. Although she may be imagining some of what she reports, to her it is real, and writing is a rich and very genuine part of what she does there. Writing helps her keep records, play school, and imagine grand schemes such as the Preppy Puppy Party. Her puppies—Brighty, Bonnie, and Freddie, who has died—are her playmates partly because her suburban house in Georgia is located far from other children. After school, however, her own world comes alive.

I usually write outside; I don't usually write in the house. I write in the puppy house, or underneath the tree with my smallest puppy behind my back. I was writing in the puppy house this winter. It is warm in there. We even have a swinging door and pictures of Brighty's great grandmother. Bonnie has a picture of tennis balls. It's very, very big.

I wrote Bonnie's record outside in the puppy house. When I write in the puppy house, it feels a lot better because no one really thinks of the puppy's house as someplace where you can talk to friends and write things. You can just do whatever you want in there. These [Bonnie's Record] are a little messy because my dog was licking my eyes when I did them.

Bonnie's Record is just written for nobody, but just to keep track of Bonnie to make sure if she got lost, then I can always have her paw print and her registered name and stuff. And this is just one of my puppy records. The Bonnie Book was the best piece of writing I have wrote in my entire life. It's important to me because I can keep up with my puppy, and in case she gets lost, I can find out who has her.

It says, "Your puppy depends on you for his personal needs but your puppy protects you so if you read this your puppy tries to tell you something. Follow him, please, please. On page 4 you will find a contract or a sheet that shows ownership so you and your puppy don't get separated on the string or whatever the world is held together by. Do fill it out. Keep your puppy out of cold weather and in hot weather take a hose or a cool water bucket and get him wet, and if your puppy runs away, put him on a leash and put the leash on a pole or a strong tree branch and wet that."

Here's the owner's contract. It includes Bonnie's front left paw— I'm going to do it in my green paint, registered name: Nicole's Bonnie Barney; Address: 3333 Old Highway. Then it has the county, my phone number, owner's signature, witness number one, witness number two, breed, color, and dog's birthday. And some of the names I call her. And pictures.

I know to put all that on there [because] I just think of it all. Actually, most of my writing I don't really have a reason. I just do them because I think about them. I wrote this for no one special, but the public. I'm going to sell it in my mother's garage sale. Sell [blank] copies of it.

This is a recipe because when I get home from school, I always make Bonnie a snack. One day I was sitting here, and I was starting to write just a recipe because sometimes I like to come home and have some cheese with different things on it. Then, all of a sudden, I think, well, Bonnie might want a snack one day so I gave her some cheese. Then I started adding things on until I started to write the recipes. I was going to make a recipe book for Bonnie, as you can see, but I don't think I got too many recipes, only about seven or eight. Every day it's a different thing.

One recipe is this: "One cup of Sprite and put it in water. Stir for 15 minutes without stopping then put in blender for 30 minutes." Oh, this is my bone thing. You take pancake mix, add some jelly to it and make a shape of a bone and a ball and on the ball pick out little pinches around the ball and put in raisins. And soak the pinches in lemon juice, cause my dogs love lemon juice, and then put them in the bone. Fill the puppy thing with puppy food and put the ball on top then fill it up to the top and put the bone on. "This chapter has recipes to treat your dog to. Most are simple if you are big, and you have to cook them, but they are rewarding." And that's all I got there.

This I used for a placemat. We had it laminated because when Brighty got water on it, it wouldn't show through. It had a pear, an orange, dog food. This was on the other side. It said, "I taste the water." This recipe was on the back of Brighty's menu. Bonnie had a menu only she tore it up.

I wrote the folders in our clubhouse in the backyard. The clubhouse is just some sticks that I made, and I put them together with rocks and mud. And that's what it is. It feels a lot, uh, cooler, than the puppy house because I can rub sticks together in the puppy house, but if I rub sticks in that clubhouse—I tried it once—some of the rocks start falling.

This piece is wrinkled because I wrote out on my swing set, at least I tried. The swing set makes me sick though because I can't write. I tried two pages on the swing set and then I got sick.

This one I wrote at my grandparents' house in the beanbag chair. When I write at grandma's, it feels like I was hugged because my cat always crawls up on me when I'm at grandma's. In my house I usually sit in my writing corner to write. That's behind the cabinet. Sometimes I even write in my bed. I wrote these in my mother's bedroom watching TV. I did it all at one time, in about three minutes. I can write fast.

When I wrote this, I think I was in my favorite chair in the living room. It's the only room in my house where the only thing you can hear is cars rushing by, and that's a loud enough noise. These are plans. Me and April have got to chasing boys. We've caught a few of them. The hardest one is Mike. This shows where the kids will go. Mike is over here. April is here. One girl takes care of a boy, calling another boy. Two other girls fight the other boy while the other set of girls take the boys that the other boy is calling and put him in the ditch and then all the other girls try to keep him in the ditch while the other boy looks for the other boy. The plan is to get boys scared. I wrote this plan for the boys in front of the television in my chair.

Here, me and Jeff were making a book. Jeff is the best drawer in the whole school, and I'm probably one of the best writers. Our mothers told us to do it. I think the idea is to make money for them. When my mother suggests it, I don't do it because when I want to do it, I do it.

I wrote these just to keep in my book pile that I write for nobody. When I say I'm going to do something, they usually end up in my book series in my living room. It's only just a few things. When I get my whole bookshelf that has five shelves—I already have two shelves done—when I get them all done, they can fit in the puppy house. I know that. I'll put them in the puppy house, and I'll read them until the puppy comes home.

The Preppy Puppy Party. That's a tongue twister for me! Here's how it all started. When I was little, I used to have something like fifteen cats in my house and three birds. I really had a lot of animals. And I started a party. I was so little I didn't really care about what it was called so I called it the Cat Walking Party. There were a lot of cats. And it was just like this, and it came [developed] on and on and on until now when I just started to do it for my two pups. We do it every once in awhile. I decided to call it "Preppy" because my puppies are like college kids: they stick their noses in the air, especially Brighty when she comes in with her duster [tail]. It dusts everything off, including tables, chairs.

Well, I've never had a sign. [See Figure 8–1, her sign.] So I hang this sign up. I tape it to the table, and whenever Brighty walks by, it goes flip. It flips back and forth when she walks past. I found the cardboard for it; it had some posters on tomatoes [on the other side]. Sometimes I just sit and look at this [sign] for hours. If you'll notice, look at the "Party"; it has a little party hat on [the P] and different color confetti is coming down from it.

FIGURE 8–1   *"The Preppy Puppy Party"*

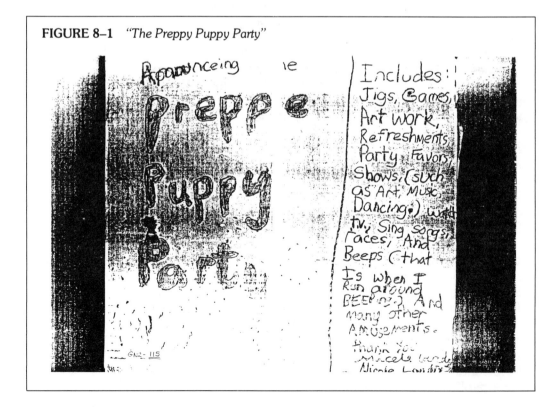

The Preppy Puppy Party is weird. I'll read what it says it includes over here [right side of Figure 8–1]: "jigs, games, art work, refreshments, party favors, shows, such as art, music, dancing, watch TV, sing songs, races, beeps . . . and many other amusements. Thank you. Nicole." The artwork is things like those, have you heard of those spin art things where you put a piece of paper on that little thing and you squirt art on it and paint on it and it goes around and it makes it splatter? Well, that's what I mean by artwork usually. A jig is when I run around the house and the puppy and I make weird noises. Sometimes I think the puppies think I'm a robot. That's what I'm trying to make them think. I make weird robot noises and sometimes I fall backward on the grass. And Brighty thinks it has something to do with my shoes, so naturally she likes untying my shoes, but she won't tie them back. "Beeping" is when I run around beeping and dogs hate it when I make little noises like that. That drives them crazy. It started out with a cat walking party and went on.

These are teaching units. I wrote lots of worksheets because I wanted to teach my puppies what their names were, and how to spell their names. Instead of having them know letters, I'm going to do it by picture. I'm trying to teach them to figure out which pictures mean their names. And when they finally do, I'll set up some more pictures that aren't their names, and then I'll ask them to point. They always do when I say, "Brighty, which one is, whatever," she'll take her nose and touch it. Whenever I call them, or I want them, I'm going to ask her to point to which one that spells her name.

This one is "Try and connect the dots." [an incomplete picture of a dog] It says, "Read all the directions first. Complete line on [dog] tag. Draw flowers around the puppy; make frame around him; make three small hairs on his head; write 'puppy' and your name; color his nose purple; complete his eyes and ears; circle the picture; color black all over him. Now only if you have put nothing on 7e. Now go back and do 1, 4, 7 and 8 only." That's just to see if they'll follow the directions first.

Here's another puppy worksheet: vowels. "Fill in the letter that starts with each word. Then circle the ones that begin with vowels. Circle the one that is not food." You can tell which one that is. "Make punctuation in this sentence: Mary went to the ball game I went too. Add 'ed' to the right word for this sentence: Bob_____ his homework—watched, studied. The review. Vowels are . . . ," A E I O U—I didn't fill that out, and sometimes Y and W.

I usually get my ideas for these from the kinds of things I do in school.

And of course I wrote my journal at school. That doesn't feel as good as all the other places I write because a lot of kids talk, and it's too hard for me to think. I write it because I have to. My teacher is the only person that sees my journal other than me, but I don't write it for her at all. I write it for my puppies because at the very end of the year, I'm going to type them down—every story—in the

FIGURE 8–2 *Vowels*

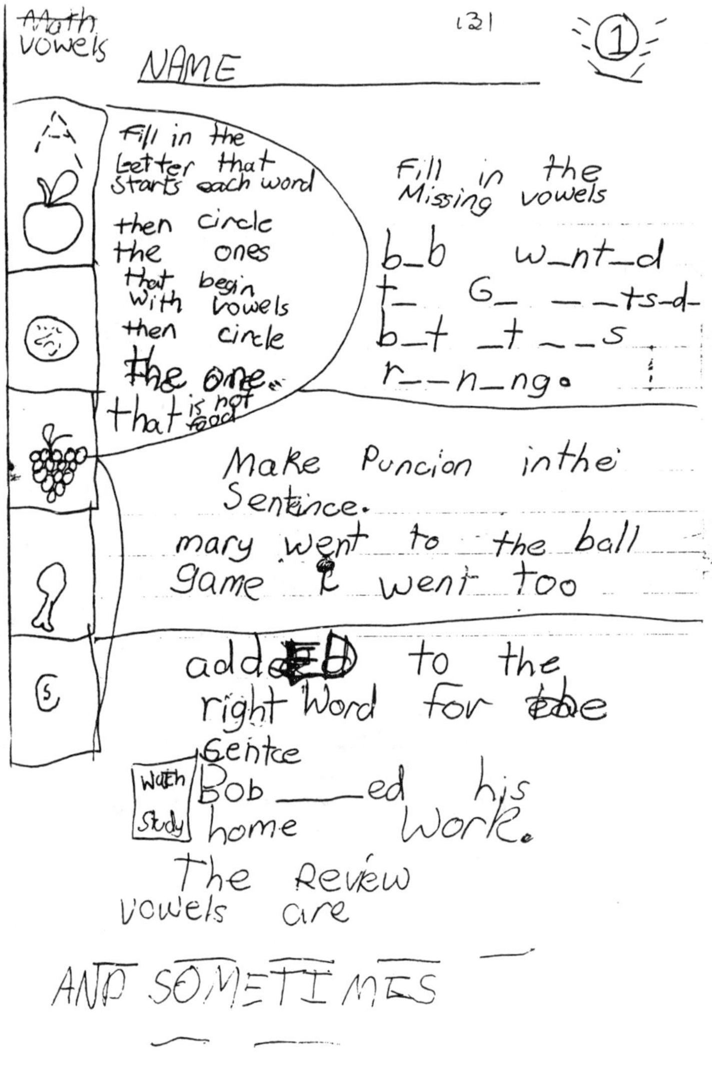

Math
Vowels

[2]

①

NAME _____

Fill in the
letter that
starts each word

then circle
the ones
that begin
with vowels

then circle
the one
that is not food

Fill in the
Missing vowels

b_b   w_nt_d
t_   G_   ___ts-d-
b_t   _t   __s.
r___n_ng.

Make Puncion in the
Sentince.
mary went to the ball
game I went too

add**ED** to the
right word for the
Sentce
with | Bob ___ed his
Study | home work.

The Review
Vowels are

AND SOMETIMES ___

___

typewriter and make a story, a storybook for them, and I'll add it to the shelf. And add another shelf.

I'm a pretty good writer because I write long stories. But I know it's not the length of the stories that matter. What matters is the way you put expression in the story, the way you use sound words. I just learned all of this off the top of my head, that's all. All the kids in my class even admit I'm the best writer in the class. But not on the entire second grade. I know I'm the best because the teacher always calls on me.

In first grade, I was the best in reading; here, I'm second or third in my class. I taught myself to read when I was two. My father would read the paper, and I would say, "Let me see, Daddy." And I would, first, I would learn my alphabet in ABC School. Then I would start to make up words and then I would start to put them into real words. I learned to write about three months later. I learned by alphabet. I made up words, and old, just crazy old words. Then I thought, I thought what the words meant, and I used real words and wrote them on paper. That's how I really got writing. Now I decide to read because it gets things off my mind. I decide to write because I just want to sometimes. Other times, to get things off my mind because it does, but it doesn't as much as reading does. That's probably because I'm reading what someone else wrote.

I write when I'm worried, mostly. Sometimes I write when I'm mad. Sometimes when I get, when I get my name on the board—I've only done it once, that was last week—I went home and I wrote "Mrs. Walsh" [her teacher] front and back on two pieces of paper and tore it up and threw it away.

There's only one part of writing I like in school. That's when I read it over and get corrections and stuff. That's the funnest part because when I'm writing, it takes me like four hours to write a three-page story, and it's hard to get the thoughts down. When you just rewrite it and get all the corrections down, you just have to write the right correction and then it's done. I know most of the corrections when I write.

Spelling isn't important to me. Not at all. Most people worry about it. I don't know. Most people don't like to write, so it's just an excuse to get up and ask to have a word spelled. You know? When I'm writing, I have the craziest spelling. And then I spend two hours trying to figure out what I wrote.

My teacher [wants] you to be the author. That means you have to write everything you can think of. [She also wants] mistakes and everything, even if you know they're mistakes. I don't know what's wrong with her. She doesn't say anything in particular; she just says, "Mistakes are okay, so write them in." Well, I don't know if she wants you to, but you know. Sometimes I go back and put mistakes in. Teachers should mainly want the kids to like what they write about and feel relaxed when they write. I would like to write things on my own.

I think my teacher is as fair as they get, but my teacher doesn't really let you write about whatever you want. She gives you topics and you have to stick with them. I think the kids should be allowed to write about whatever they want. At least a little bit more. We very seldom get to choose a topic. What I would do is I would let the kids write on what they wanted and, for the kids that don't know what to write about, I would give like four or five uncompleted thoughts and let them write the ending or make it up whichever way they want. And, you know, most of the teachers say, "If you can't think of anything, then just sit there." I would just let the kids, um, draw a picture or whatever they want.

The thing I hate about Mrs. Walsh, my teacher, is she always makes you write at a certain time. When I get all my thoughts down and when I'm doing writing, I'm nearly writing all over my math project. It would be better if you could just, um, when you started thinking about what you want to write, you can just put away what you're doing, write it down on a piece of paper and then get back to work. That's what I think would be better.

If I could change anything about writing in school, first of all I would change it where whenever you wanted to write—the teacher used to do this, but now she doesn't any more—she used to let us go wherever we wanted to write, but now she doesn't. You can get more comfortable than at your desk because in my classroom, you're all squished together. It's better when you can just go wherever you want to.

We do share our writing, but I don't like it too much. I just don't like the idea of other people hearing what I write. Except for personal—like me and you, or just one, me and someone else, one person. I don't mind that, but . . . the problem is that when kids are, when you listen to, when you listen . . . , you know how the teacher, uh, when kids laugh at the teacher and the teacher says, "Who did that?", no one says it. No one says, "Me." They, um, well, when someone laughs when I'm doing writing, I don't really know my classmates. I only know their names. I barely can remember their voices. So whereas, if I read it to one person, and they laughed, I would know it was them. Most of the time it's not supposed to be funny. But they do it anyway.

I do sort of like to listen to other people's writing. But sometimes I can't understand them. The kids in my class, some of them still talk like kindergartners. They talk too quietly and they use words in the wrong place. But the teacher makes us all read our stories. I wouldn't make kids do anything! If they wanted to read it to the class, they could.

If I knew no one was going to read something, I would change things. But when the teacher says, "You have to read this to the class," I just write what I'd never write if no one would read them because I don't want to, because personally, reading in front of the class is very embarrassing to me; I don't like the way I write in front of everyone.

I'd also tell teachers not to allow talking. My teacher didn't let you share pencils, share even a notebook. And everyone talks—that's what I don't like about it. Because when you're writing and someone starts to talk, it's just like an eraser that comes up to you and goes, "Swish," and all your thoughts go away. Even Mrs. Walsh can't stand talking when she's writing.

When I write, things just flood out and then they stop. Then they come out again, and stop. It feels weird. It's coming faster than I can think. So I get one thought and then I add to that thought and then I, then I have all these thoughts coming out, faster than I can write 'em down. Writing is sort of hard because after I get three words on paper, I can't catch up with myself. Sometimes I have to stop. Sometimes I stop because I don't want to write about it. I never change it, but I think about it.

At home, I don't really do writing-writing. I don't just sit there and write a book. Like, I write one book in a week because you know you have to get it written, then divide off the parts, decide if you're going to make a page then draw a picture, or, um, write some and then draw a picture underneath. And, um, a sentence [per] a page or whatever. And then you have to decide how you're gonna put your book together. And sometimes not all things work. Like glue doesn't work [to hold pages together]. Because then you've got to go [gestures of pulling apart sticky pages]. And staples don't work because when you open the page, usually you're writing inside the staples, and you're trying to push them like this. The staples break. The thing that works the best is, you know those little things that you tie garbage bags with? You need to use that special kind of writing paper with the holes in the side, so you put them through the holes and twist the things or tie a knot or whatever. It's like a tablet.

I'm not going to be a writer. I'm really going to grow up to be, um, something other than a writer. I have a lot of different things—singer, veterinarian—but writer isn't one of mine. I like writing, but I don't get into it as much as I do most other things. Grown-ups don't write. They may write opinions, but most of them don't write stories. My teacher writes, but very seldom. My parents? No way! I probably won't write anything when I grow up either. But in this stage right now, I do like it.

9
Reggie

"MY MAMA READ IT TO ME EVERY NIGHT"

(Grades 2 and 3

Contributed by Barbara Michalove & JoBeth Allen

We began learning from Reggie in second grade, when Barbara was his teacher and JoBeth a co-researcher who conducted quarterly interviews. JoBeth followed his development in third grade, where limited space in his trailer classroom made it hard to work with friends—an important source of help to him in the second grade— and a progression of substitute teachers did not guarantee time and choice in his reading and writing (see Contributers' Notes). It was also in third grade that Reggie began to talk about the social pressures and realities of growing up in his urban Georgia neighborhood of gangs, poverty, and the specter of jail.

As Reggie talks about the influences of his mother, other kids, and teachers on his development as a reader and writer, his insights into his own learning become clear. For him, learning takes place in an active, highly verbal community where friends help friends learn, an environment like his whole language second grade.

The major insight we gained was on home literacy events, especially the role of his mother. Reggie's family had acquired the reputation of being uncooperative with the school and unconcerned about their children's education. It was widely believed that one or more members of the family were selling drugs. However, Reggie gave us (unsolicited) a very different picture of his mother. She read to him, read the newspaper avidly herself, bought him books, brought books home from the library, wrote letters, and let Reggie add to family letters. Before we talked with Reggie, we held some tacit assumptions about home support: you either sell drugs or you read books at home—you don't do both. Reggie made us examine, and reject, our assumptions.

What follows is Reggie's talk, in response to quarterly literacy interviews, as we followed him through second and third grades.

SECOND GRADE: SEPTEMBER

I'm learning how to read stories, like them little bitty books. I can read some big books, but I don't get all the words correct. My mama is helping me. She every day leave me some books. I got to read them before I go play. Next I want to learn to read a Santa Claus book. My mama got that book from the library, but she going to buy me that book. I like it but I can't read it. I get the first word, but I can't get the second. She read it to me every night. When I'm grown up I'll read some hard books, like the book come out the mail, like the *ZooBooks* the teacher got.

I'm learning to write my book about my story. My mama make me write some words and stuff. The teacher helps me learn it. I make a book and I write what I think, and when I finish I look in the second grade dictionary and get my words correct. Next I'm going to learn to write in cursive; I can write a little bit in cursive. My mama going to help me. She tell me I can't do that. I try and I be writing fast and I took and showed her, and she said that be writing in cursive. When I'm grown I'll write letters to my uncles and my grandpa and my daddy. I'll write what they tell me at my job.

SECOND GRADE: DECEMBER

I'm learning how to spell words that I don't know and to read hard books, like *Carousels* and *Adventures* [basals]. I can help other people with words, Nancy and Bonita and Lee and Van and Wendy. When they ask me a word, I sound it out and tell them. Every morning I come in and try to read the words in the dictionary with my friend Laneal. Sometimes Van and Mac and Kathryn and Vanessa help me. Next I'm going to learn to spell my words correctly. I'll look in the dictionary and find the word and Vanessa and Kathryn will help me. I want to learn to read this thick book. It's a rhyming book, and I can't read those. Somebody will help me, or I'll try to read it every night. I got one at home; I got it at K–Mart. I don't remember the title, but it's a rhyme about a cat. When I'm grown up I'll read some hard books, like a book the teacher read in class when I was in first grade, *Tiny the Pig* [actual title, *Perfect the Pig* by S. Jeschke]; it took three days. And I'll read in cursive writing, and I'd like to read Chinese writing, no German. My daddy know how to read it and talk it.

I'm learning how to write some other people's songs, rock and roll and LL Cool Jay. And I'm learning to write neat. I got a lot of friends that help me: Lee, Laneal, Drew, Norris, Vanessa, and Fredrick. Some songs came on last night and I wanted to write it. It was Christmas carols, but I had to go to bed. I wanted to share it. I want to learn to write in cursive. I write with my friends. We look in our spelling books and copy the letters. My brother will teach me too; he taught me to do my times. When I'm grown I'll write about cars and motorcycles and a story about ABC to my favorite friend. And I'll write letters to my Grandma, if she don't be dead. She down in Florida. My mama write her, and she let me write what I want to, like "I love you Grandma."

SECOND GRADE: MARCH

I'm learning to spell some long words, like "sentence." And I'm learning to read real hard, hard books. My mama make me study. She went to a store and got some books. I read them at home; my favorite is that karate book. Next I'm going to learn to look up hard, hard words in the dictionary. I'll tell my mama to buy me a dictionary, and she tell me a word, and I look it up. In class Vanessa and David help me. They be reading with me, and Laneal. I say a word and then go along and go along and then get to a hard word like "express" and they say "express." When I'm grown I'll read some hard books, studying about karate and about jobs and stuff. I'll look in the newspaper and see about jobs.

I'm learning to write cursive, and neat too. The teacher gives us a sheet of paper, and we got to do it ourselves. Wendy can't hardly do it, so Ms. Michalove write it and let Wendy trace it, but I write it myself. I don't have to trace it. I be making 100 all the time on my cursive. Next I'm going to learn to write Chinese. I got a Chinese friend that live by me, and he goes to the Boys Club. We be looking at some karate movies at my house. He say one day he take me to Japan, but that too far; I be missing my mama. When I'm grown I'm going to write some books about karate.

SECOND GRADE: JUNE

I'm learning to read hard books and how to learn hard words. I'm learning it in Ms. Michalove's class; Vanessa and David help me. Next I'll learn how to spell and read big books; my class will help me. When I'm grown I want to be in the army. I'll read what they're going to do and sign things, and I'll read big books.

I'm learning to write neatly in cursive. I'm learning to write letters you need, and those you don't remember go in the word, leave out. My class helps me, and Chad. Next I want to learn to write a *J* in cursive. I'll study at home. I'm learning to write a play. My class helps me. When I'm grown I'll write to people. I'll write phone numbers and write to sign up for the army.

THIRD GRADE: OCTOBER

I'm learning to sound out words. I just do it by myself this year, ain't none of my friends sit by me. Well, Benton helps me sometime, and Sonya sometime, just sometime. Next I'm going to learn to do compound words, the hard ones. Somebody will help me on it. I'll ask them can they help me, like Tammy help me when I ask her. When I'm grown I'll read big dictionaries, and big books that ain't got no pictures, and the newspaper. My mama be reading it all the time. Every time she go to the store she get a paper. She read who go to jail and who be bad.

I'm learning to write real good, like my friend Benton. He write straight up and it be neat. I look at Benton and he teach me sometime, and I just start writing. Next I want to learn how to spell "dictionary," and state capitals, because they big and hard. I'll ask somebody and then write them down and then study and then spell them. When I'm grown, I'll try to write a book about when I was little. When somebody call, or I'm going to be late, I'll write a message.

THIRD GRADE: JANUARY

I can read some chapter books, like *Sideways Stories from Wayside School.* I kept on reading it, and every time I mess up, I start over. My friend Kenneth helps me sometimes. He tells me the words. Next I want to read grown up books, big ones, like the one my teacher be reading. She said at home she got a big book she and her husband read. I'll go to the library with my mama and with Mr. Williams, the other third grade teacher. He's at my house plenty of time, like when my brother be bad, and to take us to the library. When I'm grown up, I might be able to read a Bible; I can read a little bit of the Bible.

I'm writing a good story about the Mike Tyson fight. I saw it on TV and I couldn't write about it at home because I didn't have no paper. Next I want to write to rappers in New York, with hard words; we going to make a record. My brother will tell me any hard words I don't know, because he's smart in reading and writing. When I'm grown up, I'm going to write a chapter book.

THIRD GRADE: JUNE

I'm learning to read chapter books, like *Honey I Shrunk the Kids.* My brothers read at home, a lot. I watch them and I practice. My mama make us study on Saturdays. I just take out the books my mama got, then I think it over, then I write about it. My favorite at home is a karate book; it tells you the karate skills. And a Mickey Mouse book, and *Honey I Shrunk the Kids.* We got it in our class, too; I read it almost every workshop. Next I want to learn to read out of the dictionary and some of the newspaper. I can read some of it. I want to read ninth-grade books and twelfth and college. I don't know how I'll learn it, practice I guess.

When I'm grown I'll read mail and the newspaper. My mama read the newspaper a lot. We call her nosey. She like to hear somebody go to jail, my Uncle William and Uncle David and Uncle Lesley and Uncle Mike. On the other side my family they had a lot in jail. Calvin, they going to ship him off. One time I went to the jailhouse, my daddy in jail. My mama took me. They playing basketball. I hope I don't go to jail. I going to get out of this town. Police get you here, you don't do nothing. I'm going to another state. My friend go to Washington, D.C., and I might go with him, or New York, at my uncle's house.

In writing, my teacher make us write a whole page every time we have writing workshop. We don't have it that much. I want to learn to write big words like my friend Jamail. He writes in cursive, good. And like my brother, too; he write in cursive neat. I'll ask my brother or my friend to help me, or just practice. I got *three* ways I can do it. I can ask my mom to help me, too. When I'm grown up I don't know what I'll write. I'm going to be a lawyer, like Mr. Willis.[1] Or a lifeguard, like Mr. Smith[2] and teach swimming. I'm a good swimmer. The lifeguard told me how to do a one-and-a-half, and I did it. He told me one time and I did it. He told me how to tuck and straighten out. I'll write letters, and if I be a judge, I'll write down stuff. I mean a lawyer.

Next year I'm going to Ash Street School. I'm going to have to walk. I be there in no time. It's a big school. I got to go through a graveyard to get there. Lots of my friends be going, everybody on my row. I got to walk with my sister; she in second grade, and she can't run fast. My best friends Jamail and Grover be going.

My teenage brother in the gang called Colours. He do whatever they do. I don't be around them. I play a slick game on them. They call me a sissy, but I just hit that path and go home. I don't want to get in trouble with the police. Every time we go downtown, he be climbing on stuff, and riding bikes on the sidewalk.

I'm glad about going to a new school, because there's a lot of people at this school, and they like to fight. I hope it be better.

[1]Mr. Willis was the third-grade teacher's husband, who came to talk with the class about being a lawyer.

[2]Mr. Smith was the long-term substitute's husband, who accompanied the class on a swimming field trip and taught Reggie some impressive dives.

10

Katherine

"SHE'S AN ENIGMA"

(Grade 3)

Contributed by Linda Miller Cleary

Third-grade Katherine is my neighbor in a northern Midwest community. While baking cookies with her one day, I listened with growing interest as she talked about her joys and difficulties in reading and writing. In subsequent weeks and months, we spent time baking together, and then chatted over cookies and milk. At the end of the year, I talked with her "downstairs" teacher in the classroom and her "upstairs" teacher in the resource room. They have different views of what is right for Katherine, so I have decided to let them introduce her.

KATHERINE'S "DOWNSTAIRS" THIRD GRADE TEACHER:
Katherine is the lowest reader in my classroom. When you look at her reading folder, she didn't seem to have much trouble in first grade, but she kept losing her skills in second grade. I thought she had been missed along the way, but her second grade teacher had been an LD teacher, and she would have been careful with children like Katherine. Now she has passed everything, but sometimes in those tests students can guess by context. The weak areas still are vowels, predicting outcomes, verb endings. In math she has a strength, and that is how she qualified for LD; she had a discrepancy between her ability and her achievement. Katherine has spent a lot of the time in the resource room. My time to work individually with students is when Katherine is out of the room, and she's missing the extended

reading in chapter books that she needs. Katherine, I think, needs a more whole language reading program where there is a lot more writing. I don't think phonics and isolated skill work connect with her. She did a really great job with her little book, *The Disappearing Classroom,* better than her friend who is a really high-ability child. Now that it's at the end of the year, I can't check off that she is successfully reading at grade level, so I guess she'll be in the LD program again next year.

THE "UPSTAIRS" RESOURCE ROOM TEACHER:

I find Katherine to be a real enigma. She can do a test and do it exactly right, appear to understand all the facets of phonics development, score well on the test, and then turn around and not apply any of it in spelling or in reading. She still misses the "bossy 'r,' " and we've gone over that repeatedly. She can tell the rule to me, and she'll seem to understand, but when she has to apply it in a test, she doesn't. When she comes here, she works on the district reading series that is for the children that have trouble with phonics skills. If she was just to read a straight chapter book, I would assume she is about ready for fourth grade, but she slips back in phonics all the time. And yet she's a very conscientious child. I have spent a great deal of time thinking about this child. She is a well-loved child at home and even by her classmates. I have recommended that she stay in the program another year.

KATHERINE

My mother used to show me words and then ask me what they were. She'd always read the same book every night, and after I heard it a bunch of times, I'd memorize it and know what the words were. The first was *The Bedtime Book.* "Brush your teeth and get ready for your bath. It's time to stop playing and wash up. Button up your nice warm pajamas. Would you like to pick out a bedtime story? Yes, you may have just one sip of water. There you are all tucked in." And sometimes my father would silly-read a book about a boy with a tricycle that I also knew by heart, like "He put the tricycle under his pillow at night." And I'd go, "No! No!" Now he likes me to write funny too. My sister read to me sometimes; I remember a Garfield book, an Alphabet book, and one time a book she had home, *Where the Sidewalk Ends.* Now she just reads chapter books to herself. Usually we go to the library during the week, and I get a lot of books, but I don't get a chance to read them all. When I was in kindergarten, Mom used to read to me sometimes when I wasn't in school 'cause we only had to go half a day.

In kindergarten we didn't have books, but every day a teacher would read to us. Kindergarten was learning how to tie your shoes and button and zip and stuff. I guess we worked on letters, like a letter sheet, and we'd write five "a's," and then the next day we'd go on to "b," and words like "she," "the," and "and." I guess there were like three words that had an "a," and we would write that word. If we had stories, we would tell them to the teacher, and she'd write them. We drew a picture, and we'd tell her what to write. But we did write our name on it. When I wrote my name, I would write them all in capital letters, and we would hang it up on the wall.

First grade we did letters too, just small letters, like more times, and sometimes there was a special word with that letter. We had lots of people visit us, and we studied about space with a student teacher. We took a toilet paper roll and painted it black and poked holes through it, and it looked like stars when we looked in. And we used to draw a picture there too, and then we'd get a lined piece of paper and write a story about it.

In second grade we started cursive letters, but cursive was harder. There were like pictures out of the newspaper that our teacher would find, and we would have to pick one and write a story about it. Everyone in the school would do that except for kindergarten I think, and then we would send them to the newspaper place, and then all the stories about one picture would be stapled together, and then whichever one was best would win the prize and get to go to a young authors' thing. I heard stories that were better than mine in the class. I didn't get mine in the paper.

We also had to write eight lines in our writing journals, and if we filled a book we would get a sticker, and I went through five writing books. Some people did seven or ten. Every day there was like a topic on the board you could use, but you didn't have to write about that. Like this one I wrote: "What my birthday is going to be like. We are going to the park and have relays, and play on the playground and have a lot of fun, and I am inviting eight people. I'm sad because I didn't get the gerbils, and because I forgot my snack and got a stomachache."

We spent a lot of time doing sound [phonics] worksheets for reading. We had five reading groups, and each was in a different book. Sometimes we had to do a play out of the book, and we'd have to draw it, and get costumes. I liked it depending on what the play was. She was good because she wouldn't put names on the board. I've got my name put on the board twice in my life. If I was a teacher, I would give my students a free warning before the name went up on the board.

This year, if I don't like reading, it is because we have a lot to read. If I read a story and if it is four pages, sometimes I don't have enough time. If I'm reading it in school and I don't have enough time and some of the other kids are finished, you look at other people done and feel kind of bad.

Reading would come higher on my list than writing sometimes if I don't know what to write. Sometimes I write what I have done. Sometimes I take ideas off of books. Sometimes if something just happened, like I went out to dinner with neighbors, then I write about it. Mostly when I go to school, then I think about what to write about it. Or like when my grandparents came, I knew ahead I was going to write about that. In a way reading and writing are the same, I guess. If you write something, you can read it. I guess you can see the same words in writing and reading.

On Monday when we get in, we have a spelling pre-test. And then this year I go up to the resource room, and then when I come back I read with my class group out of the big book. And then in the afternoon I go back up there, and that's just a time to do your worksheets. Sometimes I like to read up there best because it is quieter, but in the classroom sometimes we get to read with partners. We get to pick a spot in the room, and we get to hear other people read. It has to be someone in my reading group, so sometimes I pick Melanie. There is a place where our teacher stores paper, a corner. We read a story from my reading book, *City Spaces*. But I like the chapter books I get in the library better. In the reading book it has too many starts, it has the story and then questions and then another story, and then questions, and sometimes poems. Library ones aren't so long, and not so many stops and starts. You can get them done, and you can read them anytime you want to.

Everyday I go upstairs twice. I like it. The rest of the class works, sometimes they get reading and spelling sheets. We just bring our math and spelling and reading work upstairs in the afternoon. If I'm just reading a chapter book in the downstairs classroom, it is fine, but if I'm reading from *City Spaces*, it's harder in the classroom because it's noisy. In the morning we have the charts and sound papers that we do, like worksheets when you had to put in the vowel or something and see if the vowel is long or short. We always have a chapter book in our classroom desk, and if we are done with one, we can get another one. Some of the Ramona ones are my favorite. We have language sheets and sometimes we write paragraphs. They tell you, "write a paragraph about a circus," but it would [have to] be on the worksheet.

This morning before school I got up and picked out clothes to wear, and then I read my homework story. The story was about a family that lived in the boat. There were some things they liked about living on the boat and things they didn't. After school they got to go on a trip on the boat because their home just moved, and they can go fishing whenever they want, and they can go swimming. They didn't like that it was small, and all the rooms were a weird shape.

At school before the pledge went on, I also needed to write my spelling words five times. I got two or three wrong on the pretest. We were supposed to have assembly, but they couldn't find the drummer, so we had to go back up, and then they found the drummer twenty minutes later, and we went back down. Then we had a language sheet. It was like "the," "a," or "an," you had to underline the one that would fit. It was kind of easy; I knew which one to pick because of what it sounded like.

Today in reading group it was kinda short because we had to read a story and answer questions. I read it to myself. We sit at our own desk. It was about John who wrote letters on leaves, invented them [letters]. He made them up by the way a person talks, and there wasn't paper so he wrote them on leaves. First he taught other people, and then he wrote letters to them. In our book there is a page with seven or eight questions on it, and the teacher calls on you, and you have to answer questions. One question was, "What did John invent?" Also he went to be a soldier, and he was gone a long time, and no one wrote him letters, and his wife didn't like him because he wasn't doing anything else except inventing words and numbers and writing, so she burnt them. But then he wrote an alphabet on a deerskin and took it everywhere with him. I answered "What did he invent?" And I think there was another [question]. I like to answer questions I know. I don't like the others.

And then we had lunch and came back and read social studies sheets. We had library. Usually we hear a book from the librarian, or a movie. Today we had a movie, and then we get to pick chapter books, science books, or kids' books. Sometimes I buy books that I've wanted for awhile, like the Berenstain Bear books, and sometimes I get books from the book orders. Today in the library I got an idea of a chapter book from my friend Phillipa.

Upstairs I had compound words. I like compound words cause they are easy to figure out 'cause you cover up half of the word. I guess I just find two words in it. I don't like words with "ght," with letters you can't hear, and sometimes I try to do the letters in the "ght" and it doesn't work. Have you ever tried [to sound] "g," "h," "t" [together]?

If I had to pick something, I would pick math to do. I get my best marks in math and writing. I didn't do any writing today except on sheets. Math you don't have to work as much, not a whole story to read or to write. I'd rather read the Bear books than do the worksheets because those are my favorite books. I like to read to my baby brother or myself the best. Sometimes it's not good to read to little kids cause they'll cry in the middle or tip over or something. Sometimes if I'm holding the book, I'm not holding him enough. At night I usually read to my parents. It's good that they don't tip over, and I don't have to hold them like that, but then also, if I'm stuck on a word, they can help me, and my baby brother can't help.

We've been writing a story about a famous person. We would have to get books out of the library about it, and it has to be a page long, and then we would have to dress up like the person. And then we have to pick either a kindergarten, first, second, or third grade class to read it in front of. I have Sandra Day O'Connor. The teacher had a robe, and it fit. My Mom still works with the PTA, and she has one of those hammer things [gavel]. I will take the sentences I wrote down and make it into a page. I hope I can read it in front of our class!

I liked doing "The Disappearing Classroom" because we did that instead of language stuff. (See Figure 10–1.) It was my first long book. I'm glad I had my own ideas because everyone else had different ideas. I read some of my friends' books, and one was about

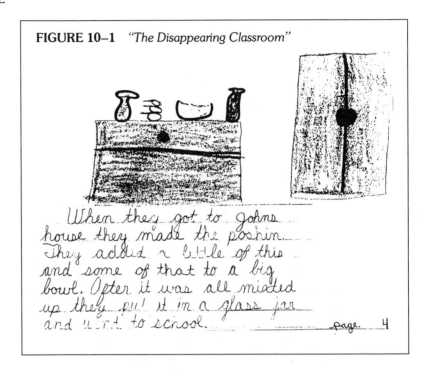

FIGURE 10–1   *"The Disappearing Classroom"*

When they got to Johns house they made the poshin. They added a little of this and some of that to a big bowl. After it was all mixed up they put it in a glass jar and wrt to school. page 4

FIGURE 10–1   *"The Disappearing Classroom"* (continued)

room 106

They got up on top of Mrs. Suns class room and powed the poshin on the class room. Son the room disappeared but with John and Katy and Katherine on it. The principle said over the inercom the next day. "Does enerbody know were room 106 is? But nobody did. So Mrs. Suns class had to have their room in the hallway. page 5 herself and another's was about pumpkins, and there weren't any other books that were about disappearing classrooms. I think my parents were impressed, and we made them right before Open House at school, and lots of parents got to read the books. I felt good about it.

This summer I will just have some things to do at home; for the upstairs teacher I have some worksheets to do. It's just like regular school worksheets. And sometimes my mom and I will take turns reading the Berenstain Bear books.

(Katherine's summer was filled with activity: a creative writing class, a trip to New Jersey, and a trip to Disney World with her grandparents. Her mother made sure she finished all the worksheets, but the chapter book reading fell by the wayside.)

11

Ashley, Nathan, Matthew, and Kristin

"THINGS YOU'D LIKE TO HAPPEN, YOU JUST WRITE ON A PIECE OF PAPER"

(Grade 3)

Contributed by Barbara Biegner Hoffman & Frankey Jones

Ashley, Nathan, Matthew, and Kristin all come from very literate environments where their families support their reading/writing development, invest in large family libraries, and read together often. They have also been together in the same progressive Georgia public elementary school since kindergarten where it is commonly accepted that each child will publish four or five books a year with the parent-run Tiger Publishing Company. Their third grade teacher, Ms. Mason, works each year to establish a community-based, whole language learning environment where decisions are made together, where children are recognized for their varied expertise, and where learning happens as a result of independent as well as collaborative exploration. Here these already avid readers and writers flourish.

Ashley leads class meetings with written agendas and an air of sophistication and efficiency that would rival any Big Eight CEO's. She is impeccably organized, and works to help others (including teachers and researchers) organize themselves. Matthew is serious and thoughtful but has a ripe, affable sense of humor that attracts friends from among both boys and girls. During interviews, his attitude is reflective; he measures each response carefully, backtracking often to get the answer just right. Nathan, the artist and the most popular student overall, is somewhat shy but is recognized by other students as the most talented writer in the class. Kristin loves school, observes intently everything her teacher does, and hopes to be a teacher herself someday. She finishes all her assignments early, often submits extra work, and plays school as soon as she gets home each afternoon, with neighborhood children, a younger sibling, or imaginary students.

In the spring of their third-grade year, these children discuss their strong needs for ownership and independence in writing, their belief in the productivity of collaboration, and the rich potential they find in a community of readers and writers.

ASHLEY

We have writing workshops this year, and we have a folder and every day we take about thirty minutes to write. We write in reading, and we almost write in every subject. Our teacher gets stories ready to go to Tiger Publishing that we write, and I just got one finished. It's called "My Soccer Career."

First you write. You write on a clipboard and then you put it in your notebook. The clipboard is just if you want to write on it; you can write wherever. I usually use my writing notebook. It's soft and easy to write on. Then you have a conference, and then you have all your periods in the right place and stuff, and she'll take it and she'll type it and then we'll do all the pasting and stuff to get ready, and then we send it to Tiger Publishing. They type it, and then they make it into a book with a binder and everything. We don't have one published yet. We're just getting a lot ready to go.

I'm writing "Our Class" and getting that ready to go to Tiger Publishers, too. It's on subjects: spelling, reading, math, writing workshops, science, social studies, lunch. I put the title and then I write what we do in that subject. I guess since we work every day in all those subjects that I should do a story on them.

We get ideas, and mostly we just think of what we're gonna write and then we write what we want to write. People give the teacher suggestions, and then she tells them to the class. Like, "write a Christmas story about a dolphin." This one boy said that. We write about animals a lot. I don't know why. Those ideas come from kids in class. "My Soccer Career" was her idea to write. I've been playing soccer for eight seasons, and she knew I liked soccer. She goes, "Why don't you write about soccer?" And I like soccer a lot, so I just decided to write about it, and it came into a big story.

Every time I write a story, I quit it. And then a few weeks later I come back, and it's still sitting there, so I decide to finish it. "My Soccer Career" went for a week and a half because some days I worked on my other stories. I just start with one story and then go back and forth, and whatever one I want to do real bad, I do.

We have partner working. Mostly people write chapter stories with a partner, so one person can do one chapter and then the other chapter. We trade back and forth. I wrote this one story with this girl, but she moved to Minnesota. It's called "Our Trip." Her name's Jillian, and in the story I go over to her house, and we sew, and we go to my soccer games. We spend the night for two weeks, so that's fourteen days we have to write. I wish it was true. I like going over to people's houses.

We write in social studies, health, science, and math, too. In social studies we have assignments, sheets of paper, like tests and stuff. And then in science we have a little booklet, and we write what we've done today in our notebook folder. In health we have more assignments to do, to write. Reading, writing, and lunch are the times I like best. In reading, you read a book, and you have this little thing [form] that you write the books you've done on. Sometimes you respond to one, and we have paper in the back of our notebooks so we write on that.

We have more writing time this year than last year. I like it this way 'cause I like to think of my own stories and stuff. Last year I got to think of my stories, but sometimes we had to write something, what our teacher wanted. Writing teachers should give us time each day to write so the kids would like writing more, because if you don't get to write sometimes, you'll never figure out how fun it is to write. Don't tell us what to write. Give us a group of time, and don't tell us what to do.

I like writing a lot, always. I write sometimes at home. I take a little notebook places and write in it. I write in my diary about my boyfriend, and I just write all different kinds of things, like my family. When something gets in my mind, I want to write that, so I just take a piece of paper and write a letter to people. Sometimes I don't really wanna send the letters. I don't think they're good enough to send.

At home I like to write in the TV room so I can watch TV. Writing at home is a lot different because I have something [activities] every day of the week, and Saturday and Sunday, so I rarely get any time when I get home from school to read or write. I wouldn't like it if I didn't have time at school to write. I get enough time to write one story in a day sometimes. It teaches me stuff when I write.

Writing is like you're dreaming. When you dream, you just fall away, and then when you're writing you just think of something and just sit here going mmmm, resting and everything while you write. And that's what you do when you dream. Sometimes I write, and I don't even know what I just wrote.

MATTHEW

We have writing workshops; we write stories. At the beginning of the year, we just started off with blank paper and nothing on it. We have notebooks that we write in, and we can write on free sheets, too. We can just write on anything. We can write any place in the room, too. We can go out in the hall, too, but we have to ask her to do that.

I've written lots and lots of mystery stories, and I've written a poem. It's about this boy, and he wouldn't eat peas. I've written books, stories for friends. I'm designing a Nintendo game now. I'm writing pictures and a story with it, and right now I'm writing the directions.

I like to write mysteries a lot. I've written them since the beginning of the school year. I was gonna write about baseball cards, but then somebody wrote a mystery, and then I guess I decided to write a mystery on baseball cards. Well, really the teacher gave me the idea. See, we have a conference so she gave me the idea that I can do a series of these mysteries.

The best piece I've done this year is, um, really two: "The Underwater Mystery," and the sequel was called "The Campfire Mystery." My birthday was about to come up, so I had a spend-the-night party—we were gonna have a campout but it was raining, so I had a spend-the-night party—and so I put a campout in the story. That's sorta where I got my idea. I got the mystery idea from Randy, and then I had read the Hardy Boys mysteries, too.

There's somebody else in my class that writes mysteries, too. You know the Hardy Boys? [His last name is Fortune, and] he writes the Fortune Boys. Last time, it was three people—me and Chad and him—who wrote one. We think of ideas, and whoever we think has the best idea, we all write. We have our notebooks, and we each write the same thing in our own notebook. We just write one story, but it's the same thing in each notebook. Sometimes we can't think of what to do, and there's just so many ideas, and we argue about what to do.

It's fun, but I can't write real good with a friend 'cause I like to have my own ideas. Ms. Mason doesn't want us to work with somebody else a lot because if we do it too much, we might not be able to write by ourselves. So you can't write with somebody the whole year; you have to write by yourself once at least.

When I think about the experts in my class, Carl knows about reading and writing and stuff like that. Susan knows about horses. Andy moved to the school, and then he moved out of the school, and he knows a lot about dinosaurs. Everybody spells good. Carl and Nathan and Chad and me know about math. I know about Nintendo. Chad and me and Daniel know about sports—specialties, really—baseball, basketball, football. Me and some girls that play softball and Chad know about baseball; lots of people know about baseball in the class. And basketball would be me and Chad and Daniel and some other people. Peter knows about karate. Nathan and Chad and Daniel and Ashley know about soccer. Chad and Brian know about football.

Nathan and me, and you could say Daniel, are the writing experts in the room. Daniel has more comedy in his mysteries than he does in his adventures. Nathan has great ideas. He reads a lot of books. He has like a whole library of books in his house. He reads one book, and he writes sorta like that author writes. He also writes different subjects a lot. There's a little group who write the best plays, me and Chad and Daniel and Nathan; we did a *Velveteen Rabbit* play, a puppet show, and then Nathan wrote a script for that. Peter writes about karate, and he's written Nintendo games, like what would happen in Nintendo games. Kristin writes something like with a friend, and one of their parents left somewhere and then they stayed at Kristin's house. A lot of girl stuff, you know, as usually girls do. Right now Ashley's writing "My Class Story." She's telling about her class. Lee wrote a story called "The Biggest Nose in School" about this guy; it was sort of like a moral story, a fable. Andy writes animal stories. Mark writes mysteries, and he wrote a Garfield story, and stuff like that.

For me, the title comes first. Then usually an introduction, like in my mystery stories, he [the narrator] says, "Today I'm gonna tell about blah, blah, blah." And then I write the story. Like I did this one where it was an Olympic mystery, "The Mystery of the Missing Gold Medal." Matt Nose [his detective character] and Daniel Fortune went to Seoul, Korea, and they tried to solve this mystery of the gold medal that got stolen from somebody. He got the gold medal, and then the guy ran away, and we didn't know where he went. The story sorta stopped before they caught the guy, and I decided to tell that in first person like it happened now. I don't know how I thought of that [first person] at the end.

We get to write more stories now than we did last year. This year's pieces are longer than last year's pieces, and last year's pieces didn't have as much adventure as this year's. I didn't write mysteries last year.

I like it when our teacher lets us write any kind of story we want to instead of just telling us what kind of story we're supposed to write. I also like it when she types the story for us on the computer. We can read it. We share too. You get up in front of the room, and you read the story. Sometimes we give suggestions. When I'm stuck, sometimes I write something else and then try to go back to it.

To write well, you need a good imagination, I think, if you're gonna write a fiction story. And for a fact story, you need a lot of facts in it. Facts come from books, encyclopedias. I like fiction because you can just do whatever you want to. Things you'd like to happen, you just write on a piece of paper.

NATHAN

We didn't write very much last year; we usually read. This year, we can even take our notebooks to lunch, and we couldn't do that last year. I like it this way. We get to write more, and I'm writing better stories. I'm reading more chapter books. I like sorta hard-to-read books.

This year we wrote about the whole class—a story about the whole class. Me and Chad wrote an Indiana Jones story. We wrote all our puppet shows; we wrote three. We just finished another play. It's about me and Daniel and Matthew. It's about "Little House by the Big River." We're all in it. We read the book, *Little House in the Big Woods,* and she wanted us to do something for the book. We might make the play into a story because there is pretty much to it. The first part is when we're a little bit older, and we run away. Then we are going through the woods and building a log cabin. We have Christmas, a birthday, and then we go to school. We're on the chapter that's called "The Troublemaker's Birthday." I'm the trouble-maker—not in school, but in the play. See, I have a slingshot.

We did a puppet show for *Velveteen Rabbit* too, and we all did parts in it. We have puppets, and sometimes we use stuffed animals like snakes because we couldn't find a puppet. We've been writing a lot together this year. Like when we're doing puppet shows, they give you ideas, and sometimes I have ideas, and I write them down, and then we make chapters or parts or scenes. Sometimes Matthew says not to write like that. Like, he told us that the story's really not about us. When I was talking, he said, it's better to say "he said," instead of "I said," because we're not really in it. It takes a long time to get it this way. Matthew's pretty good at writing, and Daniel. They write their Fortune Boys, and they write Daniel Fortune and Matt Nose about detectives. Sometimes they put me in it.

When she says it's time for writing workshops, you get out a notebook, and some people keep their stuff on a clipboard, and then we just start writing. Sharing time comes after writing workshops usually. If you have a funny part or something that you want to share, then you raise your hand, and she'll call on you. We get to write in writing workshop about thirty or fifty minutes. Five people or six people share each day. Ms. Mason likes something funny or sad. Well, she doesn't really care, she just says it's good.

Sometimes she decides what we should write, and sometimes we do. Well, sometimes we write on the same thing. She writes it up on the blackboard. Like, you could do a puppet show or a game or just write a story about a picture, something like that.

In the morning after we finish spelling, we can read books. I liked *Little House in the Big Woods*. And I read *The Good Day Mice*, which was pretty good. We can check them out during writing work-shop, too, if we need one. We have some books that people can read together. After we read, we go to our special—art, music, play—and then we come back and have lunch. And sometimes we do social studies. We read longer now than last year. Sometimes she calls us back to the back of the room, and she asks us what we've read, and she has a conference, and in the writing workshop we do that too. She talks about "is it exciting?" or something like that. She asks "what is it about?" We do learn skills sometimes. When we don't know a word in a book, we put it on the board and then put quota-tions around it, and she asks the whole class what the word means. Some are hard.

Sometimes I take my writing notebook home. I started a new chapter at home yesterday. I like to write funny stuff, and everybody laughs when we read it, like in the puppet shows. To be a good writer, you have to write funny things and exciting things. You have to make it sort of long, too. Sometimes scary.

Writing is fun, exciting. It's like drawing. You can get ideas from drawing. Sometimes I draw pictures in the stories, and it gives me ideas. Some of the stories I draw things, but not all the time. When I grow up, I'd like to be an author or illustrator.

KRISTIN

Writing is funner this year. We get to do more things. Like, in first and second, all we got to do was just sit there and do all these things that we learned in kindergarten and first. I just like third more because you learn more things like multiplication tables and lots of other interesting things. Writing is easier because I have more ideas than back in second and first. So in fifth, it will be real easy to come up with a story.

My ideas for stories just pop up. I'm writing something about this little Christmas adventure and these two little mice, and they all get to this big adventure and everything. I don't know where that idea came from. I also wrote "Freeman and Lillian." It's about these two elephants and they bump into each other and then they get married, but they don't know how to kiss and they go to this wizard and everything. Well, I don't know how I got this idea, but they put their trunks around each other, and they make the connect at the end. I haven't read it to the class yet.

If you came into our writing workshop, first you would see writing and everything. And then some people would go to the computer. And Ms. Mason has conferences with other people, like if you're almost done and you want to get it published or something. And you might see some sharing going on. And then you might see like a whole group of people working together just writing stories.

Me and Liz are thinking of getting together and doing something. We're going to write about everybody in the class. Everybody seems to want to write about the class, but I think it's kinda weird because like my mom said you could hurt people's feelings doing that. Ms. Mason has us share our ideas of what we're going to write. You just have to keep it in your head until you start writing. Almost every writing workshop we talk about ideas. If you use somebody else's suggestion, then you have to change something about it. I mean if the other person wrote a story, "The Mystery of How This Person Got Lost," or something like that, you couldn't write the exact same story. I just like making up stories of my own. I don't like writing fact stories.

When I go home, I always pretend. My pretend school looks different, but I just get this feeling that somebody's really in my class. I just go "OK, class!" I don't know why, but. . . . And I have a chalkboard and a wipe-off board. I shut my door and lock it. And then when somebody knocks on my door, I just go answer it, and I pretend. Like if my dad's saying come down to eat, then I'll just shut the door, and then I'll go "Class, it's time to eat lunch. Now that was a runner from Mrs. Benson's room." You see, I get the ideas, like if we learn how to do multiplication in class, I'll go back home and refresh my memory, and do all that with the class and everything. I go, "OK, it's writing workshop now," and I just go to my desk and work.

Some teachers just make children write the same story. "OK now you need to write a story about what you're going to do this Christmas." And the teachers give them words to jot down and everything.

And then you have to make sentences and a story out of those words and sentences. I just don't like that because I think you should just give the boys and girls a chance to make up their own stories. If I were the teacher, I would just say, "Write your own stories." That's better because you're using your mind. Because if the teacher tells you what to write, I mean that is not gonna help you at all. Like if a little kid has an idea to write a story about a mystery, and he really wants to write that real bad, then the teacher says, "Okay you have to do this holiday thing," and then, he gets hooked on that holiday thing, he never gets around to doing his mystery story. And then, after he does that holiday and everything, it's almost time for the teacher to give another assignment to write about. So, he is only doing what the teacher schedules. That's bad because the kids don't get a choice, or time to do anything on their own.

That's also why I don't tell what I'm gonna write. Like if everybody goes, "What are you gonna write?" And then I'm gonna go, "I'm not gonna tell you." And then they go, "Please." And I go, "No." Because like I just feel like they're gonna just copy me. Because Ashley and Jillian wrote about their vacation together. In the story Jillian's mom had to go somewhere for about like a couple months or something. Then they had all those days that they had fun and everything. And then about six little groups of two people in our class did that. And they all came out looking almost exactly alike. And that's why I don't want to do that with friends.

I think we need more time. I mean, I write a lot and everything. I would like an hour and a half. Now we have thirty minutes. With the extra time, I would just sit down and write and think of the chapters and think of other stories that I would like to write after I do this one, and then it would give Ms. Mason more time to have conferences with people and everything.

Writing is like a Nintendo game. You start out slow, and you get a little bit of men, and then like it gets faster. You drop down really through things. And then it turns out sloppy, and you can't even read your own handwriting. But, in my stories, I change things that don't fit or don't even go with the story. But when I'm writing really well, it feels good.

12

Mario

"IT'S MOSTLY AFTER I
READ A BOOK THAT I WRITE"

(Grade 3)

Contributed by Rashidah Jaami' Muhammad

I first met Mario when my eight-year-old son, Abdul-Jaleel, invited him to a Saturday matinee. Between mouthfuls of Juicy Fruit and Sweet Tarts, these two third graders were comfortably slouched in their seats and reading the English sub-script of *Dances with Wolves*. I was so impressed by their ability to articulate and keep pace with the film that I didn't notice that they were creating a disturbance until 'Alim, my older son, said, "Mom, Mom, Do you hear them? They are reading OUT LOUD!"

Even though Mario comes by daily to ride to school with Abdul-Jaleel, it was our talks about reading and writing that allowed us to engage in more than the perfunctory good-mornings. While he may view storywriting as little more than a schooltime chore, Mario is a well-versed storyteller, building on the movies, stories, and books that create and reflect his life experiences.

My mom taught me how to write my name before I went to pre-school. We worked on the coffee table in the den. She held my hand the first few times, 'til I could write it by myself. The *M* she taught me to make with the slanted lines. The *a* was easy 'cause my Mom told me to make a *c* then a straight line (beside it), sometimes a circle or a ball with a line next to it. She said: "Put a straight line and go over like that with a curve part for the *r*. I learned how to write my last name in kindergarten. At school we used this gray paper with big lines and a line in the middle. I don't like that kind of paper 'cause the lines in the middle are hard to see. At home we just used regular notebook paper that you buy at the store. I like the notebook paper best 'cause it is easier to write on. On the gray paper your lowercase letters are bigger than your notebook paper capital letters. In kindergarten we wrote words sometimes if we wanted to, but mostly just letters. I started writing stories in the second grade. My first story was a little make-believe about a bear.

Sometimes the writing at school is kinda boring, 'cause your hand gets tired. I like math 'cause it doesn't really make your hands tired at all, you don't have to write as much. Math is writing. Spelling is writing. You can write the time down. That's what we do sometimes at school, after a spelling test, to see if we can get it right from a regular clock. If I get it wrong, my teacher puts a check by it. If I get the time right, my teacher puts a sticker on my paper. It doesn't count, my teacher does it just for fun.

Sometimes writing at school is kinda fun. When we did the story about the dog on Valentine's Day, it was fun because we could put in anything we wanted to, we could put in a problem. But I didn't put in a problem. A problem is like somebody is in trouble, and they can't figure it out, and the solution is like they finally find out the answer to their problem. In my story: this dog had just woke up from his nap, and he got a present. The Valentine heart in his mouth was the present. He didn't eat it, he just carried it in his mouth. He had dropped it, then he picked it back up in his mouth. He put the Valentine in his bag and went to sleep.

Sometimes I write about different kinds of animals that I already know about. And I write what I know about them. I put them up in a little cupboard I got in my room. I don't take them to school. My favorite thing to write about is animals. Sometimes I write about sports. I write about the basketball people that I like on different teams. My favorite team is the Atlanta Hawks. My cousin likes them too. Abdul-Jaleel likes the Los Angeles Lakers. I like Dominique Wilkins and Spud Webb on the Hawks. Spud Webb can really dunk the basketball.

My class did a recipe book. I put in a recipe for pepperoni pizza 'cause I know how to make it. I had to put in how to make it and stuff you need.

But stories and reports are kinda different. Stories are mostly fantasy and reports are informational stuff. I had wrote a report on snakes that took me thirteen pages. (See Figure 12–1.) It took me a week and a half. My hands got tired when I was writing it; I just kept on writing cause I wanted to finish the report soon, so I could read my library book again. I got the idea about writing the story on snakes 'cause I had got this library book on them. See most people in my class know how I like to write stories about snakes, 'cause I did one before that took me nine pages. And my friend, Robert, had this book, an encyclopedia about snakes, in his desk, but he let me borrow it until I finished the report. When Mrs. Gardner, my teacher, asked me if I wanted to read it to the class, I said: "It's okay with me." I practiced [reading] it, I didn't read it much but I read it quite a lot.

When I finished it she would ask the class different questions and let me pick the people that could answer the questions. She asked me what was the main thing I learned about snakes. So I said, "Some of the most dangerous kinds would slither away as fast as they can, if they see you first. Because they are just as scared of you as you are scared of them."

You can't go to a pet store and get a poisonous one. You get those from like in the wild, 'cause in pet stores they got big snakes like the boa constrictor. 'Cause in this one story called "The Unusual Pet Store," they had a boa constrictor, and they put him in a real large cage. He had a swimming pool in it, 'cause boas like to swim a lot. They had a brick and a tree branch for when it was time to shed its skin so he could slide out of it.

Some plain boa constrictors can grow fourteen feet. Now, that's about two James Edwards standing on top of each other, 'cause James Edwards is 7'1" and Michael Jordan is only 6'6" [professional basketball players]. And they [books] got these things called pythons. They can grow twenty-seven feet long. I read about them in our library. There is this thing called *The Snake Discovery Library*. I read all of the books in Set One, except for *Cobras*. I haven't found it yet. I look for it when I go to the library, but if it ain't there I get some other book. I read all of them in Set Two.

FIGURE 12–1   *"Snakes"*

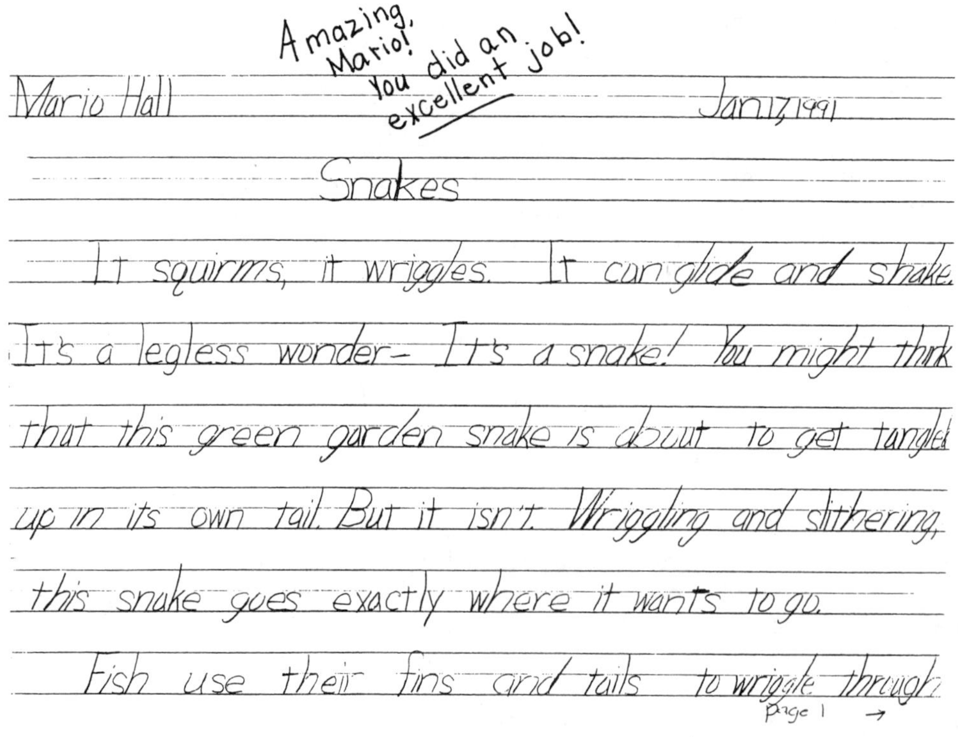

Amazing, Mario! You did an excellent job!

Mario Hall   Jan 17, 1991

Snakes

It squirms, it wriggles. It can glide and shake. It's a legless wonder— It's a snake! You might think that this green garden snake is about to get tangled up in its own tail. But it isn't. Wriggling and slithering, this snake goes exactly where it wants to go.

Fish use their fins and tails to wriggle through

Page 1   →

I like fantasy books, the problem and the solution. But they are real short and sometimes boring to read. It doesn't have to last a whole week. It can last more than one or two hours, 'cause I had one of my books last year. I was reading it and I had to go downstairs and eat, then I was back upstairs. Counting the time I had to eat it took me four hours and twenty-six minutes to finish The *Dinosaur's Paw*.

I don't like to read out loud. I only read to my friends, Delmar and Laresha. They live next door. Delmar is five and Laresha is six. They sit one each side of me on the front porch so that they can see the pictures. I read to them from my joke book, my animal books, or my RIF books [Reading Is Fundamental—a national organization for providing books to school children]. But I don't want to be a teacher.

I am going to be a basketball player. There are thirty teams in the NBA, and there are fifteen to twenty on each team. They practice every day. I practice every day, when we go outside, on our basketball court at school. I can play in my room [at home] if I don't jump around too much. Dominique Wilkins plays for the Atlanta Hawks and Michael Jordan plays for the Chicago Bulls. They are my favorites. It has to be warm to go outside to play basketball. Sometimes when we went out in the snow, we didn't dribble the ball 'cause it was too much snow, we just ran and threw it up. I wrote in my journal about the Detroit Pistons:

> Today, I feel like writing about the Pistons game. There was a fight in the game. Vinnie Johnson, Isaiah Thomas, Dennis Rodman, Bill Laimbeer were in it. They were on the Pistons team. Dominique Wilkins, Spud Webb, John Battle, Moses Malone were in it. They were on the Atlanta Hawks team. The score was 97 to 109. The Detroit Pistons won the game.

One time I wrote in my journal at school:

> If you could be anyone other than yourself, who would it be and why? I would be Michael Jordan, because I would play on the Chicago Bulls team. I could dunk [the basketball] from the free point line. I could make lots of three pointers.

I read books about basketball players like Michael Jordan and Magic Johnson. But I don't think you can learn how to play basketball from reading a book. You can learn some from watching basketball on TV. That's how I learned to dunk the ball. If I was going to write about me and my friend playing basketball, I would go home, sit in a chair in the den, and start writing: "Today me and my friend went to play basketball. We had fun." I would probably put in the score how many three pointers and how many foul shots each of us had in the game, and who won.

There are not very many black books in our library at school. I think that there is one on Martin Luther King and one on Bill Cosby. But I haven't read them. I like to read books about animals. At school, one of my teachers told me about Martin Luther King. He was this black man. And when he was young he had two white friends. But then his friends, their Momma found out about him. And she wouldn't let them play with him anymore. He was sad.

But I write mostly upstairs in my room, I got like a little desk-like thing. I like to read better than write stories. Tomorrow I might write in my journal, what I did over the weekend. I'll write I watched the basketball games and went over my aunt's house. I like to write about true stuff. I can write about the one movie I saw called the *Blind Fury.* It was about this man that went blind in the Vietnam war. He could slice an apple in four pieces when someone threw it up.

Writing means like you can do different things. Sometimes I do extra reports that my teacher lets me do. Like different kinds of animals that I like. I did one on a lion. Both kinds, male and female, and

FIGURE 12–2   *"Snakes" Book Cover*

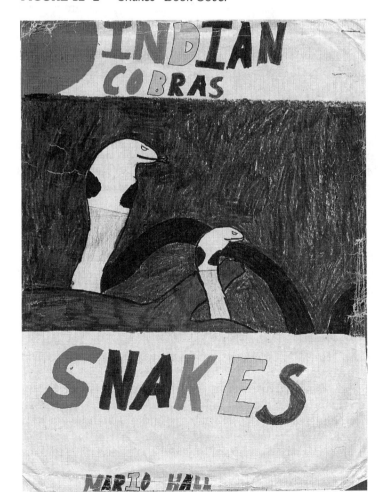

the cubs. They were in the jungle. My first report was about a snake, the second was about a lion, the third and fourth were about snakes.

You can make your own book. Like I was copying this one book *A New True Book of Cats*. I was drawing all of the pictures, 'cause I was looking at the pictures. Drawing the pictures is the best part of writing a story or a report. I drew the cover for my snake report. I got it from this book called *Snakes* (Figure 12–2).

In my first journal our teacher asked us if we wanted to do a thing about our pets or a pet we wanted to have. I did one on what I wanted to have, a cat. After that I did one [a story] on one I had, a dog. My dog ran away. I had told where I had got him from, in my journal, not a pet store. Everybody in my family, my Mom, my sister, and me took care of Bear. This what I wrote in my journal. (See Figure 12–3.)

FIGURE 12–3 *Journal Entry*

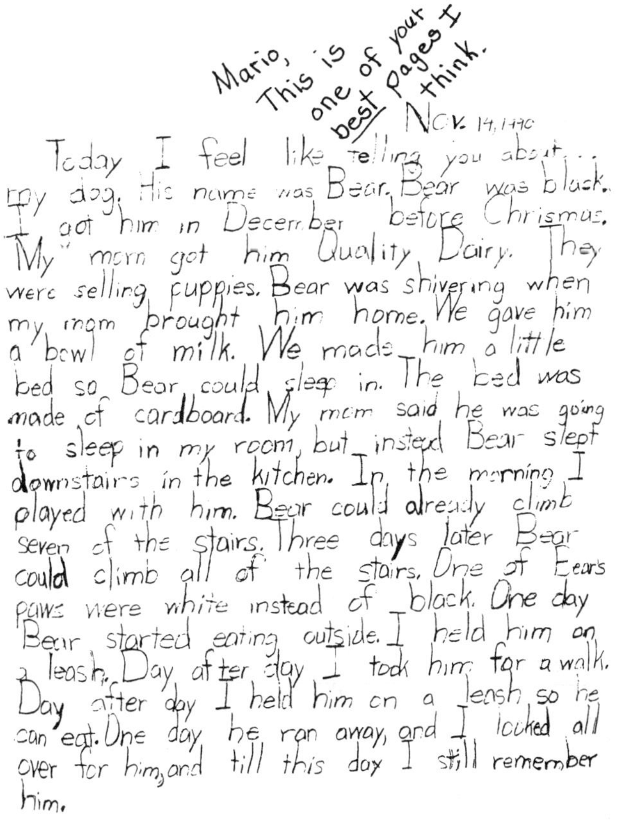

Mario, This is one of your best pages I think.

Nov. 14, 1990

Today I feel like telling you about my dog. His name was Bear. Bear was black. I got him in December before Christmas. My mom got him Quality Dairy. They were selling puppies. Bear was shivering when my mom brought him home. We gave him a bowl of milk. We made him a little bed so Bear could sleep in. The bed was made of cardboard. My mom said he was going to sleep in my room, but instead Bear slept downstairs in the kitchen. In the morning I played with him. Bear could already climb seven of the stairs. Three days later Bear could climb all of the stairs. One of Bear's paws were white instead of black. One day Bear started eating outside. I held him on a leash. Day after day I took him for a walk. Day after day I held him on a leash so he can eat. One day he ran away, and I looked all over for him, and till this day I still remember him.

I was sad when he left. He had a dish with his name in cursive on it. I was seven, but I could write [copy] Bear in cursive. Now, I'm in the third grade I write everything in cursive. Cursive is easy. I'm not used to printing anymore.

One time the teacher told us to write about a pain or a great one [small or large problem] at our house. I wrote about my sister, Eugenia. We argue a lot. Sometimes we get along. Sometimes we don't. Sometimes Eugenia tells on me and gets me in trouble. She took me to the [public] library, and she got a book about learning to drive. I didn't get any books out 'cause I don't have a library card. So I just looked at the animal magazines. My sister writes different kinds of stories in something that looks like a journal. She doesn't read them to me. Nobody needs to read to me. I read! But I don't ask to read her stories. And I didn't read my sister's driving book because it looked boring. Eugenia also reads chapter books and some on the law. She reads rap music magazines. And sometimes she listens to songs on tape, pauses it, and writes the words down.

My Mom orders *Ebony* magazines through the mail. My sister and I read *Ebony* too; I look through them to see what article I want to read and I read 'em. They got different kinds of stars in there. I write about rap stars sometimes. I wrote about Young MC before. My Mom and I read the *Lansing State Journal* newspaper. I like to read the comics and the sports section. Sometimes I read the sale papers too; I like to see what toys are on sale. We read *TV Guide* and the cable TV book to see what is going to be on TV.

My Mom reads letters she gets in the mail. Like grown-ups, she writes checks, bills, different kinds of stuff like sometimes they have to write some down to remember it. Like they write something down to go to the store to buy, so they don't forget.

Today I wrote in my journal that me and Abdul-Jaleel were coming with his Mom to the bookstore to get some books. Tomorrow, I'll probably put in my journal that Abdul-Jaleel's Mom kept trying to get me to get a different book. We went to the Book Barn and two different bookstores in the mall. And she just kept saying: "How about a sports book, an animal book, or a mystery? I really don't think your Mom wants you to get a Ninja Turtle Book." She finally let me get *Teenage Mutant Ninja Turtle II, The Secret of the Ooze.* And my Mom wasn't mad at all, she just said: "You already saw the movie. You should have gotten something new or different." But the next time we go to that one bookstore in the mall, I am going to get that big book of snakes.

Abdul-Jaleel got a baseball story book, then in the car he said: "Mom, can I take this book back?" She told him to read some more of it, then decide if he liked it or not.

I remember when Abdul-Jaleel and me went to see *Dances with Wolves.* I liked the writing at the bottom of the screen 'cause then I knew what the Indians were saying. I liked different parts of the movie. The Indians were the good guys. The bad guys were the people coming with the other weapons [guns]. I think they were the ones that killed the buffaloes. They didn't really show who killed them. They were just laying there skinned. The Indians took the hide off the ones they killed and used it for fur and they ate the inside.

I might do a story about birds next. I got the idea from reading about birds in a book, and watching them outside when I'm coming from school and stuff. And when my family rode bikes to Potter's Park Zoo. We couldn't see them because the [bird] building was closed. But we could hear them and they were too loud! All that chirping, I wanted them to shut-up. Birds talk by chirping. I'll put that in the story, about them chirping. I'll read some more informational books, some bird books, a dictionary and an encyclopedia. I use encyclopedias and animal books to write stories. If my friends tell me something, I make sure it's true before I put it in my story. I could make up something. But I don't. I'll get the books from the library. It's mostly after I read a book that I write about them.

13

REGINA: "A WORLD OF MY OWN"
GRADE 4

Contributed by Bobbie Solley

I met Regina in the fall of 1990 when she was in the fourth grade at a local elementary school in East Texas. I asked the children to write a story for me, and Regina captured my attention immediately. She was eager to write and began as soon as the activity was announced. For the next thirty minutes her attention was focused solely on her story. Occasionally she would stop, chew on her pencil as if in deep thought, then suddenly return to her story writing vigorously. When the allotted time period was up, she was both jubilant and frustrated. She was pleased with her story and wanted to share it with me. She was aware that this effort was only the beginning of a story, and she wanted more time. Regina intrigued me, and I knew I wanted to find out more about her.

During the following weeks, I was able to talk with Regina on a more personal basis. She was an avid writer and reader both at school and at home. During our talks we discussed her feelings, concerns, and perceptions of herself as a writer and reader, the content of her writing, types of reading and writing in which she engaged, sources for her ideas, and the audience to whom she wrote. It was from Regina that I learned the unique world young children can create for themselves through their reading and writing.

I like writing a lot. I enjoy it, and I think it is fun. I write when I'm happy, which is most of the time. The more I write, the more ideas it brings out. It is like a treat. I know that I can write so it's fun for me.

100

I like to think I am fortunate that I can read and write. I've always had this dream ever since I was little but never thought I would be able to put it all on paper. I've wanted to write down every word everybody was saying wherever I went and someday I could publish it. It would be about my life. And then someday I could show my grandchildren what I wrote, and they could hear a good story.

I think writing is like a sport. It's kind of like recess to me. I'm free to say whatever I feel, like in recess where you are free to play whatever you feel. When I write, everything just happens. My brain thinks up stuff and then it flows down my arm onto my paper.

My teacher thinks writing is like spelling and punctuation and grammar. It's probably boring to her. She likes to check our stories to make sure there are no mistakes.

I love to read too. It interests me, and it really relaxes me. I enjoy reading because it makes me happy.

I usually write at home just for the fun of it. I like to write there because there is usually not much happening at my house. My mom works a lot, so I write. I like writing at home because I don't have to read my story in front of a lot of people. I get embarrassed in front of people because my stories are personal. I write at school because the teacher tells me to. I would rather write at home because I can write for as long as I want. I write a lot longer stories at home because I have more time.

I read at home when I'm bored. I also read at home when I'm real mad at my parents or my brother or something like that. I just go into my room, slam the door, open the window and let the breeze in, turn on the radio, get on my bunk, and read. And that really, really relaxes me. I've got three or four boxes full of books like Charlie Brown, mysteries, and scary stories. I like to read things like the *Secret Garden* and *Peppermints in the Parlor*. I read at school when I finish all my work. I turn it all over, and I get real comfortable in my chair. I start reading until the teacher calls time.

I like to write at home in our den. It's real quiet with my grandmother sitting on the couch in front of me. I sit in my Dad's swivel chair and get out my pencil and paper. Sometimes I watch TV and that helps me think of stuff to write. I just write down my ideas and then write my stories later.

When I write at school, I have to sit in my desk. That's the only place my teacher lets us write. At school, there are lots of people around me and my teacher yells, "Five more minutes." I don't like it because that breaks my concentration. I start wishing that we could have more time for writing. I'm afraid that I will run out of time before I get my story finished. When I have to hurry, I sometimes forget my problem. So I talk to myself, and it helps me slow down and relax some. I try not to be so rushed. Sometimes it works, and sometimes it doesn't. But at home, I don't worry about anything because I have all the time I need.

I worry about time when I'm reading too. At school when I'm reading my teacher says, "Okay, put your books away and get out your work or your grammar book" or something like that. I'm in the middle of a sentence, and she interrupts me. I read the rest of the sentence, but I don't know what I'm reading. She really bothers me when she does that. But when I'm reading at home, I can just read and read and read until it's time to go to bed or do something else.

When I write at home I'm able to write about my feelings and my dreams and my fantasies. At school I can't do that because the teacher tells me what to write about. Sometimes she gives us the topic sentence and then we just continue the rest of the story. Most of the time she gives us pictures, and we have to write about what's in that picture. Sometimes, but not very often, she lets us write about whatever we want. But, at home I can do that all the time.

I especially like to write fantasy stories. I write adventure stories, too. I think I have a good imagination. I'm good at description, too. I like to write descriptive papers, but only if I can find the words that I want to write down. Like when we wrote fairy tales—our teacher let us write about whatever we wanted as long as it was a fairy tale, and mine was about six pages long. At first my story started out like, "We were in a silver time machine and then, CRASH!" But after I went back and looked at it again, I changed it to, "We were in a silver time machine with buttons, switches, knobs, and levers trying to get to London, 1886. Then CRASH!" The second one was much better, more imaginative and descriptive, so I liked it better.

What I like to write about just depends on my mood. I have to be in an adventurous mood to write adventure like if I have done something that I really enjoyed or am going to do something exciting, I write about it.

I really hate to write how-to papers. They are harder to write because you have to add everything so people will know what to do, and they won't do anything wrong. I don't do very many how-to papers unless my teacher says we have to.

Some days I feel really creative. So I write. I get my ideas from different places. I think them up, or sometimes I write about what I'm doing or have done. Like I wrote one day about when I rode my horse. Another day I wrote about when my brother broke his arm. And one day I wrote about when me and my dad and my brother went hunting and shot an armadillo. My brother and I buried it in our backyard. That was an adventurous story.

Sometimes I get my ideas from walking or looking around my house. My house is real big. It's got four bedrooms, three bathrooms, a living room, and a kitchen. I just walk around the house and look. One day I was looking at my dog back when she was a puppy. She was sleeping upside down, her legs were waving up and down in the air, and she was growling at something. I wrote about that. My dad took a picture of our dog and pinned the picture to the story I wrote.

Sometimes I write about animals. I might write about a beetle and make it be a real person. One time my cousin, who lives in Hawaii, told me she plays with cockroaches, so I wrote about that and how the cockroaches attacked her. It ended up being her nightmare.

I get some of my ideas from watching other people. They are so funny sometimes, but they don't know it. My sister is really corny, but she says some funny things. So I write about some of the corny things she says and does. I also watch people at school, especially my three best friends. They are really funny. So I watch what they do and say and later I write about them. They don't know that they are helping me with story ideas.

One idea my brother and I got together while we were eating. So we are writing a story together. He's the illustrator, and I'm the writer. It's going to be a nine or twelve chapter story. At the beginning it says, "In 1873, there was a major food fight, and all because Colonel Corn, Colonel Zucchini, Sergeant Taco, and Colonel Beef were having a disagreement. Colonel Corn and Colonel Zucchini were trying to steal Sergeant Taco and Colonel Beef's buffalo. But they didn't succeed. Sergeant Taco and Colonel Beef captured them and declared war. Both the meat-force and the fruits and vegetables were planning raids, and fortunately they planned them on the same night. Right then all the stuff from the meat-force and all the stuff from the vegetable-force hits the egg land mines, the egg carton fleet, and the egg guns. There was a clash then. It is now 1990, in Stoneybrook, Connecticut. The meats, fruits, and vegetables still have a grievance against each other." That's as far as we've gotten, but we work on it every day.

Reading different books gives me ideas when I write. Like in one of my stories I used some tricks they used in one book called *Nancy Drew: Mystery in Magnolia Mansion*. It was about a writer named Betty, and this writer wrote a lot of good books. Bessy, Nancy's niece, gets a letter and a phone call from the writer, and she's really scared. Someone is trying to kill her. In that book, there is a sliding door with all these flowers around it that looked like part of the wall. I thought about that and then I stopped and said, "Hey, I can use that." And then I wrote it down on a sheet of paper so I wouldn't forget. I used that idea in one of my mystery stories. I had a person trying to get away from someone and the person just slid open the secret door like they did in *Mystery in Magnolia Mansion*.

At home, I read what we have. I choose my own books. There's a big choice in the stores, you know. And we buy what I want to read. I like to read exciting, adventurous books. I especially like suspense. One of my favorite books is called *The Girl with the Silver Eyes*. It's about a girl with silver eyes, and she can like look at things and make them move.

I love animals too, so I like to read books about animals. *A Dog Called Kitty* is my very favorite book. Kitty is a dog, but she really likes cats. That was really the first book that got me into reading. That was the first book I ever read by Bill Wallace, and he's my favorite author.

I like reading about real lives and things that could really happen. I read *Helen Keller* during spring break, and I really enjoyed that story. I also read *Ten Boy Summer*. It's about this girl, Jill, with her friend, Toni. They started a contest of who could date ten boys over the summer.

I like a book if it's really exciting and has a point. Good books are of some use. I like reading anything except books that are real sad and pointless and those textbooks at school.

In school, we read in our *Sketches* books. I like reading from *Sketches*. We just read the stories, and it doesn't take very long. My teacher doesn't give us very many books in class. She started out with a big thing of books, but she let the students take them home. They never brought them back so now we only have three books in our classroom.

Reading is comfortable to me whenever it's on a winter night and I come in, and I'm real cold. I turn on the heater and go to my room. The heater directs heat directly to my top bunk, and I sleep on the top. So I go on the top bunk, get real warm and cozy, and start reading. I sometimes read in the den in the recliner. There's a light over it. So I turn on the light, put on a blanket, and read.

Reading is uncomfortable when I'm reading things about me or about someone like me in a story. They sometimes name all their faults, and I have the same faults as that, and I don't like it. I just throw away that book.

The only time writing is uncomfortable for me is when I write about personal things. Like when my brother makes fun of me or laughs at me. I think it's uncomfortable because I write about things that happen to me, and sometimes it hurts. But I write them down anyway. I think it helps me work out my problems. I just write the personal things in my diary and lock them up so no one can see them.

I usually just write for me, or my mom and dad. At home when I write, it's usually my mom and dad who read it. They know how I feel about writing, about where I'd like to go and all my dreams. I like to write about where I would like to go and about people in Australia and Asia and other places. I like to write about strange things like, "I wonder if the fish talk to each other like we talk to each other in just plain words." Most people would think that was dumb. But my mom understands. She laughs at the stuff I write. She compliments my writing a lot, and she knows that I don't like other people to see my writing. My dad reads my writing too. He compliments my writing and tells me how good it is.

At school, I only write for my teacher. She comes around when we are in our revision groups. She will suggest things to improve our writing if someone else doesn't. She comes around when we are writing our final draft and marks on our papers, in pencil, the things we need to improve. She writes questions to help us include more detail. She tells us to use more description or elaborate more. She helps us express our feelings in writing. My teacher really encourages us to write a lot, or at least some of the kids. Some of us don't need encouragement, like me. I write anyway, without encouragement. She taught us about drafting and revision. But, I learned about them by myself. That is just what I do.

I don't trust my teacher when she reads my writing like I do my mom and dad. She's not a part of my family. But she makes me feel comfortable about my writing. She compliments me sometimes. When I turn in a final draft, if it's a perfect paper with no mistakes, she doesn't say anything about it. But, if I need to add things or take things out, she will put a line through it or make notes that I need to change things.

I would rather write for my teacher than for other kids. They laugh a lot. Sometimes they are just kidding, but you never know when they are just kidding and when they are serious.

My teacher won't let us take the writing that we do in school home with us. She usually gives us something to write and then she likes to see what we write in class. She tells us to finish it in class.

If I could give teachers advice about how to teach writing, I would probably tell them to let the children write about what they want to write about. It gets more out of them. If a teacher gives the children a topic that they don't want to write about, then they probably won't write much. But, if the children can choose their own topic, then they will write more. Then, I would tell the teachers to let the children write freely, don't worry about handwriting. I would tell them to encourage the children to write better, not tell them, just encourage them. They should also give children as much time as they need to write. As long as it takes some people to write a story, that is how long the teacher should give them. Teachers should also be patient with children when they write.

Teachers should let the children just read more, too. Mostly, like I said in writing, teachers should let the children choose their own books and give them more time to read. The more you read, the better you're gonna be able to read. See, when I first started reading, I didn't read real good. I read slow—"The . . . cat . . . was . . . in . . . the . . . hat." And then I started reading real thick books, and I got better and better at it. Now I can read real fast. If I read really, really fast, it used to be I couldn't understand the words. But now I can. So just give them time to read about whatever they want.

I think I am a good reader and writer. I know I am a good reader because people say I am. My papa, when he comes, I read him the inside cover or the back cover of a book, and he says, "Look at that. Little Gina can read." He makes a really big deal out of it and so does my mom and dad and everybody. People tell me I'm a good reader, and I really think I am. I read a lot, and I have self-confidence. I'm not sure why I think I'm a good writer. I think it's because nobody in my family writes as much as I do, and it's not hard for me. It's a treat. It's easy. Writing helps me express my feelings. It helps me visualize what it is I'm feeling. It also helps me remember stuff that I have done in the past that was fun. The best part of my writing is my imagination. I have a good imagination. I can escape when I read, and I'm in a world of my own when I write.

14

Asuka

"BOTH IN ENGLISH AND JAPANESE"

(Grade 4)

Contributed by David P. Shea

While working in Japan for three years as an English teacher in the public schools, I found that one of the most pressing problems Japanese education faces is how to deal with children who return to Japan after having lived abroad. In general, these students have learned English well, but they have often fallen behind in Japanese and find it difficult to keep up with the blistering pace of Japanese education. Asuka [/áska/] presents a portrait of a child in the middle of this process, struggling to keep her Japanese language and culture while living in Atlanta, Georgia.

Asuka is doing well at her American school, primarily because of her mother's support and direction. Although Asuka's mom may not be familiar with all the intricacies of American schools, she knows that reading is fundamentally important. She buys her daughter books, which line the walls of the bedroom, and makes her read at night. She also provides a tutor, who reads aloud and introduces Asuka to other good books.

Asuka faces the difficult task of living in two worlds, learning two languages, and mastering two school curriculums. One way she copes with her dual identity is by working hard. She has tutors for both languages, special classes in the afternoons, and Japanese school all day on Saturday. While to American eyes, Asuka is well adjusted to school, that is not enough for her parents. Always in the back of their minds are the standards and expectations of another language and a completely different system. Essentially, Asuka leads two lives in one.

My name is Asuka, and I'm in fourth grade in elementary school. I was born in Illinois and my sister, Ikumi, was born in New York. I'm nine and she's ten. I can't remember when I came to Atlanta. I forgot when I first learned English. It was probably when I was in kindergarten. In preschool, I didn't know anything, so I just kept quiet.

At our house, we eat Japanese style food. I think our house is American style, but some things are Japanese like the vases, or the Japanese dolls my mom made. My friends' houses are different. They don't have Japanese things, but sometimes we give them presents when we come back from vacation in Japan.

When I'm in Japanese School on Saturdays and when I'm home talking to my parents, I use Japanese. I don't always use Japanese to my mother, but my mom doesn't understand English that much and she likes me to speak Japanese with her. I understand English better. When I'm mad or when I don't know how to say something in Japanese, I use English to my mom. Sometimes, I feel like I can't say what I want to say when I'm speaking Japanese, so I ask her, "How do you say this?" It's usually just one word. Even though I mix English and Japanese together, my mom will understand. Before I say something in Japanese, I always think in English because it's easier for me to speak English than Japanese. When I speak Japanese, I'm like, "What's this word?" Even at Japanese school, first I think in English, then I try to transfer it to Japanese.

My sister and I speak English most of the time. That way we can understand each other more. And Mom uses English to me when I'm studying the questions for homework. It's too hard to speak only Japanese. I would feel frustrated if I couldn't say what I wanted. But I think it's important to speak Japanese because a lot of people speak Japanese and because my mom and dad are Japanese.

I speak English with my friends at my American school. But sometimes I speak to my friend, Aya, in Japanese when we're playing. She's in the same class as me. When I use Japanese to Aya at school, sometimes I get in trouble because the other kids don't understand what I'm saying. We aren't allowed to speak Japanese at school. It's a rule. You can't speak other languages than English in school because other kids won't understand what you're saying. And the teachers might think you're saying something bad or something. Sometimes I break the rule and speak in Japanese with Aya. And sometimes, my friends ask me, "How do you say butterfly?" Or "How do you say something?" They want to know Japanese too. And so I teach them.

Once, we were having a Valentine's party in my class and when we were getting in line, I told Aya about something and then a boy said, "What are you saying?" We got in trouble. He didn't get mad. He just said, "I don't know what they're saying. They're talking Japanese!" And my teacher said, "Girls, you're not supposed to do that!"

I think the people in my class know more English than me. Well, actually, no. But sometimes I think I really understand English and sometimes I think I really don't. You see, there's a class named TAG [Talented and Gifted] and it's a group of people who take a test, all kinds of tests. Some are easy and some are hard. I think smart people go to TAG, but there's a girl and she goes, but I think she's dumb. I want to go to TAG because my friends are in there. And I think TAG is fun because they get to do all kinds of activities. My mom says maybe when she talks to my teacher, maybe I could be in TAG. I would have to take the test, but I'm not sure if I could go.

My English class is from a book. It's boring. I like to read, but the English book has nothing interesting. We do some dittos, and some writing from the book, like adverbs, verbs, nouns, and adjectives. We do common words, proper words, and linking verbs, helping verbs, and stuff like that. It's not hard, but it's hard to memorize. Most of the time, I get A's in English, but not always.

Nothing funny happens in English class. We don't do stories much. We do normal work like spelling, English, and reading. English means you get it from the English book. The teacher tells you the page and you have to write some sentences and sometimes she gives you a ditto and she'll make you do that.

Today in my English class I did adverbs, like when you use "when" and "where." There are exercises in the book. First of all, it tells what's an adverb, then it gives you some examples. Then there's a class exercise and you do them and on the next page there's a number saying A and B and Application, and you do those for your class work. Application tells you what to do and there's some words below it and it says make five sentences with these adverbs below. I make them for my work. Then I file it in a little box in my classroom for my papers. There's a box that says English and you turn it in there. First the teacher checks it, and then you need to get your parents to sign it.

I think that kind of English is helpful, because first of all, I didn't know what an adverb is, and after I read the book I knew what it is and when to use it. It helps me to write because I need to use adverbs, verbs, and adjectives and nouns in a story.

Sometimes the teacher does say to write a story. She'll change it a little, and then you'll copy it again to a clean sheet of paper and make it a story. She gives you a title, like "Why does a duck have a white stripe?" or "What if your eye was on top of your finger?" or "You had a substitute, but didn't know it was President Bush," or something. In those cases, I just make things up, and if I had a substitute but I didn't know it was President Bush, I would say that he was real nice and we did everything fun and we had a party at the end of the day and went home early.

I don't think I have a good imagination. You see, I'm not really good at stories. I can't think of what I should write. It takes me a long time to think what's next and things like that. When I'm thinking, my teacher usually has some other work to do and goes down to the other end of the building to make some copies, so we have to do it on our own. I never talk to my friends about it. Everybody's real quiet when they write or else the teacher will get mad at us and say, "You have twice as much homework!"

For our book reports, the teacher sometimes picks out a certain kind of book, and then we have to write a report on it. We have to tell what was it all about, what was the title, and who was the author. Our last book report was a biography, and our teacher said we had to dress up like the character in our book report, and really act like him or her. If I was Helen Keller, I would have to say, "I am blind."

I decided to do an adventure about Mary Jimson, which was the easiest. She was captured by the Shawnee Indians. I just dressed like her and I told my class about the book and how the book was. At the last part, I said yes, I liked the book. Dressing like the person helped me understand the story pretty much. When I said, "I," I really knew I was talking about the biography character because I had been studying about that person.

When I read, I pick a book first because the title sounds good. Then I open the book and see how much there is, how tiny the words are, and how many pages there are. I read a little bit and when I think it sounds good, I check it out. My friends tell me about books. April read *The Devil's Arithmetic* and she said, "You better read this. This is a good book!" She said that many people don't check it out, but she checked it out once and said it was a really good book.

The librarian checks books out for me sometimes. She knows how much I read and how well I read and how good the book is. If it's too hard or too easy, she won't let me check it out. If it is just right, then she'll make me check it out. The librarian knows how much our class reads, and she tells us about the book and how the book is and she will say, "You'll enjoy it."

My teacher tells us when the book report is due so we have to read it before the date of the book report. My mom knows the day and my mom makes me read the book. Every night when I go to sleep, my mom says, "If you're not sleepy, read your book report's book and then go to sleep." Most of the time, I read the books, but lately, I've been going to sleep.

I like a book if it's real interesting. I like books better than TV. Books have more detail, and the TV has less. I read *Charlotte's Web,* and then we watched the movie. I knew what was going to happen, but some things didn't show up on the television and I was like, "Where's that part?"

When I'm reading a book, in my head I will think of a picture. I will make up a person, and see their picture in my head. As the story goes on, the picture changes. When I read *Charlotte's Web,* there was one chapter where there were only two illustrations. On the pages where there were no illustrations, I just made them up. I saw a pig, Wilbur, and the spider, Charlotte. I just put them together with the rat, Templeton. The pictures I see, I put in my mind and keep on reading, and as I go, I kind of change the pictures. The picture kind of moves. It's almost like I'm watching a movie inside my head. When I'm reading sometimes, I can't just imagine the person because it's too hard to put it into my mind, with all the details and stuff. So making pictures makes me understand.

I dislike books that are depressing and sad, or when something exciting happens but then something boring happens, and the story becomes boring. I like mysteries and adventures. It's fun to read mysteries because if like someone was murdered, you say, "It's that guy! No, it's that guy!" It's real fun to guess the people who tried to murder the person. Adventures are fun because you wonder what's going to happen next. I like when I wonder because later on it's going to be a surprise and I like to be surprised. I don't care about the ending. I just go on reading and try to see what will happen next because at the end I think most books have surprising endings. I like that.

My mom makes me read books. We have lots of books we order from a book club and my mom helps me pick the books. We get a magazine and put stars on the ones we like. There's a little paragraph about the book and mom reads it. She won't buy us comics because she won't let us read those kind of books. Only books like *The Box Car Children.* Sometimes we buy books we don't really like. We don't put a star on the book, but my mom buys it anyway. She thinks it's good for us, and she makes us read it.

I like to read in my room when it's quiet, because if it's loud, I can't hear my mind reading, or if my sister is watching the television and I'm reading a book, I can't concentrate. I don't listen to the radio a lot because I have to do my work first, and I have some special classes in the afternoon, like calligraphy, gymnastics, and my English tutor and my Japanese tutor.

On Mondays, I go to Japanese calligraphy. How shall I explain calligraphy? In Japanese it's called *o-shuuji.* You have these Japanese tools: this ink stuff, well it's not really ink. It's charcoal. You add water to it and then you get a special kind of brush and hold it and you lift your elbow up. I'm left handed, but I do the calligraphy with my right hand, because in *o-shuuji,* you always have to write with your right hand. You have a thin (you can see through it) piece of paper. You put a weight on the top of it and you put your left hand on the paper and then write the Japanese *kanji.*

I do the same characters for one month. One that I did says *taue.*[1] I think it's kind of like a crop and has water in it and there's this grass piece of thing and some old people work there. I had trouble with *koinu,* because it means "little dog," and I always write *ko* (little) small and dog bigger, so it's like *koINU!*

In my American school, I don't practice handwriting, but my mom makes me do handwriting checkups for social studies and science homework. Sometimes, I have to write the question *and* the complete sentences. My mom says that it's for my own good, because when I get bigger, I'll have to write a lot.

---

[1]*taue* means "rice planting."

On Tuesday, I have my American tutor. I have one hour and my sister has one hour. After that, we change to our gymnastics suits. We play Nintendo or do something for a few minutes, and then we go to gymnastics. Mrs. Takagawa takes us. She has two kids: one is Ella and one is Erika.

In the car with Ella and Erika, we sometimes do pattycake, both in English and Japanese. Sometimes we tell jokes and talk about things that happen. I teach them things like pattycake:

> *Ladies and gentlemen, children too*
> *Us two chicks gonna reebop for you*
> *Gonna reebop shibot shibot shibot*
> *Gonna reebop shibot shibot shibot*
> *When I was little, I played with spiders*
> *Now I am older and drinking apple cider*
> *Gonna reebop shibot shibot shibot*
> *Gonna reebop shibot shibot shibot*
> *When I was little, I played with toys,*
> *Now I'm older and beating up boys*
> *Gonna reebop shibot shibot shibot*

And sometimes we make things up:

> *When I was little I used to be a dork*
> *Now I'm older and eating with my fork*

And there's the one,

> *Went upstairs to say my prayers,*
> *Came downstairs and the boogeyman's there.*

And stuff like that. I mostly learned these from my friend, April.

After dinner, my sister and I have to do our work. If we're finished, mom says to read a book or watch television. Well, she doesn't *tell* us to watch television, but we sometimes just watch it and when my dad comes home, my mom says, "Turn off the television!" because my dad doesn't want us to watch television. At night, my mom says, "It's night. Now it's *our* turn to watch television." So they watch a Japanese show. To me it's boring. They have swords and stuff like that. It's on video my grandparents tape for us. Or sometimes my mom borrows them from a friend.

Mostly, I watch American TV, but sometimes I watch *Folktales from Japan*. My grandparents send us the tapes. I like it because the characters have square faces and potato heads, and they speak funny. Sometimes I watch it, but I have no time to watch anything because my sister always watches a Japanese cartoon. Uggh! It all started when we went to Japan. We go every three years. When we went last time, my sister just turned on the TV and started watching this cartoon. She told my grandmother she wanted a tape, so my grandmother taped it for us and *ever* since then, my sister's been watching it. I don't like it *very* much.

My sister doesn't really read books. Probably she doesn't like books. You see, my sister likes television *a lot,* more than her work. I think that books are better than TV because books tell you more things. But I think TV is useful. When we don't know the weather, my mom gets it on the weather report. Watching television is also useful for language because when you hear something and you don't know what the meaning is, you can ask your parents and learn some more words.

I think Japanese Saturday School is fun because we get lots of recess, but I really don't like Japanese language class. It's boring. I don't know Japanese much, so I think it's kind of hard, and I really don't understand.

But it's important, and I would go even if my mom said I didn't have to. It's for my own good, even if I don't like it sometimes. Japanese language class does me good, and sometimes it makes me learn things. I like *kanji* and reading Japanese books for homework. When I know what it's saying to me, then I know what it means and I feel good about it because I don't get stuck on the words.

My mom helps me read the stories. If I don't know the *kanji,* she will tell me. And when I don't know their meaning, I will ask her and she will say, "It's like this or that." I can't read the story if I don't know the *kanji.* They fit into the story, and if I didn't know the *kanji,* I wouldn't understand the story, and it wouldn't be any fun.

I don't talk much at Japanese school. Well I do, but . . . Sometimes we play jumprope, or sometimes we play tag, or sometimes we just stay in the classroom and do things like origami. I talk to Aya a lot. We talk about English school. We say, "Do you like English school? Do you think the teacher is nice?" It's kind of hard to speak English at Japanese school. There's a rule against it.

I had to write a story about my mom for Japanese school. I wrote about how she gets angry when my sister and I don't do our work, but she's real nice when my sister and I do something real good, like wash the dishes. That time, I thought in Japanese because I was afraid that if I would think in English, I'd write in English. So that time I did, pretty much, think in Japanese.

15

Ben

"IF YOU'RE DIFFERENT, YOU'LL ALMOST PROBABLY BE GIFTED"

(Grade 4)

Contributed by Mara Casey

Ben lives in Southern California with his mother, Peg Syverson, a fellow graduate student with whom I do collaborative research. He is an unassuming, witty, gifted fourth grader whose interests are art, physics, chemistry, and electronics. He also composes music and songs and plays alto sax, recorder, keyboard, and Little League baseball. Before Ben was seven, he had over 230 inventions, including a pocket-size coffee maker, a pocket-size vacuum cleaner, and a time machine. In third grade Ben's teacher turned over all science teaching in the class to him.

This profile, based on three, hour-long audiotaped interviews conducted at his kitchen table, gives Ben's perspective on what it means to be a gifted child. He values being different, but claims to be just a little smarter than the rest of us. Unlike many of the children I've talked to, Ben likes writing so much he doesn't care whether he's given assignments or not. Also, unlike many other children, Ben wants help only with mechanics; he doesn't want to be told what to write and how to write. This may be because he thinks there's no such thing as good writing.

I'm gifted. You might say that. If you're different, you'll almost probably be gifted. You can't be just the same old everyday person. People will notice you. That's the way I've always thought about it.

I may be ten percent above average—around there, just a little smarter than the average person, you know, like my mom is. That's

113

like the only big part being a GATE [Gifted and Talented Education] child is going to play in my future life. I won't walk down the street and say "Ha Ha, I was in GATE school in the fourth grade."

I have a theory: If a reporter was looking for one person in a crowd of New Yorkers, and all the New Yorkers were wearing black suits and a tie, and you're wearing a fluorescent pink shirt and green trousers, who do you think he's gonna pick? I don't want to be your everyday person, you know, that time-to-go-to-work kind of person. Life would be kind of boring. I mean if you were just walking along being an everyday person, not standing out in any crowd, nobody would say, "Now look at him!" Or, "Look at the shirt he's wearing!"

I want my stories to be different because if I was the same as everyone else, then I could never really be really good at writing. If I grew up and got to be a famous writer, and I wrote books just like every other person and his grandmother, then nobody would really buy my books.

Writing has always kind of come easily. As long as I can see words on the page, I'm satisfied. I like the fifteenth and sixteenth century because of the sword fighting. That's why I joined fencing. I'd probably pick that to write about, or something really wild. Weird stories like: "The boy was walking down the street, and he found a little egg. He wondered what was in the egg, so he cracked it open, and it was a spaceship. And then he flew to Mars and there he found people, and they had all these different eggs. He could go to different galaxies."

I sort of like science fiction, but not in a serious way, just funny and light. I don't like stories like: "The Martians came, and they ripped everybody to pieces." More like "He met the Martians, and the Martians were really nice, and they had candy bars." I like my stories to be unexpected, really unexpected. A surprise everything, beginning, middle, and ending: talking gorillas, a steamboat that wouldn't stop even if it started about two or three fires, the gorilla touching a shark.

I learned to write through my mom; she was constantly writing things. When I was in kindergarten, she was making a dictionary at the publishers where she worked. So I made a little book of my own, and I typed it.

When I first started writing, I had to really think about it. You had to write in really big letters, and you could only fit like three words on a line. You'd go, "The cat went"—next line—"to the"—and then you'd have to start a new line. I'd put all that effort into writing something, and I'd go back, and it'd be only four sentences long. Writer's cramp would come after about five sentences.

My first grade teacher was kind of a regular teacher. I wasn't really interested in writing, but you usually didn't have a free choice of topics. They'd say, "Write about Thanksgiving and give the ten things that you're thankful about." Sometimes they still do that, but at least we get to write it on the Mac now.

I didn't do a lot of writing in second grade, except for the play I wrote at home for the talent show. It was just seatwork, seatwork, seatwork! We'd come in, and we'd have like five pages of seatwork.

It's lunch time by the time we're done. When we'd come back, we'd have to do like a little bit of math. That takes up an hour. We learned how to write a letter in cursive each day. We started with A, and we'd write it about twenty times. That was about an hour. And then we'd go out and have P.E., and that was the end of the day.

In third grade I had kind of a tough, really weird teacher. About ten times that year we copied from the board every single word on the first two pages of the medical thing in the encyclopedia. It taught us how to write cursive better. But it didn't do a lot for our writing. But if you don't do it, she yells and screams at you. I wanted to be taken out of that classroom.

She wanted us to be really prepared for fourth grade, but she was teaching harder stuff then they'll ever teach in fourth grade. Doubling and multiplying and really heavy dividing like 3,928 divided by 400 or something. I was really awake in math class, but it was like really easy stuff for spelling and all the rest of the things. They'd show you a word and say, "Find another word that means the same thing in this sentence." And Health was especially weird 'cause they'd say, "You should brush your teeth every day. Plaque builds up on your teeth." Stuff you would learn in kindergarten.

Most teachers, they're just teaching writing. They don't really think much about all the stuff behind it. My second grade teacher just wanted to get work done. My third grade teacher just wanted to yell and scream. But my fourth grade teacher, Miss Miller, is good all around. She's organized. She gives the right amount of work. She's like one of the gang to the kids, to all of the kids. She's very peppy and stuff.

Writing in a GATE class is a lot different than in a regular fourth grade where writing is just another subject. With my teacher it's a whole other experience. We have a lot more writing. I mean we have to write a research paper two or three pages long. That's longer than my mom had to write a paper.

We have creative writing every Friday. We have one Mac for thirty-two kids, so we do our creative writing by hand. She passes out the paper that tells on it what you have to write. This is an example: "Alien invaders have invaded. They say, 'We want all the money in the city.'" And then you have to write the rest of it. We have to finish in a limited amount of time. Our teacher says it has to be twenty sentences long. If you don't have twenty sentences, it'll lower your grade, so you go back and count your sentences. If you see "The cat won the race," and that's only nineteen sentences, you put, "The cat was happy." Then you're fine.

We don't always have assignments. Sometimes when our teacher has a lot of stuff to grade or something, she just says, "Write about whatever you want." It doesn't matter to me whether I have an assignment or not. I just like to write stories.

Each kid has a certain time to write on the Mac once a week, but not creative writing. It's a little harder than writing by hand 'cause I can write as lot faster than I can type right now, at this stage. When

I can type as fast as I can write, I'll do creative writing on the computer. Everyone has the same assignment. She tapes a little index card on the desk where the Mac is, and then when the kid comes up, it says, "Write about Easter" or something. But it's more free, not like, "Write ten things that you like about Christmas."

It isn't usually too long. Sometimes we have a twenty-sentence requirement on the Mac, but it's not as strict as creative writing. If it says, "Write ten sentences," and you forget two, oh well, it's like no big deal. You just type it up. And then you print it. Sometimes I write the whole story or secret messages in my secret code. It's a really complicated secret alphabet. My teacher writes on my paper, "Strange story" or something, but she'll accept it as long as you type something.

Sometimes we have oral stuff. That's when we have to stand up in front and read our story to the whole class. You have to finish writing your story really quick so everyone in the class has time to read. Some kids get it real sloppy, or they don't get it finished and get a really bad grade or an incomplete. When you read your story to the class, nobody would say, "Oh that's a weird story." They might laugh, if it's a funny story, but they don't usually ask questions or make suggestions.

When I'm doing creative writing, I just start writing, and I go into this kind of trance. I have all these thoughts, and my hand will write it. Sometimes I forget what I've been thinking about, and when I go back to read it, it seems pretty interesting. The stories I write by hand probably have more imagination or more creativity because I don't go into the same states when I'm typing on the Mac. But when I get better at it, I probably will.

This trance only happens when I'm writing about something I really like and know a lot about and when I'm writing songs. It's kind of like a little voice back there telling you what to write, like the central chip on the computer. It never happens when I'm writing spelling words on a test because I'm concentrating on writing them correctly. If I have to write a paper on the study of frogs, then I couldn't just go into a trance because I can't get the information right at hand. I'm not like a computer that can read all the disks. But if I already had the information, I probably would go into that same kind of state and just keep writing.

Some of the kids my age probably go into these trances, some of them don't. Maybe ten more in my class. A whole bunch of other kids keep trying, I guess, to write something really good. But when they're trying to write something, they can't go into it. It only happens when you really like to write, and when you don't really have to think a lot about a subject, when it's kind of free. You're kind of relaxed and you just write.

That's kind of what happens. I can't help it sometimes. It's eerie, like tooth decay. It starts out right around near my brain, just floating around. Then it starts eating away and goes into my central brain, and then it controls my muscles. "Oh, no!" The first time that happened I thought it was a dream. They call it subdreams because you're still awake. It's like when you're in bed, and you think you're falling off a cliff, and you get the same sensation. And when you're about to hit, you have a little muscle movement. It's that same kind of trance. Then when I go back to see what I've written, it's like someone else has written it. It's like a handicap sometimes.

The gifted class is just regular stuff. It's not like perfectly prepared students that are so well organized and everything. They're just a little above average. It's not like they're zombies or anything. They get in trouble sometimes. I mean, they're kids. Some GATE kids are very smart, but still they laugh and everything. They know how to do a couple of subjects better. And that would pass them through the GATE test. It's one of the easiest tests we've ever taken. Sometimes you guess, and you get lucky.

I like being a GATE student because I know it's not very different, and, especially in math, it's a little more challenging than the everyday "two plus four" they'd teach. The only difference is that you might have a little more work, a little more activities, 'cause they know that in regular class you get bored. In third grade I was really bored even with all that work 'cause it was real easy. It was like waiting for something to do. I kept on looking things up in the encyclopedia.

I'm not bored any more. But still I'm zipping through the work. But when I'm finished, then I have maybe a center to go to, or I have the CTBS test to do. Or I can go to the library. There's so many things to do.

But science is really pathetic. The kids love doing all those little experiments, but they teach so little of it. I'm disappointed because I love science. So I set up a whole big lab in my room. The kids call me Ben Franklin.

Science probably takes the biggest part of my life, but writing comes in second or third. But still you have to write a lot in math and science in school and at home. I have to take notes on my experiments at home. You know, write hypotheses up. Then conclusions. Sometimes I save my notes because I might go back to that experiment. It's like police records.

Writing songs and creative writing play a big part in my life, too. I bought a synthesizer with the money I had in the bank. I didn't know how to play it, so I started a band. Nobody knew how to write songs, so I kind of taught myself. I have to think of all of the melodies for all of the instruments. I memorize them and stash them all back there in my head. I think up a little part of a song, and I say, "sounds good." And then I think of some words, and I say, "sounds good." And then I say, "Hey, I've got a little bit of a song." So I keep on writing more of the song, and then, finally, I have a song.

Writing is always going to play a gigantic role in my life, especially in high school and college 'cause I know you have to do a lot of writing then. All those term papers and things. I know it's not going to be that hard. Kids say, "Well, fifteen pages. That's going to be real hard. How am I going to write that?" But as you get older, you learn more, and you're able to write more at a time, and it seems like less.

Miss Miller doesn't really help me with how to write. She doesn't say, "OK, you ought to make it more adventurous," or anything like that. I think that can get obnoxious if people tell you what to write and how to do it. She just tells me where to indent and stuff.

I don't think there's any such thing as good writing. If you say, "Well that's good writing," it can be appalling to other people. I know a whole bunch of people say, "That's a good writer," but you can't just really say, "That's good writing, and that's not." I don't think that's really a good way to think.

16

Lisa, Rosa, and Paul

"I'M GLAD I WROTE, INSTEAD OF JUST TELLING IT TO SOMEBODY"

(Grade 4)

Contributed by William McGinley & George Kamberelis

For the past several years, we have been working with Victoria Rybicki and her fourth-grade children helping to create a literate classroom community where children can use reading and writing in ways that they find personally meaningful and where their voices can be heard and celebrated. Within this community, children have been encouraged to discuss and write about their lives, their families, and the community in which they live. Indeed, children have responded to this invitation with excitement and enthusiasm, sharing with one another many of their experiences, aspirations, and visions for themselves, their families and friends, and their community. They have been particularly enthusiastic about getting their ideas and experiences "down on paper" and helping each other out in all aspects of the writing process. At the end of each year, children have published an anthology of their work, leaving a trace of themselves in the larger world.

Our work with Victoria and her children over the past several years has clearly shown us that writing is much more than the ability to communicate a particular message. The talk and texts produced by the children with whom we have worked have provided us with insight into the many ways that children use writing to understand themselves in relation to other people and the world in which they live. In this chapter, the voices of three children illustrate some of the personal and social functions that underlie and motivate children's writing.

We begin with Lisa whose vision of family and community life is embodied in her essay "Living the Black Life." In this piece she envisages possible worlds for herself, for others, and for society, while remaining naively yet painfully aware of past and present social injustices. Next, Rosa discusses how she came to write the published piece she called "My Mom" and how the story has functioned in her life. Particularly intriguing is Rosa's use of writing to externalize difficult emotions and to create openings for social exchanges that help her to work through those emotions. Finally, as Paul talks about his essay "Enslaved," he shares his sense of joy at thinking about himself as a writer, the importance of self-expression through writing that he has come to believe in, and his perceptions about the potential power of the written word to transform social meanings and practices.

FIGURE 16–1   *"Living in the Black Life"*

Living in the Black

It's nice Living in the Black life. I haven't been harmed in Detroit. Back Then Blacks were treated bad and beaten and spat at. But right now it is better and I am happy that I am living in the Black life. Some people don't like living in the Black life. Back then white people hated Blacks but now White people really like Blacks. We communicate with each other and it's a wonderful life being Black. And I don't hate for being Black and other Blacks shouldn't hate being Black. They should be happy who they are and no matter what Whites do to Blacks we are good people still.

So love who you are don't hate yourself and thank God for making you a person. It doesn't matter if you're White or Black, Just Know who you are. So living in the Black life is a good life to Live.

———————————————

LISA: "PEOPLE SHOULD LOVE WHO THEY ARE AND STAY TOGETHER"

I wrote about how Black life was, and how it is now, and stuff. I wanted people to know about the history of Black people, and stuff like that. Probably people want to know how I knew about how it was back then. When I read in the history books, they said that Black people were slaves and they was treated bad. And then I thought, I'm happy that I'm living in the Black life because White people are treating me right.

My cousin gave me a suggestion to write about Blacks and how they were treated. And Ms. Rybicki was reading us stories about how some White people didn't like Blacks and how some Blacks didn't like themselves. So I thought of some ideas . . . that's why I wrote my story. Some of it was in the 1950s. Some of it was in the 1850s. In the 1950s was Alabama and stuff like that, and some was in the 1800s, about like Harriet Tubman. A lot of Blacks were treated bad, like Martin Luther King was treated bad. Harriet Tubman and all other Black Americans were treated bad.

Some people, some White people are prejudiced of us, like in Mississippi, like the Ku Klux Klan. My mother said that my great grandma, she didn't like being Black. She wished she was White so people wouldn't beat on her 'cause she was a slave back then. But she got free, and she wished she was White, so she wouldn't have to be hurt during the troubles.

I wanted to tell the world don't hate who you are—don't hate being Black. If some people don't like being Black, don't hate being Black too 'cause God made you a happy person. So be happy with who you are. A White person could have that message if they don't like themself. . . . So don't hate who you are and thank God for being alive, whatever color you are. Jesse Jackson was preaching that on TV one day. I want the world to know that. So, I'm glad I'm Black.

When people read my story they can feel how it was painful living in the Black life, how Blacks was beaten, and beaten on, and beaten on like we was just animals. And they can try to stop it [racial injustice]. The message is for Whites too. I want White people to get the message not to try to start killing. If you don't like Blacks, don't just beat on them. Try your best not to do nothin' bad to them. If they read my story, well, the people who don't like Blacks will probably change their ways. It makes me feel sad when I read my story, but I got to get it out and show other people how it is, how I felt.

I want people to understand how I really felt when I wrote about the Black life. See, I said the Black life was nice. But back then [during slavery] it was very painful. So, I want people to see how Blacks stayed together so they can understand how it was. They stayed together and tried to get free, 'cause if they got separated or fell down when they were trying to run away, they just got beaten and everything. So you [people] should stay together as a group so you'll have friendship, and won't break up, and you'll stay together to help each other get free, and stay together for many other things that I can't think of now. So I hope they [readers] can understand what I meant—that a person should love who they are and people should stay together. But it's gonna be a struggle.

I'm glad I wrote my story instead of just telling it to somebody. If I was just to tell it to somebody, they'd probably just forget it and not remember it any more. And they couldn't pass it on to the next person.

ROSA: "MY STORY BROUGHT ME TO HOW IT FEELS"

For my first story, I wrote about Martin Luther King. I found he was a hero. Even though he died, he's still in my heart. I was already

---

FIGURE 16–2 *"My Mom"*

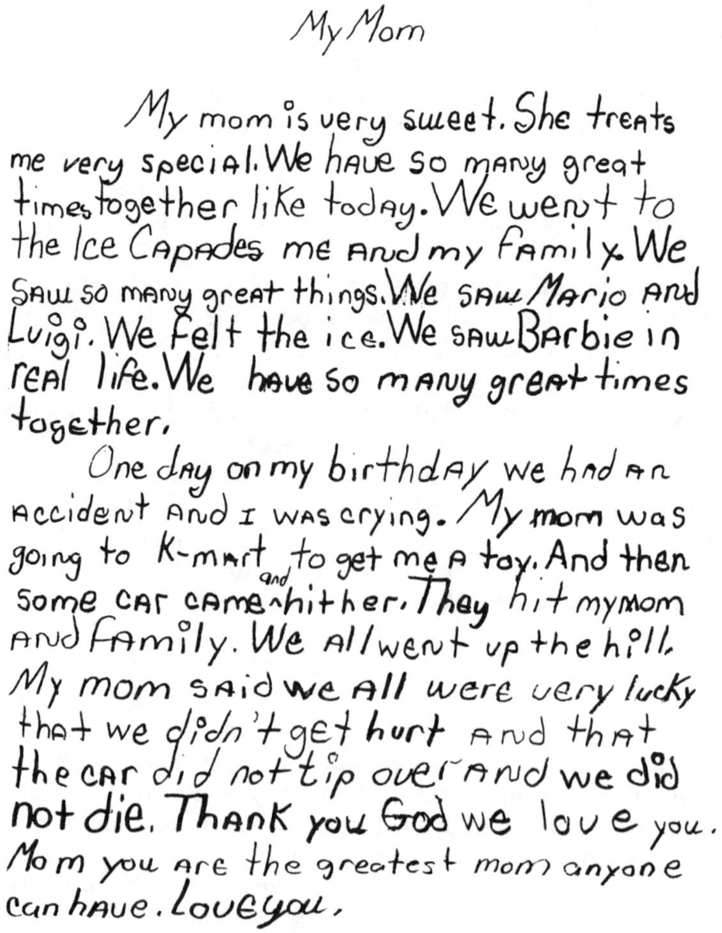

My Mom

My mom is very sweet. She treats me very special. We have so many great times together like today. We went to the Ice Capades me and my family. We saw so many great things. We saw Mario and Luigi. We felt the ice. We saw Barbie in real life. We have so many great times together.

One day on my birthday we had an accident and I was crying. My mom was going to K-mart to get me a toy. And then some car came and hit her. They hit my mom and family. We all went up the hill. My mom said we all were very lucky that we didn't get hurt and that the car did not tip over and we did not die. Thank you God we love you. Mom you are the greatest mom anyone can have. Love you.

writing stories and poems—really poems. I had no stories. But then, I was gonna write about my friends, but they were most of them already in the book [the class anthology]. So I started writing about my brother. I did my daddy first, my brother and sisters, and my family. Then I said, "People on TV use to get in accidents or crimes," and then I brought that into writing about my momma. Me and my mother are family. So then I decided to write about that.

Um, I just tried to write about my mom because, um, every time we have so much fun together I always write about it, and so when Ms. Rybicki told me we were gonna write a book, I decided let's talk about my mom, my dad, and my brothers and sisters. So I just picked out my mom, and I decided to put "we have lots of fun; we have so many great times together" because we do.

With this part, I don't know if I wrote that down all right because my mom did get hurt bad. They rushed her to the hospital because where we got hit at was right across the street from the police station. I was crying, and my auntie told me not to cry, but my momma did too. And then my momma was in the street 'cause she couldn't walk. I mean she could walk but really slow, and she was in the street walking really slowly, and I was crying in the street trying to help her. She was saying "get out of the street," but I helped her anyway.

I decided to write a story because I felt like getting it out. Getting this part out. The part about my momma and about how they hit my momma badly. Because everyday I would wake up and think of the accident. So when Ms. Rybicki told us about it [the student anthology] I thought about this again. Then I was for sure I was gonna write about my mother and all my feelings.

When I wrote about the accident helped. It helped me to learn that the day that my mother got hurt that she would be all right, 'cause she was telling me that she would be all right. I know because I thought something. I was scared, so I ran behind the what's-it-called where everybody was sitting [bus-stop shelter]. And I was so embarrassed because for a minute I thought it was my fault because my momma was going somewhere to get me something. And then my auntie, and my cousins, and my mother, and my little baby brother even told me that it wasn't my fault. After I wrote my story, I felt like it wasn't any of my fault, really. It was just slippery, and the car slipped into us because we was goin' down a hill and this other car was turning, and then my mother stopped, and then the other car came, and then we all went up the hill.

I was going to put the part about the accident into my story, but I thought that some people would say, "Why would she want to put all of her private life in it?" I thought of putting something in, but I thought that wouldn't be good writing. I decided not to put that part in. My friends were telling me, "It's up to you," but I didn't put it in. When I read my story back I think of why I wanted to put it in. If I wrote the story again, I would tell about the accident and how I thought it was my fault and how my mom and Ms. Rybicki and my friends were helping me, saying it wasn't my fault.

Writing my story made me feel good. I didn't think of the accident too much anymore—about how it happened and I was so scared. The story helped me think of my mother as always there for me when I need her, and it brought to me how it feels. When other people read my story I would like them to know that me and my mom have great times together. And my family, that we spend lots of time together. It's important to me because I like telling about my mother a lot.

I think my story gives other people ideas—to talk, be together, and have fun with their mother. If people don't have fun with their mother, and they don't do a lot of things with their mother, my story may give them ideas. Sometimes when my mother's sick, I still be tired, but I still help my mother. Sometimes I get on my mother's nerves 'cause when me and my brother and sister be playing together, I be just going down there to play with them. And then when I go down there they start making noise, and then I may get in trouble, and they may get in trouble. But I try to get along with my mother and be good to her.

PAUL: "IT MAKES A BIG DIFFERENCE TO WRITE"

I never thought about writing about what happens to me. Before, I would like tell about stuff that happened. I'd tell like a story. But I would never have dreamed about writing it down. It never came into my mind. I'm the same person I use to be, but I can write. I knew like I could copy something down and write it really good. Something like that. I could write up on the board. I could write what the teacher writes about. Now I can write about something that happened to one of my family. My aunt was telling me about when my grandma and my other aunt was little girls, and they were chased by the bull. I could tell about that. And when I do write it, I can make another copy. It changes me because I can write about and other people can read it.

I got my ideas for my story when I was over at my cousins' house, and they taped this movie about Dr. Martin Luther King, and then I was like thinking about it. I got some more ideas from movies that I've seen about slavery. I saw *Mississippi Burning* and some about Dr. Martin Luther King. And then it was Black History Month, and I was wondering what could I do for it. And we were talking about slavery about that time, and then I just went on to write a story about slavery.

I wanted to know why people be treated that way, and why did they have to come to the northern side, because they didn't harm White people so why should they harm Black people? I wanted to know like why they hurt Black people? The laws was prejudiced 'cause they was back then when there was slaves, but then like in the sixties when the White people met Dr. Martin Luther King, they was like . . . Dr. Martin Luther King was showing them the right way, and they didn't like that, so they try to do everything they could to get them away from Dr. Martin Luther King. Like if they see somebody

FIGURE 16–3 *"Enslaved"*

Enslaved

Slavery was unfair because they were beaten and taken from their family. And I bet you that the hardest part is to be taken from your family because they took care of you since you were born. And most of the White people did not care about how the Slaves felt. Those White people were too lazy and they wanted to take Slaves from their home in Africa.

All the Slaves were on a ship. The ship was on bigger than the classroom. The slaves were dying because if somebody got sick then the others will get sick and they will die too. When they made it to the south they were to sign a contract to do service for twenty years, but they got tricked to serve for life! I don't think that was fair, do you? But that's how it was.

Now, I want to tell you about Nelson Mandela. He was a leader in Africa. He showed them the right way for a long time. Then he went to court and lost the case and he was in jail for twenty-seven years. He's out now in 1990. He is all around the world. I'm

drinking out of the good water fountains, they would arrest them for nothing—something like that. But don't you see, I'm not so sure of that of what really happened.

First, I wrote my feelings to show other people how it was . . . to show kids how it was back before our parents were born, and before we were born. And I wrote it mostly so they can get around prejudiced people like the Ku Klux Klan. We can turn around, and we can join each other. It's like this because the color of our skin. Like if we

> **FIGURE 16–3** *"Enslaved" (continued)*
>
> glad he's out to turn the idea of Blacks getting along with whites the right way.
>
> Now I want to tell you adout Harriet Tubman. I learned this in a book and in a story that my teacher read to our class. Harriet was a slave since she was 4 years old. She had take care of one, two, and three year olds when she was only four or five years old herself. And if She didn't do right she would get locked in a box for a lot of hours or for a day. I know Harriet was treated bad but the white people did not have any feelings for slaves. They had no feeling for slaves. All they wanted was to get their house cleaned. Some of the slaves didn't know how to read. Some of the slaves had to sneak to learn to read. Back to the story. The part I did not like was when She had got hit in the head with a weight. She was out for a week and then She was not feeling right. Nobody wanted her but she started the underground railroad. she made it to the free side, but She was not happy because she was thinking about her family. She went back to the South to free her family, She tricked everybody

take off our skin, we both look . . . if we take off our skin, we look the same way.

In my story I think I was trying to explain, to say something about the family in times of slavery, because they took care of you, fed you, clothed you, had a house, had a roof over our heads. And then all of a sudden somebody would come and take it all away from you and have you working out in a cornfield somewhere. I was thinking about like what if my aunt and uncles were in this position, of being a slave, or my grandma or grandmother, or my grandmother's mother, or mother.

I started with this story and I just put it in the back of my writing folder. I wasn't even thinking about doin', uh, 'til we got into that

FIGURE 16–3 *"Enslaved" (continued)*

on the south side. They wanted her dead or
alive. But they could not find her
because her family was free. But you are
still a slave to drugs because drugs can make you
a slave. Say like I was on drugs I will be a slave. Because
drugs is telling me what to do. Drugs can
be harmful. There are steroids, Crack, Pot, Weed
alcohol, and cigarettes. Back to the point. How
can drugs effect your life? They can kill you
in a week or probably a day. I don't see why
people do drugs. It's killing our city. People
kill each other over crack. You are addict
to crack. You are robbing and killing, smoking
and dealing. Crack is stupid. But people think
it is fun, and they get high off it, making
people go and kill each other, because drugs is
telling them what to do. I hope that the
world will stop killing because I don't want
my family to get killed over drugs because
I will die before my family.

discussion about guns and about violence, and all that stuff like that.
Then it just made me remember about how I would be watching
shows like Dr. Martin Luther King, and videos, and I just started
thinking about it, for a *long* time. Two days. And I just thought about
it, and I said to myself, "I think I should get back to my story, that I
wrote." So when the next day came I started working on it. Then, I
realized that's all I really knew about slavery. That's when I asked
Michael, Dr. Johnson [a local university professor]. And then I got
most of my information from him.

At the same time I was writing about drugs. I forget why. Then
once we started getting on to slavery on Black History Month, I didn't
know that drugs could make you a slave. And then when we was
talkin' about Anthony's story about guns and drugs and stuff, then I
just added that into the story—about how drugs can make you a
slave. 'Cause I was thinkin' about my own uncle. My uncle was tellin'
me how drugs was affecting his life, and Ms. Rybicki was tellin' us
how drugs can tell you what to do, and I was seein all this stuff on TV
about how drugs was killin' people. I had a little help from Mrs.
Rybicki, and she was showin' me how drugs can make you a slave

and how you can add drugs onto the slavery paper. She was telling me how it could take over your life. You would give anything to get it, and my uncle he did it. He did anything to get him some, just to go around the corner and get some drugs. What she was telling me was true.

I wrote my story because I don't want anyone in my family to use drugs, cause my uncle he was using drugs, but he helped hisself. He went to this clinic, and he stayed there for five months. Now he only smokes cigarettes. He don't drink nothin'. He recovered hisself. And he be at meetings and stuff, and he's havin' speeches and stuff. They can't be doin' it anymore, and stuff like that.

When someone reads my story I like them to think about it. And if they're on drugs, I'd like them to think about it and see how they could turn theyself around and become a normal person like my uncle. Hmm, it's like a new version of slavery. What if drugs is telling you to do and stuff. And you gonna do it! It's a different version. It's still the same. You could get like addicted to it, and then you could do like stupid stuff 'cause it's telling you what to do.

I felt like I really could write it. Then after I wrote it, I felt great . . . because I wrote something that I could understand and get around. I don't know. I would hope that people will actually read it. And I felt happy. If I meet more friends and stuff I could show them and maybe I could turn them on to being a writer, but that is only if they want to be a writer. It makes a big difference to write because if you write about it and you put it in a book, more people get to know about it. People that don't even know you. Everybody could get the message that people all over the world should stop doing drugs. Maybe they'll stop crack houses, and that's good enough for me. Now I can write something, like when something happened to me. It's like very important to me because I never thought I would write about something—never thought I'd be a writer.

17

Mary Elizabeth

"I'M AN ORIGINAL"

(Grade 4)

Contributed by Sally Hudson-Ross & Susan Allcorn

The real world, as well as fantasy worlds, intrigue fourth grader Mary Elizabeth. Science is her chosen field, one in which she can dream, plan, and imagine mechanical ways to alter things around her to better fit her own taste. Not many of her projects or expansive dreams ever translate into reality, but that fact doesn't bother her at all. As one project falls by the wayside, others quickly consume her mind with possibilities. For Mary Elizabeth, the plan is the thing. Sometimes stories—written or told—emerge in the same fantastical ways.

Mary attends a magnet school emphasizing foreign languages in an inner city in Pennsylvania. The teacher of her gifted, or Scholars, class in fourth grade found ways to challenge her in science, but sadly, school has rarely helped her see how books and the written word can provide another outlet for her extraordinary imagination. For her, reading is generally boring; writing is something the teacher makes her do. On her own, when given time and freedom however, she finds many ways to use writing and drawing to organize both her life and her dreams.

The interviews upon which Mary Elizabeth's profile are based were conducted in a variety of ways: with her mother, Susan Allcorn, at home; with her aunt, Sally Hudson-Ross, while walking in a home-town park and over the phone; and most interestingly, on her own. When her mother didn't have time for a follow-up interview, Mary Elizabeth took the tape recorder and final questions up to her bedroom and gave a lengthy, personal monologue explaining the world of reading, writing, and planning as she sees it.

My ideas come from my head mostly. It all does. My teacher for science will give an assignment; ten minutes after that I'd have a plan for it. Like we had to do a simple machine out of pulleys, stuff to raise flags, wheel and axle, and all. Well, I made the ally-up dog feeder for some dog food that's all gooey and yuckey and gross, and you don't want to end up touching it. So what you do for that is take the dog food, put it on this cardboard platform that is attached to two wheels, and the rest of my Capsela set [a toy with hundreds of parts for building moveable machines], turn it on, and the food will go from the platform, over and down into the dog's dish.

Or like if it was too hot, or I was real sick and burning, and I didn't have a fan, I'd make a triple fan-a-crane. It'd be special gears that I could make three fans with and then on the back I'd have a crane. Like if I was sick and I couldn't get out of the bed, I'd hook a bag of chips to the crane, and I'd pull it up. I made plans for that with the parts and everything.

For the planning, I draw some how it's gonna look. I group all the parts so I know what I want to use, and I label all the stuff I'll need, all the pieces. Then after that, I do another plan and check it over. It helps me know what I'm gonna do and what I'm gonna need. Sometimes I could picture it in my head, what it's gonna look like and all, but I usually don't just do it in my head. The [written] plan helps me build whatever I'm gonna build. At the end I'd have twenty plans, at least, and most of 'em are different. I don't know why I do several plans; they'll be almost all different except for the parts I need. At home, I give my mom all the plans I made. She checks, tells me which one would be better to do. Most of the time I make 'em 'cause I'm building something, or I just make 'em 'cause I don't have anything better to do.

When the teacher gives us free time to do anything we want for our class, I don't play or color or anything like the boys do. They play hot potato; I make the plans that I am gonna use. Other children don't do that. I'm unusual in lots of ways. I'm about the only one that keeps the guinea pig. I'm the only one that would build all kinds of things and all. I'm about the only Girl Scout in the school that sells Girl Scout cookies. Like I'm real unusual and stuff. I'm original, my mom says, and all because I do stuff nobody else does.

Sometimes on my free time in school I will conjure up poems, stories, maybe some of my own imaginative book reports, and at home I would do mostly the same thing but a little bit more of stories and reports. Imaginative book reports would be like this report I made up of Napoleon F. Catochini who invented salad, and he eats cabbage, and everyone thought his invention was great until lettuce came. 'Cause he didn't know what lettuce was or anything. 'Cause a poor farmer found it, and then everyone hated his invention. Then

Napoleon F. Catochini changed his invention into a salad with lettuce, instead of cabbage.

Then there's this story I wrote called "Santa's Sick." Santa was out on snowy hill playing snowy golf, and he just stayed out too long and caught a cold, and he couldn't ride his sleigh and give presents to kids on Christmas Eve because he was sick, so Mrs. Claus took his place, but she couldn't go either because she was sick, so one of the elves, the French elf, whose name was Mo and who just got out of Junior High Santa School, took Santa's place and Christmas was saved.

Imaginative stuff is fun because of the fact that I made it up from my head. In my opinion, what makes writing really good to me is that it doesn't have any sense in it at all. It has no animals that exist in this world anywhere in it. It's all unreal, no matter what it is: a story, a poem, a phrase. As long as it's not supposed to make sense. That would be what really good writing would be to me, in my opinion, of course.

Good writing would have been done fast but neat, and it has that [feeling of] "what in the world is this animal doing in this story or this character in this story? Who is this animal or character?" That's the kind of writing that I like. The kind that as you read you start to figure out a certain character you wonder about. Like that striped cat that could disappear in *Alice in Wonderland* because he was real strange, and as I read through the story a little bit more, I started to find out stuff about him. And that's the kind of story that I think would be good writing.

If I was supposed to write an imaginative story for homework or school, first I'd sit down and think about what the story would be about, think up some characters from my head. If it's an imaginative story, everything comes from my head. And then once I get the ideas down, I write them. I don't have any certain order. I just write down what comes into my head at that moment. And then once I have it all written down, I proofread and make sure everything is spelled right, if spelling counts, make sure that my teacher will be able to read it. To do that, I'd have my mother or father read it, and then I'd turn it in. If I didn't know how to spell and didn't have a dictionary, I would ask someone if they knew how to spell the word, and if I had trouble writing something, a letter or something, they would help me.

But I hate it when people hover over me. That really annoys me. Sometimes they will just ask me so much stuff and talk to me so much; that really annoys me too. It's comfortable to write when I know that I can take as long as I want and as much time as I need. Whatever I'm writing just gets longer and longer, and it gets more enjoyable for me to write that long stuff. I feel good that I'm able to write, really good because I know that I can do all this.

There is no just one right way to teach writing. I'd have to say, let students' imaginations go free, write a few things imaginative down and let it go into one subject, and then put them together into a whole paragraph. Then take that paragraph and put it into a story or a poem or whichever. Then either have a story or something, a poem or anything to be proud of to write. Let them go freehand. Let them write what they feel. That's the procedure I use. I just let myself go free, just write what comes into my head, and then I put it all into one story and that's how I get all my stories written.

But usually in school, there's work the teacher gives us and all. In science, you write reports, observations, sketches. For book reports, you read a book, a story or something, then you write a report on it, tell about the characters, what the characters are like, and what the story is about. In spelling, I write words and paragraphs and everything. Spelling is important, if the teacher says it is. If the teacher says it matters, then I worry about it. Like spelling supercalifragilistic-espialidocious. Then I'd really be worried. If I'm just writing a letter to my aunt, I don't think it matters too much 'cause I try to spell it out as good as I can, and she doesn't usually end up reading it wrong. For homework in spelling, I sometimes have to write a paragraph on a certain subject. This last one I did about a doctor; I called him Cure E Us, and he found a fossil.

I also have to write in my reading workbook, write answers to my building skills in vocabulary studies, and my teacher gives us fun sheets to do when we're done with our reading stuff that deal with writing and art, such as the Winter Wonderland Worksheet. Then I do my math packet 'cause we have to. What my teacher does is she makes these packets which are all math so we won't have to take home math stuff. Instead, you do certain work, keep it, and put it in the packet for the teacher to check.

I hate to write the book reports, homework, that kind of stuff, because it always takes me awhile, and it's so hard. It's hard on my shoulders if I have to take a book home to do it. And there's so much of it that I have to take home that I never have time to do stuff I want to do, except on the weekends and on vacations. Mostly I don't get to make up imaginative stories in school because there's too much work that I have to do. It's just [in a slow, bored voice], "Read the book. Read the book."

When I go to school, I eat breakfast at school, then after two bells ring, I go to my safety patrol post. I have bus patrol and lunch patrol. I have to watch the kids, tell them what to do—"Sit down, be quiet, put a sock in it," all that. That's real good, but that doesn't work. So I just write their names down. I have to write their names on a list and turn it in to Connie Corliss (she's the captain of the guard), and then she turns it in to the principal. If I don't know their names, I hire a secret guy to find out. Like my safety's helper, Linda. She goes around and asks about names and all that. But she only helps me on bus patrol because everybody—every other safety—has to go help teachers on that bus. So I have to hire a safety's helper. I don't pay her, but she gets to be a safety. I said, "The gooder you are, the more you get promoted." Like she'll be assigned to get a badge I made.

I'm also supposed to write a report on the kids who are bad. I describe their behavior—his or her behavior—how they act on the bus, how I see them acting at school, and all that. The principal calls up the kids and suspends them, or does something so they won't do it again, like he'll put 'em in hot-house suspension. In there, only the teacher can drink ice tea, ice water, all that. All the other people write, write, write until their hand falls off. Like, "I won't run in the halls again," "I won't say swear words," "I won't be a graffitier." All that stuff. So they won't do it again. I don't know how many times they write it because I've never been in hot-house suspension. It used to be called in-house suspension. Kids call it hot-house suspension now 'cause you sweat your heads off. Too hot. I've been in there because I had to bring up the work load.

I did have to do writing like that once. I wrote: "I won't forget my math packet ever again"—fifty times at least—because I forgot my math packet. I only forgot about twice. I was so furious I could murder my teacher. Writing for punish assignments doesn't help because it's just painful to whoever is writing it.

At home, I'm usually at Nintendo, playing Super Mario and all. I only read because I have to. Like my mom'll make me when I need to. I hate to read school books then write a report on it. Yuck, I hate it. I did like *Nancy Drew: False Impressions,* but it had big words. It was good because it had mystery and all. It's like there's murder that's threatening Nancy and all that kind of stuff. I've only read that one, and I'm not really planning to read any other. I sort of like joke books too. Like, the scientist mixed cow milk with sheep wool and got a cow that had wool, but it doesn't make sense. I mean it doesn't tell how he did it or that kind of stuff. I like stuff that has directions on it.

At home, I write for my mother, sometimes my father, even my sister once in awhile, and I send letters to my aunt, some with a secret code. I'd rather not reveal how it works, but the numbers correspond with the letters. I write the same for everyone, but I try to write a little neater when I'm with my teacher. For her, I try to do the best I can. I'd have to say that I'm more comfortable when I'm writing for my aunt than I am for my teacher because my aunt doesn't give me a grade for what I write and my teacher does. It makes me feel about the same when I'm writing for both people, but when I'm writing for my teacher, I'm just a little bit nervous because sometimes I get scared that she won't be able to read my writing and then I'll get a bad grade. But with my aunt, I trust her with my writing.

One thing I just wrote at home was the Kid Mall. It's like my dream mall because that's what I'd want in my kind of mall. [See Figure 17–1.] No adults are allowed in the mall, unless they're my relatives, and kids don't have to spend money for anything except for the clothes and stuff. The Wave Pool is my favorite place. And there's boys and girls clothes—one store for girls and one store for boys, not both kinds in the same store because boys might try peeking. At the free restaurant, Free Food Forever, the store's open all the time and going to be there forever, and you can get whatever food you want for free. Even if it cost two hundred dollars for one pound, you can get it for free. At the malt shop, you get all kinds of malts and ice cream, and if you happen to be with a boyfriend, you can get a real large one only with two straws.

There's an arcade, most definitely, with all kinds of video games and all my favorite games, that's for sure. It says "one cent cheap" for the Arcade because say you have two dollars, that's two hundred pennies for every single game. There's a Nintendo Outlet, too. You just go there, and you can get *all* the stuff for Nintendo: shirts, movies, all that.

At Make Your Own Parents, you make your own parents. Just what the sign says. You key it in or draw what kind of parent you want, and if it's a bad drawing then, you know, you could make a test drive and see how it would look. If it doesn't look too good, then you draw it again and again and again until you get the right kind of parent. Then you just program in what kind of guts you want. It's gotta be a living person. If a kid can't draw good, that kid can rent parents.

For Science Time, you go there and you spend some time doing science. There's books and everything, and depending on what it is—say if it's instructions combined with equipment on how to make

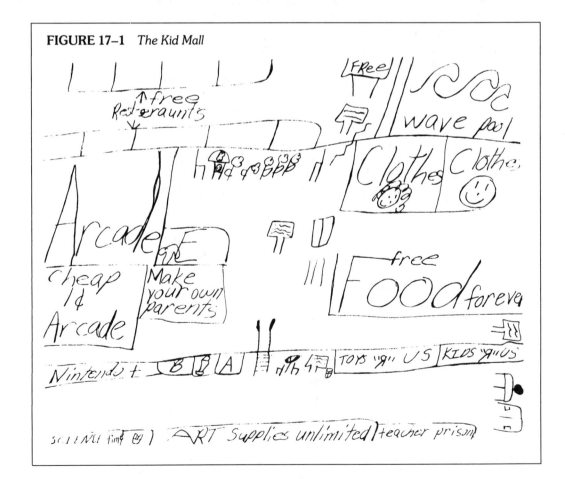

FIGURE 17–1 *The Kid Mall*

a nuclear reactor, or something like that, something real science—if it's too dangerous, like if that store just couldn't have little kids playing with it and only a real big teenager kid could handle it, the teenager would have to get permission to try it. But for everything else, you're allowed to try it. If it's a book, there's chairs to sit and read.

At Arts Supplies Unlimited, you just get all your art supplies. If you're a drawing fanatic, that's where you go. The prices are all different. Some are free, but say if it's stuff that's real expensive, it goes in the range of the average allowance, about three dollars, because that's what I used to get.

And then there's Teacher Prison. Say you're sick and tired of your teacher, you stick her in there. Like my teacher, she was giving punish assignments—like twenty-eight spelling words, write 'em twenty or twenty-five times each—if that mall was real, I'd trick her into coming there with me. You know, like I could jump her or something and throw her in there. Or I could call that place, and they'll come and get her, and she'd serve a life sentence for assigning too much homework. Yeah!

18

Hobbes

"I PRESS REWIND THROUGH THE PICTURES IN MY HEAD"

(Grade 5)

Contributed by Linda Miller Cleary

I met Hobbes through the Special Education Coordinator in a Maine school district. I was interested in what elementary reading and writing were like for children who went to the resource room every day. When I went to his house for our first interview, Hobbes was plugged into his Walkman, playing out the beat of music with his sandy head and his restless feet. At the moment, I wondered whether his shyness and restlessness would wear off when his mother left for work. Hobbes kept his Walkman near at hand during that first interview, but to borrow Hobbes's Maine dialect, halfway through that first interview we began to have a "wicked" (very) good time together as he talked about reading and writing, about being "held back," about the book he was writing that summer, "Sea Hunt." During those interviews in the summer of 1990, I gained entry into his world of literacy and insight into strategies that he collected to deal with being a visual learner in a fairly traditional elementary school.

When I was wicked little, I don't really remember what reading was like. I thought my parents reading to me was pretty weird 'cause when they were reading to me and my brother, I didn't really know what most of it meant. I remember Dr. Seuss, and I mostly understood everything there. Later when I read, I didn't ask any questions, 'cause my mother would say, "Do you know what it means?" and I would say, "Yes," but I didn't really know what it was. I was afraid

136

they would put me in summer school or something like that, but I ended up going last year anyway.

In kindergarten we had to do five letters of the alphabet: five *A*s, five *B*s, five *C*s. She'd have you do your name at table one, second table was the activity table, the next one was the letter table and special occasions, and last one was like the workbook table for circle the cat, like which picture didn't go with the other, or like write your name without looking at your card. We had a week to make a Mothers' Day card. I wrote "Marvelous Mother." It was hard. We went to the activity table, did the picture, and then to the letter table.

Then we had reading group, and she had a screen around the group so no one would bother you. We would sing songs, and then she would read us a book, and, "Does anyone know what this word is?" like an "and" or a "can." Usually no one could answer it. And she had letter people, like "C" for Cotton Candy Man,"R" was Rubberband Man. She was nice if you needed help with anything. Some times I would skip reading group 'cause I just wanted to go with the blocks. I learned how to tie my shoes right away, but some kids had trouble. I had some trouble reading; they had trouble tying their shoes.

In first grade there were like three groups: bears, goats, and something else. We would have to read something like Paddington Bear, "Look at Paddington run down the street." I finished that and went into *Sunshine,* a big thick book like that, and that's when I got into trouble. I was behind some kids in reading. I didn't like being in a group that no friends were in. I didn't like that book at all, and I used to look over at others' papers, and they were ahead. Then they put me into two reading groups, and I didn't like that either 'cause I didn't get a study period, so I didn't complete my work, even though they told me it was okay not to finish it. I used to pay more attention to the clock for recess to come than to reading. The clock should be in her desk instead of on the wall. I don't like reading much, I don't know why, but I'm good at drawing and roller skating.

When my mom told me about staying back, I kind of wanted to stay in first grade 'cause I didn't understand stuff, but I thought I'm not going to tell anyone I'm gonna stay back. At first it was pretty scary. I was afraid I was going to have to stay back again and again and again, like a teenager in first grade. But I didn't really 'cause I ended up doing pretty good. Like in first grade, I didn't do that good. I wasn't in the high group at all; I was in the lowest, with difficult kids. Like they weren't that good either, and they would have to count on their fingers. I used to look over and copy theirs but realized that didn't do me that good.

I think parents and teachers should ask the kid if he wants to stay back. They should ask the kid, and they should tell him to try to be honest, and if they don't [stay back], they will eventually end up in a lot of trouble in sixth. If they're asked, instead of told, that'd make them feel comfortable. It was good my mother told me, but I sort of gave up. I thought I was never going to finish a paper, and it took me two days to finish a paper, and I just stopped, and then I had to go to another paper. And I ask myself why did I give up? Why didn't I just ask for help? Teachers should tell kids not to give up. The teacher told me a story about what happened to her when she didn't understand it, and then I just thought I don't want that to happen to me, so I started to work harder; I started to understand it more.

Ms. B., a teacher took me to the resource room, gave me a test and found out I had a little trouble, and I kept going there until fifth grade. It was kinda embarrassing to leave the classroom for the resource room when I was the only person, but now I know the others didn't really care. At the end of the year, she gave us a beach party, and we only had to go to school for like an hour and a half. Next year some of my best friends left class too. And they thought Ms. B. was going to be strict too, but I went there in first grade, and I told my friends she was really nice. Ms. B. was strict to other kids that I'm not going to mention. We would do our homework, read a book, or play computer games. And my friends ended up liking the beach party too. All teachers should be like Ms. B. and teach reading and writing the way they think students will get it. This year I don't get to go anymore. That's okay; Ms. B. is getting married, and she won't give beach parties anymore.

I like books when I like the stories. I get into the books. Most times when I read, I read slow, I wouldn't read that confident. It's hard to explain. When I really like the book, I read a chapter ahead of everyone else. But when I don't like the book, I'm always behind. My mother picked out this book about Jonah Twist. Like Jonah Twist reminds me of me. He wanted to be very good at reading, but he was always last at everything. Say like he would be the first one there, but he would be the last to finish something. Like he had to write about his summer vacation. He wrote his name in 3D and then he drew a picture of a jet, and then he started the story, "This summer. . . ." and his time was up. I always felt like that.

In third grade, sometimes she'd make us read a sentence, and sometimes I'd have trouble. She would make us write it out on a piece of paper, and then we could read it. I ended up learning words like "dog" and "he can run that way," and even though I wasn't in a very high group, I did pretty good.

Sometimes my buddies and I get each other in trouble. It's hard to pay attention to something that doesn't interest you. In the last four months of fourth, that happened when we had a substitute, so I didn't go to the resource room sometimes, thought I could get away with it. The substitute didn't notice it, but then Ms. B. started to come and get me. Then I had to go most every day. But with the sub and missing and my buddies, I was behind. So I had to go to summer school, but that's how I got my fish tank though so I didn't mind. [My parents said] I could have had a VCR or a fish tank if I went to summer school, and I got a fish tank. I like fish. In summer school I had to read three books and I read *Super Fudge* in two weeks, oh, and I loved *Mark and his Marvelous Medicine,* I read that in two days. My mother would go "would you put that book down," and I would put it down, and like five minutes later I would pick it up again.

In fifth grade writing was kind of hard. When your arm got tired, you'd still have to write to get it done. We had to take notes, and we had trouble keeping up, so we had trouble on the test. I had to write about an Indian; we had to do fifty fact cards, like the first day we had to do ten, the next twenty, thirty, forty, fifty. Like we might have to write fifty facts about Pocahontas; that was too much work. Then we had to write down about your Indian. I couldn't wait 'til the last day of school when I ripped those cards up.

Then we had whoops slips. They are for not finishing your home-work, or if you forgot your notes, or notebook, or your work. If we didn't finish our work we had to bring these slips home, and we had to do more work that night. I got seven of them. You had to do it at night or stay after school. I read *A Wrinkle in Time, Trouble River, How to Be Perfect in Three Days,* and *A Christmas Carol,* and we did a play on it, and I got Scrooge, and I had to memorize twenty lines, and I did it! I wrote a story about my puppy. I liked her, but we had to give her away. But we might get another dog if I'm responsible. I just thought in my head what I used to do with the puppy, and wrote it out. Like I used to put a little tiny sweatshirt on her.

I like the reading books best, I think they're easier. I don't like the stories in the big books that only have three to five pages. I like the ones where you do chapters. The ones with short stories are boring because they're so short, but with the books, you go to the same book every day. I like reading books, except when we get to the book reports. Sometimes I forget to read, and sometimes I tell my mother I read it, and I didn't. In fifth grade I'd just read the last chapter, 'cause I didn't have enough time. I would just go like read the beginning, "He started his motor bike," and then read the last chapter, "He won the race." Some kids make it up. I'm not that bad. At first we had to write it all out, but then she gave us something like draw a picture, least favorite part, most favorite. That was easier because I like the drawing.

I started hating what I call "the goody two shoes" group. In social studies last year, I'd get about a 75 or 80, seventy is passing, and they'd get 110 or something, and they'd go around and show it, and that didn't make me feel good. I wanted to say, "Why don't you sit down and stop making people feel bad?" I felt like I was last most of the time, like Jonah Twist, but in racing I'd be first most of the time. But in school work sometimes I'd be last, and sometimes I wouldn't be last. Jonah Twist isn't always last either. He was first to school, but last with work. And there was this girl he called "the announcer" in the book; she said out loud when you were last, like what I call "the goody two shoes."

The best teachers make jokes, like: "What is the ghost's favorite food?" "Booberries!" Teachers shouldn't make students do some-thing they don't want to do. If kids don't understand something like

I didn't back then, like if the teacher explains it a hundred times, maybe they should be in their own little group. Maybe if it's just one person he can work by himself—better than making a kid do something he doesn't understand in front of other kids, or making him do something that he doesn't think that he can do. Like if he's going into fifth grade and he didn't get some of the stuff in fourth grade, let him go back and do some fourth grade stuff at the beginning of the year, so he can get it back, and maybe staying back another year to learn the fourth grade year isn't so bad an idea. I'm still friends with those kids when I stayed back. It's not like they aren't my friends any more, in fact some are my best friends. I thought everyone was going to call me stupid and stuff, but they didn't at all. A couple of other kids stayed back too, so I didn't mind that at all.

This summer I got the idea for writing my story "Sea Hunt" from first playing around with the computer, and then I came upstairs and tested my fish tank and watched the fish for awhile, and then I got the idea. So I went downstairs, and I printed out the cover with the title "Sea Hunt," and then I went upstairs and wrote one sentence, and then another sentence, and then I went to play Nintendo, and then I got more ideas, and then I went upstairs to write it down, and then I went downstairs to watch TV, and then I got punished for watching TV, so I couldn't watch TV, so then I wrote another chapter. When I'm playing Nintendo, some games are adventurous, and there was one with a submarine in trouble, and so in one chapter my character got in a mess, and in the next he figures it out. One time I got an idea from the *National Geographic*. Like my Dad would call me if there was fish stuff on, and I'd see how divers would do things, and I decided to write a story about it instead of me doing the real thing by diving.

It seems like when I'm writing the story things are happening right in front of me. In ways that's better than doing the real thing. Sometimes when you do something wicked fun, you forget it. Like I don't remember going to Fun Town with my cousins. My brother told me I did, but I don't remember it because it was a long time ago. But I remembered my kindergarten writing thing 'cause I looked at it. So I decided the other day that writing is better in ways 'cause I will be able to remember it. I'm going to save the "Sea Hunt" story. When I'm twenty-one, I can search around a bit in a box and find it, and then you can remember, and you can see how sometimes you messed up, how you're better when you read it later.

Remembering periods gives me a hard time. But when I read a book, I notice those things, like "The boy ranned," and then there's a period. Reading helps me a lot with my writing 'cause sometimes you can tell if another kid made a mistake, and you noticed, and you know it.

When I have trouble reading, I'll ask my mother to help me by reading the first chapter. I feel better because I know she will help me with the words, and when I get into it, I can do it by myself. Sometimes I have to read the whole half-hour, but sometimes I only do twenty minutes 'cause the book got really boring. But if I read a

Stephen King book—but I never read one, but I will in sixth grade—
it is going to be wicked scary, but I will read for the full half hour,
maybe longer. Sometimes I would like to read a book that is not too
kiddish, you know, a grown-up book. I did read a little of my brother's
Stephen King book, and I didn't have too much trouble with it.

If I can listen to my Walkman, I can get my work done in around
ten minutes, and I would be liking it because I could get it done. But
my mother doesn't like the idea, but when I do, then she looks at my
papers suspiciously and says good, but she doesn't say anything
about the Walkman. So sometimes I get to listen to it, and sometimes
I don't. Like my friend's sister, her father gave her a math paper to
do, and she did terrible, and then she did it with the Walkman, and
she got it all right. Sometimes I sneak and put my Walkman on my
desk and put it on high, and I'll listen to it, put my head down on
my desk. It helps me a lot because I think the work is much more
fun. But if I had like classical music on, I don't know whether that
would be so hot.

Writing and reading are different things. Reading is like listening, or
listening in your head, but writing is like writing stuff down. But they
are kind of the same really, 'cause if you write stuff down you're
reading it while you're writing. Like the writer will write it down
how other people will read it. But they're kind of diverse. That was
in "Word of the Day": use "diverse" instead of "different," "abrupt"
instead of "sudden." I can concentrate on writing more than reading.
You're doing more, and you're thinking of the things right in front of
you. Like if you're doing pictures, then it is right in front of you. You
get good ideas. But if you're writing first, like I'm doing in "Sea
Hunt," then if it's a tricky part or an exciting part, you're just writing
it as it happens.

If another person is into the story, if they really like the story a lot,
then I'll probably work more on the story to make them like it even
more than they did before. But it bothers me when people read my
writing and correct every little thing. You want to make it so it's right,
but it doesn't matter if there's a couple of things wrong. I like using a
pencil because I can erase it. A pen kind of makes you more shakier,
but it never gets dull, but sometimes the ink squirts out in blobs.

I wrote more on "The Sea Hunt" this week. Writing a story you
want to is much more different, like you're not doing it from the
worksheet or anything, and you can mess up on the words, and it's
okay. And assignments, if you don't have time, you have to either
stay in from recess or get a whoops slip, . . . or a detention. Only my
family, and my grandparents, will see "Sea Hunt." I'm going to wait
until it's done to show them. In school, like if another kid is a good
speller or something, the teacher will go, "Why don't you go check
your work with him?" So then it wouldn't take as long because they
would skip some stuff, 'cause you're friends, and they don't write on
the paper. If the teacher writes on it, then you have to write it all over
again. But if your friends tell you, I just ask, "Are there any corrections?" "Yeah, there's a couple." And then I just correct them.

When I'm writing a story, if I don't have pictures in my head, the story isn't going to make sense or anything. The pictures in my head help me when I write stuff down 'cause then I can get ideas from my pictures. Every night I draw on my pad, and it's pretty fun 'cause then I just get ideas for what I could write about it. Like I draw sharks, anything I can draw. If I like drawing it, getting a picture in my mind, I usually write something about it.

When I'm writing, it makes it easier to write, 'cause you know what is happening. I would just look at the picture I drew for awhile and see what is going on. If I start with the pictures in my mind, I write about the picture. Sometimes if I forget the picture and I go back in my story, I'll see what I wrote, and then I can usually get most of the picture back in my head. Sometimes the picture would change if I get off my subject, like talking to a friend about movies, but then I would really forget the picture, so I would have to go back and read, and change the picture again and again.

It's like a movie in my head. In "Sea Hunt" I'd go, "The guy was swimming away from the piranha," and I would have the guy's arms and legs moving in my head, and I could describe that, and I could see the piranha chasing him. I don't know how I get the words to go with the picture. I just do it somehow.

The resource room teacher told me about using pictures for reading. For practice, she would go, "Picture an elephant sitting on a pie. Is the pie sitting on the elephant?" And I would have to make a picture in my head, and then I would tell what was happening. That was for reading, to help make pictures in your head while you are reading. And she used to tell me, "Picture a VCR in yourself." So you can go back, or forward, record it in your head. When I'm reading, like when we were reading *A Wrinkle in Time,* you had to do questions, and I would go in my head and pretend to press rewind through the pictures in my head and go all the way back and answer the question. And if there was another question, I would have to go forward from there through the pictures and think what happened to Meg in the story, and then I would have to tell what happened.

I hate reading for social studies or science. I hate it. Science I like doing the experiments. In social studies it's boring 'cause I don't think I'm going to need that stuff in my life. I just don't like the George Washington stuff. They didn't have cars back then; I think their life would be pretty boring. It's like harder to make up pictures in reading 'cause I don't know what it looked like back then. Like we see drawings, but how do we know that's what it really looked like? But some things I do believe, 'cause we went on trips. Like we went to an old school, and I had to sit on the chair with that big thing on my head, and I didn't like the way they treated kids then.

My Teacher Is an Alien was the best book I've read in a long time. I didn't picture the main character the same as they show him there on the cover though. He looked like a nerd to me in my head 'cause he was weird, but when I saw the picture, it wasn't the same. That wasn't the first time. When you buy the book, you don't know what anyone is like in the book, like I would read the first chapter, and I would picture the kid, but when I saw him in the pictures in the book, that wasn't how I'd picture him. Sometimes the pictures argue, like it doesn't look like him at all compared to my mind picture. I would like to be an illustrator and put my own pictures in the books. Or maybe an architect or a computerist. When you're an architect you have to know what this wire looks like or that, but when you're a computerist, you're writing every single day on computer disks, like how to play that game and this game. I'll probably have to use writing in the future, but not history.

19

José

"IF I CAN'T SHARE THE BOOK,
I FEEL LONELY AND EVERYTHING"

(Grade 5)

Contributed by Julianne Elliott & Mara Casey

José is a very verbal, friendly, talkative ten-year-old boy, one of those kids who can't stop talking no matter what the circumstances or consequences. He loves to have adults' attention and to organize and manage activities with his peers. He is being raised in a low SES (socio-economic status) neighborhood in Southern California, in a small, old house in which whole families share bedrooms as if they were small apartments and cook in a common kitchen. José writes and reads at school only when he has to.

Julianne interviewed José during summer session at his elementary school. During the previous school year, when he was in fourth grade and she was a first-year teacher, he had spent a lot of time trying to engage her in private conversations while she was trying to teach a lesson to the entire class. Not having to share her with other students at first seemed to overwhelm José and make him a little awkward, but he soon warmed up to the interviews.

José is a slightly taller than average boy of Mexican descent. He has friendly, dark eyes and thick black hair which he combs straight back and secures with styling gel. He is a casual dresser and a charming, outgoing boy.

When I was a little kid, I got my sister's crayons and wrote on paper so I could be like entertaining myself while my mom was in the kitchen. My sister didn't mind because she knew that keeping me busy helped my mom. I used to draw fishes and animals on books, paper, and tags. Animals are my favorite. Sometimes my mom saved my pictures and sometimes I saved some, too. Even now when my mom is doing something, I draw cartoons. In school I love to write and draw comic strips because it's like you get to do art and writing, two lessons at a time.

I learned how to write by my sister teaching me a little bit and my mom teaching me, too, because she used to go to night school to learn English. My mom would take me to a desk, grab my hand, and teach me how to write by moving my hand on paper. I learned to write and read in Spanish first. My grandpa taught me how to write names and stuff like that. He lives with us. Sometimes my grandpa didn't work, and sometimes he did.

Before I came to school my sister helped me read comic books and regular books. My dad was studying English so he taught me to say a little English before I went to school. He got books from the school where he was going, and he would read a little bit to me, like a word, and I would repeat it. I learned to read the meat packages at the market, and when I would go with my grandfather to see a baseball game, I could tell which of my favorite foods, like nachos, to order by looking at the menu.

I share a bedroom with my mom and dad and two sisters. It's a room just for my family. I am usually alone in there in the afternoons with just my two-year-old sister and some cousins. Everybody's working. I feel lonesome because nobody's watching me.

There's a store right here on the corner, and I like to go play video games there after school. It's like a hobby. My dad says, "Where are you going?" I goes, "I'm going to the store." And he goes, "You're gonna read now. Turn off the TV and get in the room and study." And I go, "Okay, okay." So I go in and study. I have to read for like one hour or thirty minutes so I can learn to read better. When I try to read, my little sister jumps on me.

I sometimes read to my dad, and sometimes he still reads to me. When he corrects my homework every night, he checks a couple of problems, and then he just gives the okay. Usually we just have dittoes that take about one hour. My mom doesn't help me with homework that much.

My other sister is twelve years old. She reads comic books and girls' things, like what to buy. She looks at the pictures. I don't know if the other grown-ups in the house read, or the other kids, but my cousin Esmeralda's mom puts her in their room to read, and Esmeralda teaches her little sister.

Grown-ups write different stuff. Like if they are a teacher, they write assignments for the next day for their students. They write on the chalkboard. Moms write recipes and grocery lists. Husbands can write stuff for work or for their wife to read. When I grow up, I will probably write invitations for when I get married. I'll say like, "I'm getting married. Will you please come?" I will write about what's happening in my life. I will be able to be a manager if I can write good. I will get to write checks when I'm a manager. When I'm a husband, I could write a note if I am going to be late for dinner. I'll probably do stuff like that until I'm old, then I will write stuff like a will. When I'm really old, I might write a letter to my friends to ask them to come see me in the hospital.

At home I see my parents write stuff like grocery lists and maps to go places. I help my mom with the grocery list, when I go to the store with her, I like helping her read English. I read the gallons of milk in the basket sometimes and see how much they cost. I read bags of potato chips to tell if they have a lot of fat in them.

My parents read English books and recipes and write bills; they do math for the bills. When my parents go to school, they have to do their homework. My mom writes recipes and things about the kitchen, like about an oven, so my dad can get her one. I help my older sister with writing some assignments they give her for homework. I help my friends write their homework sometimes, too. Like if I know some hard words, I could show them, and if they know some, they could show me.

My dad is in school now to get the certificate that says they know how to talk in English. He works as a carpenter, but not no more 'cause they closed down the factory because they don't have no work and everything. So now he's not working, only my mom. She does like calendars, folders, and pencils. She makes them with a machine.

If I didn't know how to write, I couldn't write to my family in Mexico. I'd have to just call them on the phone. Most of my family lives right here in California, but when we went to Mexico one time, my grandma stayed over there. My parents and me and my sister send a birthday card, or a letter to my grandma and aunts in Mexico to see if they are getting along good. They write to us, too, and tell us stuff about what's happening there. But I haven't gotten any really important news from them because they call us on the phone with that. I have written them news about what I'm doing in school and am I studying good. I like to get letters back from them. It makes me feel good.

I like to read stories and art books and like a card when somebody sends you a message. My favorite time to read is like reading a map or when I have to read signs when I drive around with my family in the car. I like that kind of reading because I can help people find a place they're going. Sometimes my dad doesn't see the signs, and he passes the exit he wants. I tell him he passed it, because I can read the signs.

I hate writing when I have to write like two pages. Like in Miss Dunn's class, I had to write big words five times each. There were one hundred words that she gived us. Some were easy but some were hard, too, and we had to write them five times each, each one. That was a hard assignment.

I haven't been doing writing at home, except for homework. Now that I'm ten, the kind of writing that I do at school is cursive and writing my name and the date and assignments. My friends do pictures and assignments the teacher tells you, but they also write inside their school books where they aren't supposed to, gang stuff for fun, like the name of a gang.

We had to write a thank you letter to Officer Bob, a policeman who came in every Tuesday at eight o'clock to teach us about drugs and gangs and everything like that. He taught me to say no to drugs and what drugs would do to you. And what gangs do to you. We also had to write to the soldiers over there fighting in the Persian Gulf. I had to say my name, school, grade, and do we like to come to school and our family size. I asked the soldiers how is it in Saudi Arabia. We had to write about why the soldiers are probably over there. Five or six kids got letters back so far.

I don't like to write fiction. I want to write about stuff that actually happened. The way I decide what I am going to write about is by thinking about what we did last week or yesterday or what we are going to do today. In my journal I like to tell what happened that was exciting so maybe the person who reads it will be excited, too. Like last time I wrote that my family went to Mile Square Park for a picnic. I wrote everything that we did, like my dad said, "Let me see who can run the fastest." And me and my cousin ran all around, and he beat me. I dropped down over there, "Oh, I'm tired. I'm tired."

In my class we don't do our journal that much, but we do it. The teacher reads it, then she writes back. You could just answer her back. I think the school district orders us to do journals, but I don't mind. The teacher gives us ideas for what to write about. At the beginning of the year when we first started school, she just said, write five or six sentences.

If I had to fix up something that I wrote, I would put it in order and then copy it over again. I would read it and look for mistakes and fix them. My mistakes are spelling and if it doesn't rhyme or something like that. Like if I put double words, like *the the*. We do a rough draft, like on a piece of paper, and then we do a clear one on another piece of paper. The teacher has already corrected it and everything, so we have to repeat it sometimes like three times. In third grade I did one on Halloween. Like if you like Halloween, or if you don't like it, or like are you going trick-or-treating? And what's going to be your costume?

I get uncomfortable with writing when I get too-hard-of assignments because I can't think in my mind how to do them. I feel comfortable when I get not-so-hard and not-so-easy assignments, like writing easy words, because I can do those easier. I hate to have to copy stuff out of a book.

I write stuff in different ways for different people to read. If I was going to write to the President, I would tell him to send money to our city and to stop drugs and prevent gangs. In our house we have a big wall, and they write on it their gang names and their nicknames and everything. If I was writing that to the President, I would write it a little different than I would write about it to my teacher because if I wrote to my teacher I could tell her about things, like with gangs, that have happened to me.

I think teachers could help you more than they do. They just tell you, "Do this," and then maybe they just go to their desks. I'd like directions how to write, like what to write about. They could have helped me write better by looking at my assignment with me right away when I finish it. Instead she said, "Put 'em right here, and I'll correct them." She said that before I went to Mexico for three weeks at Christmas, and she still hasn't corrected them. If she'd look at my assignments right away, I could redo it. Then I could finish faster and start doing another thing.

When I am reading, other people help me with words I can't understand. The teacher could have helped me more with reading by having us in small groups so everybody could read to her by taking turns. She could help all of us at once.

We got a new student teacher in our class now. She has us doing different stuff, like writing recipes about cooking and making a magic potion, a brew of ingredients for how to disappear teachers and principals. You just invent things. She told us we had to write three nasty things and put many other things in the potion, like a pound of sugar, bread, water, and milk, too. My nasty things were Kenny's brains, one thousand pounds of ice, and three thousand pounds of boogers. I got the ideas for the nasty stuff from brainstorming with my friends, and I got the other ideas from a cooking book that I read. I will have to write the recipe for this brew in my composition book, and the teacher might make me get rid of the booger part. If she does, I will put in monkeys' arms instead.

The student teacher sometimes puts ideas up on the board, and we have to write about that idea in our journal. Like she asked us to tell her what games we'll play in the future. My favorite thing is playing video games. Another time we had to say what kind of pet we'd like to have and how would you feed it. I didn't like to have to write about what she said because I wanted to write about what I done over the weekend that was special.

We've been reading *Dear Mr. Henshaw*. Beverly Cleary wrote that. She wrote the Ramona books. They're like funny books. It's about the right hardness. The student teacher has the three tables in the front take turns with the books, and we read out loud for about a half hour. We don't just go in order around the group, she skips around. We have to do questions on worksheets for that story. Like I have to describe Mr. Henshaw as good or bad and do you like him. The student teacher has us write a character analysis, too, with one or two sentences about each character. I have to do book reports, too, and I have to tell how each character feels about a divorce that happened.

For silent reading we have been in a contest called "Book It." This month I have to read two picture books, three chapter books, one important person book, and a mystery, then I'll win a pizza. The chapter books and mystery books have to be long. So far I have read about Paul Revere, and I'm finishing the *Black Stallion*. I read a picture book about sharks, too, but mystery and adventure books are my favorite. I like action, excitement, and scary stuff, like when someone is killed and no one knows who did it. If a book doesn't have excitement, I might stop reading it before I finish it, like if they are just talking about something. When I'm reading, I am thinking things in my head, like what it would look like as a movie.

My favorite place to read is inside the classroom when I am reading and sharing the same book with a neighbor. I don't mind reading silently, like in silent reading, when you have to read for twenty minutes or something like that, but I like to share the book with someone while I'm reading it. If I can't share the book, I feel lonely and everything. It makes me feel like I'm not hearing nothing. When I can read out loud to somebody else, I don't feel lonely.

20

Butch, Jane, and Bobby

"WHY I READ"

(Grade 5)

Contributed by Jamie Myers

Their teacher helped me pick Butch, Jane, and Bobby because he felt they were very different as readers. Butch was "in the middle," Jane was the "best reader," and Bobby was "at the bottom" of their fifth grade class. As a reading educator, I wanted to find the reasons children would give for reading. In a large midwestern elementary school, in a town of fifty thousand, I visited the three fifth grade classrooms that Butch, Jane, and Bobby moved between for English, science, social studies, reading, and study time. During nine visits over the course of eleven weeks, I watched them work, and I recorded all the different types of reading in which they engaged. In four interviews in the library, we compiled a list of all the different texts they read at school and at home, helped in part by a home reading log they kept for one week, and we discussed why they read each of the different texts.

Butch taps his pencil and looks around the room during lessons after quickly finding the answer to the teacher's question. He always has a book nearby that he can read before and after lessons. Jane is the quickest worker, so quick that it often appears that she isn't even following along with the lesson. This is largely because she hunches over her desk and begins work on the next assignment while the teacher is still reviewing the current one. Sometimes she leans over to talk to her neighbor during lulls in the lesson. Between lessons she'll read and often share parts of the book with a girl at a nearby desk.

Bobby is older than his classmates because he repeated an earlier grade. He is very dutiful, using every bit of the time available to complete papers or worksheets. The other students and activity in the room seldom distract him.

BUTCH: "I AM READING ALL THE TIME"

I am reading all the time. Often, I don't have anything else to do. Plus, there is this thing at school where you win a free pizza if you can read four books a month, so I want to finish a book every five days. Last month, I read three Encyclopedia Brown books and one called *Operation Dump the Chump*. Right now, after four days of reading, I am on page one hundred of *Otis Spofford* by Beverly Cleary, who is one of my favorite authors. Next, I plan to read *Chocolate Fever* and another Encyclopedia Brown book. When I read at school, I like to read the good parts aloud to my teacher, and show him how far I've read.

I really like these Encyclopedia Brown books because my dad is a lawyer and to me it is always a mystery around the house who is going to win each case. These mysteries give an answer in the back of the book, but I never read that until I'm done because I like to try to figure it out myself. But, I don't like all mysteries. I think those pick-your-own adventure books don't make any sense.

I read books between TV shows and for about a half an hour each night in my room. I think I deserve to watch TV after reading each night. Of course I keep reading during commercials because I don't like them. Sometimes, instead of reading, I will play my drums or eat. I like to eat; that's why I like pizza.

My mom also tells me to read when I go to bed because it will help me go to sleep. I also learned to read in the bathtub from my mom, but I play first for a while before reading. I see my mom reading great big books with five hundred pages and real small words. Dad reads mysteries too, like me. He stretches out on the couch and reads all the time. He also has his own library of books. About the only time I stop reading a book is during the seasons that it is nice outside and the days are longer. In winter I can't go out as much.

I'm also always looking things up in the encyclopedia. The other night my sister was doing a report on Egypt, and I saw one of her books open to a picture of King Tut. So I looked him up in the encyclopedia. I like to figure out stuff that I see, or hear, or think about. I like knowing about the stuff partly because it will help me when I have to write reports in future years in school. I'm just curious, I guess. My friends are always asking me about stuff, and I'm telling them about stuff that I find out. A lot of times I use the encyclopedia to study the states and capitals for the tests, instead of taking the school book home. I like the encyclopedia because it doesn't give me every detail like the textbook. It gives all the important stuff first, so I get a real clear understanding.

I figure about half the time that I read, I have to read school books. I really don't read in my English book—just work in that one. With my reading book I sometimes like the stories, and sometimes I don't. We just talk about my science book. The social studies book gives me information that I have to learn for the test. The teacher wants me to learn this information so I can use it later in a job application so I can get a good job. I want a good job too, so I can be happier making more money to get the things I want. The teacher grades me on what she wants me to know, and the grade tells me what I know and don't know and what I need to look up in my encyclopedia over the summer. I don't get into trouble over my grades. Mom and Dad told me that my grades show what I know and, if I do bad, they say I should just study harder because I might need to know this in the big world.

I don't like the way we do vocabulary in social studies. I think we should just look up the word in the back when we need to. Some of the time I like to flip through the social studies book and look at the pictures. My favorite picture is one of a huge mining truck that is so big that the people look like ants and the regular size bulldozer looks like a toy. But other pictures, like the maps with all the states and capitals I have to memorize, I don't like at all. The stuff I read will stay in my head if I like it, but the other stuff is gone in half an hour, especially after watching TV.

JANE: "I GET MY ASSIGNMENTS DONE SO I CAN REALLY READ"

I think reading is fun, so I have books at home and at school that I read every day. My favorite books are adventures about girls my age that go to school, like *Nothing's Fair in the Fifth Grade* and *Your Former Friend, Matthew.* At home, when I'm not ready to do my homework, I'll watch TV and read until Dad gets home. Then I have to do my homework or get into trouble. Sometimes, Dad finds something interesting in the newspaper, and he gives it to me to read. I also listen to Dad read stuff to Mom, which is usually when people die.

Once in a while when I get tired of reading a book, I'll read one of my sister's *Young Miss* magazines. I find these magazines and other books by snooping in her room. I like *MAD Magazine* too, and some others at school, but I can't remember their names. Mostly, though, I like to read books. My sister gives me books to read too. I pick books by reading the back cover. With *Hearts Don't Lie,* the back cover had questions on it that I answered, then read to find out if I was right. But the main reason I read this book was because the characters in the story had my name and my sister's name.

Just recently I was reading a mystery at home and someone got murdered. This bothered me, so I looked on my shelf and found *Ralph S. Mouse* by one of my favorite authors. I decided to read the mystery at school and *Ralph* at home. I like mysteries because I have to figure out what happens. Really I like all books partly because I have to keep reading them to find out what will happen next and in the end.

At school, I find extra time to read at the end of English, after spelling, and on the bus. One day I read *Nothing's Fair* at the end of every class and before every class began. I also read parts aloud to my girlfriend. I have read eight books the last two months and have won two pizza coupons in the "Book It" contest.

Even though I like to read books, I spend more time reading for school assignments and tests. I work really hard to get all my assignments done so I can have my time for reading. Since I can figure out the directions myself, I always begin working immediately. Often I look ahead after each page to see just how far I have to go yet. Sometimes the teacher changes the directions in the textbook, adding some or crossing out some, so I have to read along when the teacher gives the assignment to know just what to do. But most of the time I can figure out the directions myself. This is especially true with my reading workbook. But, my English assignments have more changes; once I missed a change, and I got all the answers wrong.

I don't have many assignments in my science book. We read that to find out about stuff like the body and measurement. But with social studies, it's tests! I have to answer all the questions at the end of the chapter, write out the vocabulary definitions, and study all of this so I can get an A on the test. If I get straight A's all year, I will get a TV or something like that. Plus, all my friends want to see the grades I get.

In social studies we read the chapter aloud, but I don't like to read aloud. I read along and answer questions if I get called on. To study for the test I review all the questions from memory and look back if I have to. Then I'll read the chapter and make up questions that I think will be on the test for each section of the book that has a heading like "How to make steel." When I'm done, Mom will go over it with me and ask me more questions on each section of the book. Sometimes my sister does this for me. I really don't remember for long any of the stuff I read in this book or study for the test. I really don't like nonfiction. Sometimes I'll find something interesting.

BOBBY: "READING IS WORK I HAVE TO DO"

Reading is like work. It's not like the fun I have riding my cycle on my dad's farm on weekends. I also have about twenty metal toy tractors and boards that I use to build things to play with the tractors on.

I really don't spend much time reading at home. It depends on where I am at and what I am doing. A little more than half the time at home I read so I can get the grades I need to pass and not waste another year. The rest of the time, I want to read about sports. At school, I read 'cause the teacher tells me to do assignments and take tests. This reading is hardly ever interesting. Most of the time it's just work that I have to do.

I read on my own about sports because I want to be a sports star when I grow up. I even told my mom that I'm going to play for the Cincinnati Reds. My favorite sport is baseball, so I look for things to read about all the players I know, especially one Cincinnati outfielder. I don't want to tell you his name. My grandma got me hooked on the Reds by buying me stuff at the ball games and bringing it to me.

If I go to the library, which isn't very often, I look for books about sports, especially baseball players I know. I signed out two books, *Mickey Mantle Slugs It Out* and *Willie Mays* to read for the pizza chart. I had to sign them out again because I didn't get them done. I would like to win a pizza coupon, but I haven't read any books yet for the pizza chart. I might be able to if they are thin books. I don't read thick books. I was reading one thick book, *Halloween,* because I was at home looking for a book, and it was an old one of my mom's. I also knew something about the movie. I was reading this at school when I got to this good part where snakes started coming out of a person's head. My teacher yelled at me to stop reading and pay attention to how to write a friendly letter. I quit reading it later because I'd never have finished a book that thick.

Sometimes I will look through the newspaper for something in the sports about somebody I like to watch or know about. Sometimes it's a football player, but usually it's a baseball player. I always read the little square about sports on the front page above the headlines. Just the other day I was looking through the newspaper ads for a cycle race my dad and I heard about. I found the ad, but it didn't tell where the race was going to be at, or give any phone number.

When I go to ball games, I like to look through the program. I spend a lot of time looking at the pictures. I read the names of the players and match them with their picture. One time Eddy Miller wasn't in the picture, and I still wonder why not. I'll also read stuff about the players like their height and weight. After that there is usually not much else left to read, and it's not very interesting anyway.

I have a collection of baseball cards that I read a lot. I read the number of years played, height, and weight. I have cards sorted by teams with the manager card on top. Each team is wrapped in a blue piece of paper with the names of the missing players written on top where I can always read them, so I know what cards I need. Whenever there is a game on TV, I get the two teams out and look at the players.

Like I said, I read at school because I have to do all these questions over everything. In the reading book you have to do the focus questions. In science you have to do the questions in "think about." In social studies you have to do the questions at the end of the chapter. These questions really aren't reading to me. I know the teacher wants me to learn so I can get a good education. I want to get a good job and get good money, so I try hard to do all the assignments right. I check with my teacher, or a friend if I'm not sure how to do an assignment, like what I'm supposed to find, or how to mark something, or if I should write the questions and answers.

I know when an assignment doesn't seem right, like doing the crossword puzzle on the chalkboard in social studies when I noticed right away that one word didn't fit the number of blanks right. In group work in science, I check to make sure our paper looks right and find out what we need to do yet. Some cry if they don't get an *A*, and some it doesn't bother. I try to get an *A*, but I usually don't. In reading I do a lot of vocabulary words and skill pack workbook pages and focus worksheets. I usually get *D*'s on the workbook, *F*'s on the focus, and *B*'s on the vocabulary.

Sometimes in reading, when I finish my work, the teacher tells me to work on the card machine that has math and reading problems. I don't like this machine because it has a lot of buttons, and I have to look down and back up all the time. But I work on it because if I didn't my teacher would have me do more worksheets, and I don't want to do that. I wish I could just stay at my seat and draw pictures of four wheelers and sports fields.

My teacher wants me to read in the reading book so I can learn to read better. I find it hard and uninteresting to read silently to get the story. I guess I'm lazy. But I like it best when the teacher reads aloud or has a tape of the story. It's more interesting on the tape recorder, even though it's not really interesting any way you do it. We do read every story aloud in class. When I read aloud in class, like social studies, I usually have to have help from the teacher to pronounce all the words in my paragraph.

I read in my social studies book because I have to, but once in a while I find something I want to read about. I like learning about the states that are around me like Indiana, Illinois, and the state that has Detroit. And I know that in our book we are going to Florida next, then Texas, then back up to Indiana and Ohio. I want to read about Indiana because that is where I want to live and because I like farm ground. I also like the maps in the book. I don't read all the words on the map, but I like looking at them. Sometimes during class when the teacher asks a question that I think will be on the map, like the name of a river in Pittsburgh, I will look through the book to find the answer. I know the teacher wants me to learn about what happened long ago, and today, and in other places. But then you take the vocabulary quiz, study for a test, and she grades the test.

21

Nicki, Andy, Abigail, and Paul

"THE SEEDS AND THE SUN"

(Grades 5 and 6)

Contributed by Penny Oldfather

Avid writers Nicki, Andy, Abigail, and Paul thrived in the rich environment of Sally Thomas' whole language fifth- and sixth-grade classroom. They attended Sycamore School, in Claremont, California, a site of progressive educational leadership for many years. Predominantly student-centered, experiential, and humanistic, Sycamore has served a diverse community, including a population of approximately thirty percent minority students and a number of children of college faculty.

Under the shade of the trees in the grassy playground these students shared their thoughts and feelings through a series of informal, indepth interviews focused on conditions that supported their continuing impulse to learn. Learning was not always easy for them. Nicki, a very able bilingual student, struggled to meet the extremely high standards she set for herself. Andy literally suffered in classroom settings which restricted his physical movement and energy release, but had developed ways to cope, and to use his gifts for visualization and problem solving. Abigail had difficulty with math and spelling, but was a gifted writer who eloquently described her ideal school or her grasp of the complexities of the evolution of technology. Paul had dealt deeply and painfully with personal and philosophical issues, and had emerged with a wisdom beyond his years. These co-researchers and their classmates taught me many things, especially about the importance of self-expression and choice in nurturing student motivation.

NICKI (SIXTH GRADE)

Writing is part of me. I like it a lot. Once I write a paragraph I always go back and read it, and I always flow through it real softly because I want to make sure that it sounds nice. It has to flow itself, you know? With no jumps to things.

I remember in the fourth and fifth grades, I started to get feelings about my own type of style. When I first started, I would write about something that happened to me. Later I started writing things that I would make up. What I like now is to write stuff that is fiction, but is still about real life and real feelings.

If you don't know what you're feeling right now, you can write it all down and make a story of it. Then maybe when you go back to it, you understand. It makes you understand what that feeling was exactly. Where it came from. When I have to write something for social studies, I don't feel in myself, "I like this. I like how I've written it." Because in social studies you write about someone else, not about how *you* feel.

Recently I've been trying to write humorous poems. It's really taking a risk for me, to see if I can do it, and to see if I like it. It's more risky for me because I have more of a relationship with serious things. I like humor a lot, but I have decided I like to hear it more from other authors than myself. I write better in the more serious form. I like to dig down deep and find out about myself. It sounds like it might be more work, but if you enjoy it, it's not at all.

Another risk I took was in my reading log. Everyone else just loved the *One-Eyed Cat.* I just didn't like it at all. It went too far. They never let you know if he did shoot the cat's eye. He just kept thinking about it every minute. He just kept saying, "Oh, did I really do it? I feel so bad." It was hard to say I didn't like the book because all the other kids liked the book. I decided to take a chance and write about it. All I knew was that I didn't like it. But when I started doing the reading log, and wrote about it, then I understood why I didn't like it. I kind of felt bad telling Mrs. Thomas I didn't like the book, because she liked it so much. But I knew her talents and she knew mine, and she accepted that. She accepted my judgments and opinions. You can't teach an opinion.

When I wrote my book, *Brush Fire,* we had been studying about art and great artists, so I was thinking about that for the theme. When I first started, I was kind of confused and frustrated, but it was just a matter of teasing the story out. Some people plan writing, and make a chart and work it out ahead of time. I wrote *Brush Fire* as it came to me. I would think, "If he was doing this, then he would be feeling this way." Then I knew what would be coming next.

For me, if you have an idea, it's not really hard. I was really excited about working on *Brush Fire.* I took it home, sometimes, to write. Sometimes I wrote lots, lots, lots. Other times I had to stop and think.

Sometimes I would really go blank. You want to start writing, but you don't know what to put.

Sometimes the very words come into your head. Sometimes just the *idea,* and then you have to *find* the words. When I try to think what to write next, it just depends on the feelings the character is getting. I communicate with the characters in the story, if they are feeling sad or greedy or confused. To get a picture. Like it's running through you. You're so scared you kind of feel like crying. You kind of get—the vision looks up to you. You almost get that same feeling. It goes through you and down to the page.

ANDY (FIFTH GRADE)

You get to write whatever you want here at Sycamore. I like to write stuff that's like fiction. The person is fictional, but the place where he lives is real and what happens around him is real. I don't like fairy tales as much. I mean 'cause nobody knows where they came from or anything, and so it's hard to know who wrote them.

I like real books better than textbooks. Textbooks have stories about "Jill went to the store. Jill came back. Jill forgot the butter so she went again." That's really it. I like to read the newspaper and magazines.

I kind of feel like that guy who wrote *A Brief History of Time.* He tries to figure out why we're here, and stuff like that. And I always try to figure that out and come to conclusions. I just don't know how to explain it, so I don't like explaining about myself much. Sometimes I can really picture things. I can do a lot of stuff in my head. Instead of writing on the paper, I put the paper in my mind, kind of, and I can do it off that. I want to be the first person to fly to the moon and around it and then back, or the sun or something like that. Like the first person kind of thing. You get to be written down in a book, and that's kind of fun. It's kind of hard these days because everybody's taking what hasn't been done, and so I don't know if I'll get anything.

I'm worried about going to middle school 'cause I don't read very fast, and I think they have lots of homework. Sometimes when I'm trying I get really nervous and my hands start shaking and I can't read so I just stop. It's when the book is too hard for my level, or I get tired of reading, if I've been sitting for a long time. I have to get up and walk around. Too much energy or something. Once I couldn't read because I couldn't get my hand to stop shaking. When I do Hebrew school all I do is sit in the chair and I don't get to run around and get rid of my energy, so I have to keep moving. Now lately, when I'm at the table I have to switch my legs.

At school if there are different stations, with different places to work, that helps. In some classes, teachers don't have stations, so you can't walk around. You just basically sit in your desk and do work. If a room has learning centers it kind of shows me that there's lots of good stuff to do, and I can move around. And that could help in a way, 'cause there's more to do to fill the mind differently. Like they say Lego's build your mind, so Lego's are good.

On a rainy day I set up an Olympic course at home where I have to jump over chairs and stuff. 'Cause I can't do anything else. At school when I can't move around I have a hard time. Sometimes I just wiggle my toes.

ABIGAIL (FIFTH GRADE)

Writing is my favorite thing. It's fun to write because you have all these ideas and stuff about what to write. If you don't write, you just sort of don't do anything, and it's kind of boring. Everything else is kind of boring. I write at home, and I write on vacation, and I write at school a lot more, and I write a lot of places. Everywhere I go—I just write.

I think of story ideas, like it was real life, like if it was really somebody talking, like if it was a king ordering somebody. I think of it in real life, and I find characters. I made up a story about how it's quality not quantity. It's about two little boys and chocolate bars. And one of them gets one *delicious* chocolate bar—and the other gets fifteen of these *yucky* ones. And they are the same price. And the boy with the fifteen chocolate bars says, "Yuck. These are yucky." And the boy with one, said "UMMM. This is delicious." And so it was quality, not quantity.

It's like that with books. It's good to find a little small book with really good words in it, and not one that's just long and boring, and it gets you stuck when you read it. I like it if a book flows. If you're reading something and it goes "This-is-a-dog," it doesn't sound so good. But if you have something that's like "Juliet jumped off the balcony and danced her way home," it sounds better.

I love fairy tales. I heard some people wanted to take away fairy tales, so I wrote a letter to the *L.A. Times:*

Dear Censors:

I have heard about banning fairy tales, and I don't like it!! These parents think that it is "lying to children" and "making them believe black magic," but it's not! Fairy tales are a part of growing up and learning how to cope with real life, and it's also our imagination! If they get away with banning fairy tales, children are going to be boring.

Also, fairy tales are everywhere. The only way to get rid of fairy tales is for kids to stare at a blank wall! And still they'll get away with imagining. No matter what you do, fairy tales will live forever. And if fairy tales are gone, there won't be such a thing as a kid anymore.

Disagreeing young reader,
Abigail
Fifth Grade

When I'm doing math, I'm really bored, and it's kind of dull because it's not words. It's like somebody saying [mumble, mumble]. In writing you get to decide the whole thing about what you're gonna write. When you're doing math it ends up the same, no matter what. Well, it's the same unless you get a wrong answer. Unless you have a math problem that you make up yourself, and you get to answer in a different way, 'cause you made a new kind of problem. Like Albert Einstein found something in math. I forget what it was. He changed it. Then it gets fun.

I like to read *National Geographic*. At school we barely get anything to compare to *National Geographic*. In the textbook they have just plain facts. Nothing that you want to know. In *National Geographic* they show the digs where the archaeologists have last been, and stuff, and what they found. And in textbooks, they just have boring stuff like the names of people and what they did for the last fifteen years, or something, and it's really kind of boring.

In *National Geographic* they tell the person, and what they found, and they take pictures of what it was, and tell how they did it and what years it was from. Not just how many years they have been working or something. They show things that you more likely *want* to know, than what you *have* to know. What you want to know is usually funner stuff. Some kids think archaeology is really boring, but I want to be an archaeologist.

At school they make you have to do it all. They don't really tell you about what you *want* to know. They just kind of give you an idea about what there *is* to know. They just give you a couple of basic things. And some things they go in too deep that you don't always really need.

It's kind of hard, because everyone is faced toward their own thing. Like there's a couple of kids at my table who are faced to this math, and I will face to archaeology and history. Some people are faced to writing. It's what they really want to know. A school could have everybody think about what they want to be, or do, or want to know about. And they could have separate rooms for each, and split up the grades and the knowledge and everything. It would be kind of hard for a school to do that, but if they wanted to get everybody's exact interests and mostly base a classroom on it, they could.

But then they would get just a little bit of everything else. Now they give a touch of the things that we want to know, and then they give more on things we don't quite really want to know. So they just do the opposite way around.

PAUL (SIXTH GRADE)

I think the only thing you can own is thoughts. Just thoughts. The way you say things. I think that's the only thing you can really own and say that's how *you* said it and that's *your* saying.

My best subjects are writing and literature. I like writing because I can express how I feel and how I felt before and what other people feel like. And how the world is and how things work. This year I've started to write more about how things *are*. All the other years they just told us to write a story. I'd make it like "Someone walked down the block and went somewhere." But now I'll write a story, and it'll say "I saw the butterflies as I walked around the corner, and then I saw the trees in front of me."

When I'm writing I can really think about what I want to put down. When you're talking, you don't have time. You can't sit there and say something and then think about it again and say the right thing and then it will be perfect. In writing you can put exactly what you think with no flaws. When I write something I read it over a few times and I pretend I didn't write it, and it's by Ray Bradbury. And I think if it's a good job by him or not. A lot of times I try to compare my work with Ray Bradbury's. Of course I'm not as good as him, so maybe it'll make me better. I just think about every word, if it fits perfectly. And usually it fits perfectly. Usually when I write something it's exactly how I want it. I guess I edit in my head as I write. I don't really try to. It just comes out that way.

Going to Outdoor School [an environmental education camp attended by the class] made a difference in my writing. It was one of the best experiences of my life. I really started noticing things. You just learned about everything, and got a feeling about the whole world, and learned you should take care of the world. You could just find the inner feeling inside of you. And you just felt different through the whole trip. I have a whole new outlook. Now when I see grass, I see it as something living, instead of something to run on.

Here at Sycamore you can kind of do what you want. Not exactly what you want, but you can kind of do what you want. What's life without choices? There's not a life without choices. And even if you're younger you should still have choices. Students at Sycamore are different. Instead of not wanting to read, they'll read. Instead of not wanting to write, they'll write. They want to write.

I like it when the teacher and the kid are equal. Like a kid can stand up and go throw something away instead of having to raise their hand and ask if they can go throw something away. If you have a piece of scrap paper, you can just take care of it. You don't have to get permission to do every single thing. It helps the kids to understand that everything's equal.

I love when Mrs. Thomas lets us get out all of our ideas. What she does is, she lets all of us talk. Most teachers say, "If you have any ideas raise your hand." Mrs. Thomas will start us to say stuff. She'll give us examples or give us ideas and then we build off of those ideas and say our ideas, final ideas. I don't think they are really final ideas because *every* time you think about something and then you think about something else for it. Then you think *that's* your thought, but then there's something else about *that*. So we do that many times, whenever we get something. You can express yourself.

There aren't a lot of places like Sycamore. You know, once you've dipped in you can't get it off. Once you're in a school like this and you have my teacher, you can't make it like a regular school with that good philosophy. If there was a student in Sycamore that was in Mrs. Thomas' class, and they were going to be a teacher, they couldn't be just normal like everybody else saying, "I before E except after C." They're going to be like Mrs. Thomas. Good and open-minded, and with a good philosophy.

On the last day of school at Sycamore, I gave Mrs. Thomas a poem I wrote about her. I tie-dyed a shirt in pastels and wrote this poem on it for her.

The Seeds and the Sun

*As the colors of the hill run up the horizon,
the sun creeps down, sneaking, hiding.
The wind mill turns and creaks from the wind that
blows and blows, never ending, never beginning.
The moon wakes up, opens its eyes.
A tear runs down for it is happy it is starting.
The stars twinkle and shine,
burning their last breath of life.
The people marvel and wonder as it opens their heart.
A teacher picks up her wand,
Implanting huge imaginations in young children.
She picks only the plump
to be in her wondrous class.
Then a miraculous magical beam of new light
breaks the barrier.
Another tear runs down the cheek of the moon,
for it has come to an end.
As the colors of the hill tumble down the horizon.
Thanks, Mrs. Thomas.
We were the seeds and you were the sun.*

22

Adam

"MY MOUTH IS FULL OF WORDS"

(Grade 6)

Contributed by Judy Storeygard

Adam is a bright articulate eleven-year-old boy who has Tourette's Syndrome. His condition was diagnosed when he was seven years old. Tourette's Syndrome is a neurological disorder characterized by involuntary multiple motor and/or vocal tics. The symptoms come and go and change over time. Adam has fine motor difficulties, particularly with handwriting, a common problem for children with Tourette's Syndrome. He copes with his condition with courage, grace, and humor. Other children accept him, and he has some close friendships. Adam participates in all school activities and is active in several sports. His special interest is math, and he is planning to be a mathematician when he grows up. He has always enjoyed writing. Since the onset of his Tourette's, Adam has developed a writing process that allows him to utilize his creativity.

I know that I dictated stories to my mother a long time ago. I think I was about four. I don't remember why I started because it was a long time ago. There may be a number of reasons. I might have wanted to because my brother was writing in school. I may have wanted to just to do something. I didn't think much about writing these stories. I just wrote whatever was in my head. I mean there's always something in someone's head.

When I went to school, we wrote on big lines that were an inch tall. I remember one of my first stories was about a movie theater, and there were people in the movie theater, and it turned all rainbow colors or something like that. I probably liked rainbows when I was that young and could picture one in my mind. I have a very visual memory. I remember left and right some very strange ways. When I was taught pedestrian safety on my Big Wheel, I remember that left looked dark and right looked light. I did my own writing in first grade, but then the teacher proofread it. There were a lot of mistakes. Again there wasn't much thought going into my stories, but more than I had when I dictated to my mom. I wrote very silly stories back in first grade. They made no sense. Because I was young, I wrote what came to my head in kindergarten and before. I did a little bit more planning in first grade, a little more in second grade. By the time I got to fifth, I did a lot of planning.

I remember in kindergarten, we had these books. I know I made a lot of spelling mistakes. I was only in kindergarten so they didn't care about spelling. I don't think there was any theme to the book, except for holidays. I wrote a Halloween book and that had to do with a holiday. Other books I made up like "The Case of the Missing Marble" didn't have to do with anything at the time. The book is about how a boy loses a marble and it goes to the dump, and he finds it there. I loved garbage, and I collected little pieces of garbage and stuff. I think that probably influenced it.

I think I liked writing because it was something new; it was something different because I wasn't introduced to it before. Writing by myself was fun. I probably felt proud when I read back my stories.

I had a wonderful teacher in second grade. We studied different historical periods and countries all around the world. She read us "Tiger, Tiger," a very famous poem. Then we had to write a poem about another animal. I wrote, "Hippo, Hippo":

> *Hippo, hippo, wrinkled mud*
> *Why are you like a just mopped floor?*
> *Where did you get your ivory teeth?*
> *Who gave you that bowl of jelly?*
> *Why do you pose like a round submarine?*
> *What makes you waddle like a colossal goose?*
> *Do you know your tail would be proper for a pig?*
> *Hippo, hippo, shuffle, trudge*

She gave us like a special sheet and I started the first and last sentence with "Hippo, hippo," and I used a lot of questions. I really copied "Tiger, Tiger" with a different animal and a few different questions. Another one I wrote was "Whale, Whale":

> *Whale, whale gigantic creature*
> *Why do you squirt and spout?*
> *What makes your fins glide through the water?*
> *Why did they make you so mighty?*
> *What gives you the power to wallop the waves?*
> *Whale, whale, slippery, huge*

It was another one like "Tiger, Tiger." One of the things I remember about it was I used meaningful words. My favorite sentence in the poem was when I said, "Why did you wallop the waves?" And my teacher liked it and so did my Mom, and that made me feel good. The word "wallop" is powerful, and a whale is powerful. I feel good when I find the right word, especially when I have to think about it a little bit.

I wrote two other poems. One of them was completely on my own. It was called "The Desert." I think I wrote it when we were studying about desert countries or sometime after. The main factor in my deciding to write the poem was that I could imagine myself in the desert. I was having a great time writing poetry because I had already written "Hippo, Hippo" and "Whale, Whale." I think it was fun because again it was having something of my own, having something that *I* did. I think I thought, "Hey, why don't I just write another one?"

I really loved poems, and I was practically craving to write another because it was my "in" thing. I think it was something new and it was sort of like art and I like art a lot, because it is sort of graceful; it flows. It's not just like a story. A story is sort of the same, but it doesn't flow as much. That's why it's more graceful.

One thing I liked about my teacher was that she gave us a lead in. I hate it when teachers say, "Just write a story." They give us no idea of what to write. It is really hard because you have no guidelines.

That year was the biggest start of the writing process for me. The year before and before that we maybe only wrote a few sentences. That year we really started going on writing, second grade.

I remember one other thing I wrote in second grade. She gave us this writing format: one paragraph about the setting, one about the characters, one like the body of it, and the closing. I wrote a spoof, called *MacFeather*. It was a parody of *Macbeth*. She did a lot of literary stuff with us. I liked the story because I said, "The ghost called," and it said, "eat fish and chips" instead of "boil, boil, toil" and whatever it is. I like making funny things in my stories. I love parodies. Like I love the movie, *Spaceballs* [a Mel Brooks movie]. It's fun. Again you have something to start off with. Writing the desert poem was probably harder because I just thought up the idea. I thought of *MacFeather* because she told us to write a spoof. I think it was because we were doing cultural stuff with Macbeth. She was telling us all this, and I thought it would be incredibly funny if I did *MacFeather*. I ended up the story by saying he was going to be a King because he ate fish and chips, but the crown was too heavy for him because he was MacFeather. He became the elevator or lift man, you know lift as a joke because he was so light and in England they call elevators lifts. To show us how to write a spoof, she probably gave us an example of a spoof. I think she took somebody famous and made a parody out of it, like Cinderella.

In third grade I found out I had Tourette's Syndrome, and the first real symptoms started. It made it very hard for me to write. I still had the ideas, and they got better as my academic career went on, but the actual putting it on paper was hard because of my tics. It was very slow. A very hard thing for me was that we *had* to write in cursive, and that was one of my very worst points. If we hadn't had to write in cursive, I think I would have done at least a little bit better. It hurt my writing process, not only because I couldn't put it down, but I had so many ideas, and before I could put them down and now I couldn't put them down, so I remembered the ones I just thought of, and I forgot the ones I thought of before. I was annoyed. It was very slow. I would start to write, then I would do a tic, then I would start a tic, then I would write again. It was just very slow in general, and then I would do a tic once in a while. A tic would interrupt my thought process some, but mainly it would interrupt my writing process. In third grade, a teacher tried to teach me the keyboard, but it wasn't working. For anyone it takes a long time to learn typing, but for me it has taken an especially long time. It's because of my Tourette's. I don't have the motor skills, and I have bad muscle tone; my muscles are weak.

We had to write a daily journal in third grade. It was very boring because of the topics. I like topics when they're pretty general but not as general as what did you do on your vacation. I think topics should be kind of funny. I like topics that are not too broad, but not too exact. If you have to write about what you did yesterday, most of the time you are in school. So it's like saying, what did you do for six hours, and that's an incredibly small portion. If it was only a paragraph, that would be ok. There's no way you could write two pages, unless something really exciting happened, and ninety-five percent of the class probably nothing happened. That's why I think it's a really stupid assignment.

One of my favorite stories that I wrote that year was called "Mr. Turkey." I liked it because it was funny. At the end of it I put something that I really liked, but the teacher took it out. I was really mad about that. She didn't understand it. I said that someone in the story was someone's sister's friend's mother's sister's nephew's former college roommate. She thought that didn't make any sense. I really liked that expression; I remembered it from a movie I had seen. Because she didn't understand it, she said, "That's not good." I handwrote it myself, but it took a long time. It was slow.

Another thing I liked that year was a poem called, "The Underwater Palace." I made it up, and what I liked about it was that I made the words into a shape. I had seen that before, in a poem book, and I thought it would be neat in this poem. I made the shape into a castle.

I can't write rhyming poems. "The Underwater Palace" was the only rhyming poem I wrote. Part of the reason I can't write rhyming poems is that you really need to think about it for a very long time. If you write a rhyming poem, if you say rhyme two things, then the poem doesn't make sense. But if you don't rhyme it doesn't sound as good. But I had to write nonrhyming poems because it was too hard for me to rhyme. You have to have a built-in thesaurus in your mind if you rhyme.

My least favorite assignment that year was when we just copied poems. In reading, for a very long time near the end of the year, we just copied poems and put it on paper. It was supposed to be a writing assignment. I don't understand why it would be considered writing because all we were doing is copying poems that other people already wrote. I liked funny poems and stuff like that, but these weren't my cup of tea. At that time I didn't learn anything because I wasn't thinking about anything, but I did learn how other professional poets put their stuff together, if they rhyme or don't rhyme and that sort of thing.

One great thing about fourth grade is that we did a lot of typing at home, my mom and I. I don't know who had the idea of dictating for me, but whoever did it was a real good idea. I got a chance to think of more ideas and write better stories when my mom was typing. I pretend I'm there or how it would be when I write. I sort of picture it. It is a lot easier for me to write by dictating. In the beginning, it was hard because I couldn't see what I wrote, and I must have made a lot of mistakes. When I wrote myself, I made a lot of mistakes, but I could erase them because I could see them. The mistakes were grammatical or not what I wanted to say. At least now I ask my Mom, "What did I just say? What did I just say?" If I do that, it's just easier. I don't think that the way I get ideas changes when I dictate or my thinking about what words to use is different, except that my Mom sort of helps me sometimes.

In class, though, after I got Tourette's, I would start wandering off and thinking about other things when I wasn't even trying to. I kept practically slapping myself in the face, I mean not actually do it, but I kept saying, "Keep to the task." It was really hard to keep to the task. In class, if they gave us guidelines, I would probably start writing right away and then have a few tics and then saying to myself, "Don't think about something else," but I'd keep thinking about something else for almost five minutes. Or if a teacher was talking to another reading group, I'd keep listening to that sometimes. I don't know why it happened. I would think about completely different things. When I dictate I don't have trouble concentrating because my Mom's there, and that keeps me on my toes.

I think the longest story I wrote in fourth grade and my favorite one was "The Adventures of Twabby and Babbitt." It was a complete spoof. I used a lot of different things I knew. I had read a book by Daniel Pinkwater, and most of his stories took place in Hoboken, and my story took place in Hoboken. My father and brother were reading stories by Douglas Adams called, *The Hitchhiker's Guide to the Galaxy, The Restaurant at the End of the Universe,* and *So Long and Thanks for All the Fish.* I put those in the story. I just spoofed a lot of things. This is the story that took me three class periods to write less than a handwritten page. Then, my Mom took over on the computer. Part of those three periods was getting the idea because I don't think she gave us any guidelines. As I said before, I don't really like when teachers do that. When teachers do that, they only give you two days to write it, and it should take at least a class period to think of the idea.

Then the teacher had this special format of thinking of ideas. What you did was put a circle in the middle for the title or topic, with little lines going off; that's a semantic map. It's supposed to help you get organized, but it didn't help me, I was already organized. I just thought of my ideas, and I don't know how; I thought of the story as I wrote it. I probably thought of the names first; they were Twabby Twertle and Babbitt the Wabbit. I used a lot of other spoofs. I had the Blitz Barleyton instead of the Ritz Carlton. I just heard about this really weird animal, I think on *3-2-1 Contact,* called the wombat, and I put that in the story.

"Twabby and Babbitt" was funny. It was the first time I wrote such a long story. I was really amazed. It was three computer typed pages, doublespaced. I had a lot of ideas for it. I don't think you can really stretch a story, except really good authors. Unless you have a lot of ideas, if you just stretch it out, it's not going to be a good story. It will sound boring.

I think when I write a story, I mainly write for myself and a little bit for other people. It's more for me. I want to write a story I will like.

I wrote a poem called, "Colorful, Crunchy, Fall." It was very short, only five lines. I think I didn't like this poem. I couldn't think of anything to write about. I mean, what are you supposed to say about a poem about Fall? I like a topic, but Fall is sort of too narrow and sort of too general. I really can't explain it. I just like it when it's not too little and not too much, and this one was too little and too much at the same time, even though that's impossible.

My favorite thing in fourth grade was not really writing a story. It was a game of how the real world of publishing works. We tried to write, edit, sell, and publish stories. Each student was assigned to one of these jobs. It was really fun. Everyone had to critique the writers' stories. I remember my favorite story. It really sounded like a professional mystery. It had a clue and then another clue. I don't remember if the word selection was very good, but I mainly loved the idea and the plot. I *wish* I could write like that one. I was a publisher and didn't have to write anything. Because of my Tourette's, that was good.

We did a lot more writing in fifth grade. Writing a lot made me better since "practice makes perfect." I used better words and mixed around my sentences. My fifth-grade teachers helped me with my writing because they gave us neat assignments. We had a journal every day. It wasn't like in third grade when it was very boring because we had to write what we did every day. The teachers gave us a topic which was usually sort of interesting and had a little bit to do with what we were studying.

One of them was when we were doing a little bit on slavery, and we had to pretend we were escaped slaves and we learned to write, and we had to write the story of our life as a slave. We learned a lot about slaves. So I tried to imagine I was the person. I tried to make it realistic. It was supposed to be like a true story. I wrote down all the things my teacher taught me about slavery and other things I know myself.

All of the topics were reasonably good, like what it would be like to be blind, comparing a worm's body to your own. That one was really weird, very interesting, and it was neat. There are so many differences that you can think of. One of my favorite topics was "What it would feel like to be a paper being corrected by our teacher." Our teacher was pretty strict so I wrote it and really tried to pretend that I was a piece of paper. It was a fun assignment because teachers don't usually do assignments about themselves. I didn't have to think about it a lot, but I really liked what I did. I thought about what a paper would think, but I only thought a little bit because I don't know anyone who has been a paper! I liked this assignment because as I said before, I need a topic. I can't write by myself. This one wasn't too much or too little; it was just enough.

The longest story I wrote in my life was about slavery. The assignment was to write about a gift. It was a little too broad, but I was able to find a topic. We had been talking about slavery in Social Studies, and I thought that would be a really good topic for a gift. I thought the greatest gift there could be was the gift of being free from slavery. I wrote a nine-page story. I knew what would happen at the end, that he would escape and meet a nice man who would free him. It ended up being sort of a myth, a crazy myth, because at the end they write a letter to President Lincoln, and that's how I said the Civil War is started. It's a myth and a story of friendship.

That year and this year, more and more, I'm trying to use better words. Like instead of saying "good," I say, "fantastic" or instead of "he went," I'd say "he drove," "he walked," or "he biked." I think the teachers helped with some of this. It wasn't until fifth grade that I really improved my word selection. With my poems I only had one or two good words. The teachers didn't talk about it before fifth grade; they probably thought we were too young to understand about words. In fifth grade, we wrote a lot more, and they talked about the words. I was maturing.

A lot of times I can't find any good words, but I know a lot of words. I think that helps. I learned words from people using them, and I found them in books through context.

I read a lot of adventure books. I love *The Prydian Chronicles* by Lloyd Alexander and *The Chronicles of Narnia* by C. S. Lewis. They are exciting, and they are both in a series. In between books, you can be in suspense about what will happen in the next book. When I was younger I read a lot of biography books. That was almost all I read. I liked them because they were true. I didn't like fiction because I thought stories should be true.

When I wrote in fifth grade, I did a first draft, then a second draft, and the second draft had three changes, so I had about three drafts. That is something I hated about writing that year. My teacher who was the strict one and who teaches language, made us pass in the first copy, and we had to write the changes on the paper. Because I write on the computer, it is more work to do that. Usually, I didn't want to make handwritten changes on my first draft, or maybe one or two.

She graded us on grammar, content, changes. She graded the changes part on how many changes you had, as long as they were good changes. I do revise some on the computer, especially on the Gift story. My writing sounds better because I can make some changes when I dictate to my mom. The changes are grammatical, and I remember taking away three sentences. They were pointless sentences, and they weren't needed. I made the changes, and my mom typed them on the computer.

I wrote a reasonably short paper on a mythical beast. We had to make up an animal. The first thing I thought of was the name. In order to do the rest of the paper, I had to make the picture first. On a descriptive story, you can't really do the writing without the picture. It's hard for me at least. My drawing influenced my story. I like making up animals or worlds and things like that. It's fun.

In fiction the amount of prewriting depends on how much of a lead in the teacher gives. If she gives us a very general topic, then I have to do a lot of prewriting. I don't do much jotting down because I can't write very well. I just sit down and think. If she gives us a very exact topic, then I practically have to do no prewriting because she already did the prewriting for us by giving us a specific topic. With nonfiction, the way I begin is different from what I do with a story. When I start a report, I look at resources. I might sit down in the library or with a book.

With fiction, you have to have all the parts in the right place. In a story, you can't have the setting and character description after the plot, and you can't have the climax at the beginning. In nonfiction, if it's a report about an animal, for instance, you don't really have as much of an order. You probably want to have what it looks like maybe first, and then maybe where it lives. The computer is a great tool for putting things in order. You can cut and paste and copy and put different things in different places.

I like writing nonfiction, but fiction is also fun. It depends on the topic. In fifth grade, we did a math paper on estimation, and that was great for me because I love math. Sometimes I'm surprised when I get a good idea for a topic. In sixth grade we had to think of an invention. The thing I liked about ours (I did it with a friend) is that it really would work. Some kids did things that were powered by air, but they gave no thought to how it would work.

We invented a personal miniplane. My friend did the writing. We both thought of the ideas. He made up the idea of the personal miniplane, and I thought of the actual controls. I would say something, and he would say, "Maybe we should do that." I might say, "How about this?" and he would say, "Let's write this." We started off with a sketch, and the sketch built the beginning part of the story. It was a fun assignment. It was a broad topic, but I love inventions.

We haven't done much writing this year. We had to write a letter to a soldier in Saudi Arabia. I didn't like that assignment because I don't like writing letters. I don't know what to say, and I know a letter should sort of be like a story, but it's really more talking than writing. A story you're writing, when you're talking, you're talking, but in a letter, you're doing both, and I don't like that.

In one of our book reports this year, we had to describe ourselves. I wrote that the most important thing about me is "my mouth is full of words."

23

BECKY

"WHY DON'T *YOU* TRY IT SOMETIME"

(Grade 6)

Contributed by Kathy Knight

My daughter Becky is a bright, articulate eleven-year-old with a ready smile. She loves math, swimming, playing baseball, writing poetry, and computer games. She has always had difficulties with reading and writing. In third grade a low score on a standardized reading test put her into a reading lab for fourth grade. She felt stupid, ashamed of herself, and afraid she had disappointed me.

As a new teacher myself, I felt I could learn why Becky has trouble in reading and writing by working with her on this profile. I discovered she enjoys reading with someone because it makes the story more interesting and helps her express her ideas and understand difficult parts of the book. She also has less trouble with punctuation and spelling when she reads what she writes to another person and gets the personal attention she needs and desires.

Although Becky knows good writers need to use proper punctuation and spelling, she does not like to write this way. Many of my students also want to express their ideas, but don't want to take the time to make their paper into a quality product. Should I squash creativity and make these children slaves to proper punctuation and spelling? Or should I continue providing good examples through reading and writing and hope that someday my students will understand why writers must use mechanics as well as put their ideas on paper? Becky helped me explore these issues.

Sometimes I pick up a book for fun and when I can't get to sleep, but I don't on a regular basis. I'd rather go over to my computer and play Indiana Jones. I read the newspaper a lot because I like sports, and I like to see what the weather is. Sometimes if a magazine article catches my eye, I'll read it.

I enjoy reading with my mother because we read to each other, and we do other comprehension stuff on it, like our reader-response journals. I have more understanding when I read the story to her, and she reads to me. If I have a question, she's there to answer it for me. But when I read by myself, I have no one to read it to or tell how I feel about it or anything.

I had to take the reading lab in fourth grade because of low scores on the basic skills test. When I found out I had to go, I felt like I was a failure at reading. I wasn't smart any more. I was so mad at myself. I felt like a lower educated person. My classmates didn't kid me; they were pretty nice about it.

I don't like sad stories. I like exciting things like scary mysteries, people getting killed, a sword fight, something that will pop you out of your chair. I don't understand romance or slower mushy stories very well. They stop me, like something is pushing me back. If I can't understand the book, then I lose interest and don't do the work. I don't want to answer the questions that go with it because I couldn't really do it. Like one trimester our teacher assigned *Journey To Topaz*. It's sad and depressing, and I couldn't get into it.

It's the same in writing. I don't like romances or when the teacher says to me, "You have to write about a Gypsy Queen and what she does on her travels to Nowhere Land." That's like when your mother buys you a pair of jeans you don't really like, and you have to wear them around school.

I love writing. It's one of my better subjects. Out of a scale of ten, I'm an eight or maybe a seven. I use writing to communicate with someone, to just write down my feelings, like in a journal or something. I write notes to my friends to ask them a question. If I have questions about my assignments, I put them on paper and ask the teacher when she's finished with the lesson. I also use writing to remember things for a social studies or science test. My goal is to be an accountant, and they don't do much writing. I probably won't write as much as I do in elementary school, or will in junior high next year.

I could write all day when I don't have a topic, and I just write by myself. It comes real easily to me. I'd write about monsters, mysteries, real freaky things, something like Indiana Jones, something exciting. They grab my attention more.

I feel excited when I get into my writing. "What's gonna come next?" You can pick what you want to do. It's like designing a home, you get to pick what you want to put in, like what kind of carpet. It's more exotic, neat!

If it was up to me to design a writing program for my class, I'd like it to be just free. I could write whatever I wanted. I wouldn't have to be pressured on having a topic sentence. I'd give students unlimited time to write, to express theirselves and their feelings. Like if you give them only ten minutes to write something, they might not have it all finished and want to express more, and sometimes kids have real bad problems, and they need to get it out. But after it got a long time, I'd make them stop. I couldn't have them doing it forever.

I really have to be careful when the teacher gives us a topic to write about. It stops my ideas, like "Oooh, I lost my idea." I feel like someone is taking away my freedom. It's like she thinks you can't write by yourself, like you're a little baby or something. And then you don't know what to write about any more. My second-grade teacher always did this to us. Like on St. Patrick's Day she told us to write about what you would find at the end of the rainbow. I didn't like that as well as me creating my own writing.

I don't enjoy our daily journals this year because our teacher gives us a topic every day; she doesn't let us express ourselves, like about what happened yesterday or today. She gives us a topic like "what's your most favorite food?" or if it's like Columbus Day, "what's your favorite explorer?" And maybe she gives us a beginning sentence. It's never creative writing. I just wish she'd not tell us what to write about, unless I need help or something. If I could write whatever I wanted in my journal, I would probably write more than I do now.

My mother lets her class write about what they really want. They use letter form, like "Dear Mrs. Knight," and then they write their letter, and then Mom writes back to them every day. I think that's the best way, and I wish we would do that in our classroom.

I like it when the teacher reads my journal because when she doesn't read it, when she tells me just to put my writing in my folder, I feel like maybe she doesn't like it, or didn't have time for it. I hope she likes it. I know it's hard looking at thirty people's journals, but I'd rather she looked at it. I want to impress people. If I don't get that attention, it makes me feel like bad.

I find I'm more enthusiastic about my writing when the teacher asks me to read my paper to the class. I'm proud that I'm up there doing that. A lot of people are real shy, but I'm not. I'm different. I don't feel foolish when I stand up in front of the class. I'm excited, "Oh, yeah. People like my story." I'm proud of my work. I think people should have to hear what I say. I don't care if it was aliens coming down to earth in a doughnut. It's nice to me.

I wish I could just write and no one would check my punctuation, and no one would check how I wrote it and my grammar. In life you can't do that all the time, so why should we have to do it in writng? Writing is putting your mind into space and just writing down what you feel. I don't think writing should be about punctuation. Life wasn't made to worry. I mean, how would you feel if every time you speak to someone, they would correct you?

I would like to improve my handwriting because I don't have that good handwriting, and I would like to learn more about punctuation and stuff. In first grade our teacher would give us a sentence that was not correct. If there wasn't a period at the end, we would have to put a period on it. If there were words that had to be capitalized, you would correct things.

As a result, I love writing, but I hate that everything has to be corrected. I don't know where the commas go, or if it's an exclamation, or if it's a question, or where I need quotes if someone says something. I've tried, but I just forget it all in my mind. I mean I'm a real talker, I could go without a period for a real long time.

I'm pretty good at writing, but I don't spell very correctly. My teacher always asks, "Did you check all the spelling?" I'm never correct. The words don't get into my head. It helps when my teacher goes over my paper individually. I just don't know why I can't get it when she is talking to the class, but it's easier to do it when she is talking to me. I usually do put periods, even on my rough drafts, but I wish I didn't have to put them there, and could keep on writing.

When she demands a perfect paper, with perfect spelling, punctuation, and handwriting, it stops me. It limits me. I can't get any ideas in my head. I just go blank! I'm busy thinking I have to get an A or B. You are expected to be perfect, and nobody's perfect! It's very hard.

Every time we write, we do rough drafts, and the teacher and students fix it for me. I don't feel bad. Everyone makes mistakes. It's my rough draft, and I can always make another one. The rough drafts help the most because now I won't make that mistake again.

Writing teachers need to know probably about all their quotation marks, how to correct a paper, how to look for run-on sentences. When you correct a paper, you must know all about grammar, like if it isn't slang or something, and if it's correct like a period or capital. They should teach all the basic things to know about writing, how to write properly. That should be all you need for writing. Also, making your letters correctly.

In fifth grade last year we did a lot of writing, but we haven't done that much this year. We've done poetry like limericks, and we had to write a poem five sentences long that rhymed. I made a couple of them. And my teacher said that they were real good. One of them was called "Where, Oh Where Is My Teddy?" It's about a little boy trying to find his teddy. And he says:

> *I feel something wiggily and jiggily under my bed.*
> *I can't find my teddy.*
> *I think he is dead.*
> *I looked under my bed, and guess what I found:*
> *My teddy right there on the ground.*

In the poems she always makes us a limit, like five lines with only five words. It has to be a rhyming poem. I like writing poems and words and stuff, but I'd rather write poetry that comes into my head free. I wouldn't have to indent or put in a period because I expect people to know this is a sentence. Poetry is meant for people to express themselves. It should flow freely like a wave. You can't make a wave stop at five centimeters high.

In third grade our teacher was into creativity. Every day she would write a poem for us to copy down. She made the poem herself, and she wanted the class's opinion. She tried to improve it the next day. In her class *every* idea we had was a good idea. No idea was bad to her, and I think that encouraged me to write more.

I like the teacher to help when I'm stumped. I just stop. I can't think of anything. My brain says, "No." But when we're writing, my sixth-grade teacher just sits at her desk and corrects papers and tells us what she wants us to do or not do and gives us the topic. I've never seen her write while we do. We don't know much about her. If she wrote, then we'd know how she feels. It would be fun to know about her because she always finds out what happens in our lives, like in our journals. Lots of times she thinks it's so easy to write, like she thinks, "Oh, this is easy poetry. Just write five lines and make it rhyme." I'd like to say to her, like why don't *you* try it sometime!

24

Robert and Joey

"EVERYWHERE THERE WAS ENGLISH"

(Grade 6)

Contributed by Thelma A. Kibler

When I asked a friend who teaches ESL and science at a middle school to recommend some second-language students who wrote well, she introduced me to two sixth-grade boys. They were eager to share their stories of becoming bilingual.

Robert is quite articulate, reflective, and confident in himself and his opinions. His parents are separated and, as the oldest child at home, he takes on responsibilities for his sisters and helping his mother. Although born in the United States, he attended two years of preschool in Gaudalajara, Mexico, prior to kindergarten in southern California. He moved to a very small southwestern town and then to the university city where he has attended fourth through sixth grades. Like many children in the southwest, he has strong family affiliations on both sides of the border although he sadly notes that he doesn't get to see his Mexican family much. Robert and his mother value education, and they actively seek out literacy resources in the community.

Joey is a wonderful blend of sophistication and naïvéte. He has lived in two countries, two cultures, and he is proud to be "equal in Spanish and English." He is fortunate to have the support of a close-knit immediate family and a large extended family on both sides of the border. Although he went to kindergarten in the United States, he attended first through third grades in Mexico, returning to the U. S. for fourth grade. He found warm support at Madison Elementary, a school that nurtures a population that is approximately eighty percent Hispanic.

Certainly, all second-language learners do not find success with English literacy in such a short time as these boys did. Commonalities in their stories provide insights about second-language development. Both boys had very close, nurturing families that provided great security and happiness in a less than affluent lifestyle. Both talk of early uneasiness in an "English world" and focus on the social relationships, peer and adult, that eased them into this new world. And in a society where "English only" is advocated by some as the way to force English use, I note that both of these boys, who found relatively rapid success with English literacy, had some Spanish literacy first. These stories then become a child's eye view of literacy in two languages.

ROBERT

When I first came to Hastings, I was in the middle of first grade. It was scary 'cause everybody was talking in English, and nobody talked in Spanish. My teacher started teaching in English. I didn't speak English, only "yes" and "no." It was all English; it was real scary, and that's when I really learned to speak English.

When we had lived in California, I went to a special kindergarten; the other kinders were English, but mine was a special one for kids who spoke Spanish. My parents and all my neighbors in California spoke Spanish. There was a Spanish TV channel, and that's what we mostly watched. I knew that everywhere there was English. I saw it a lot, signs you know, and other channels, but I just didn't know how to speak it. I think my dad knew how to talk in English, but he mostly talked in Spanish at the house. I never got interested in English until I was in Hastings.

At Hastings, the school was very, very small. There were only about twelve kids in the first grade. My teacher was a little bit of Spanish; she knew a little Spanish. So whenever I would get to school, she would put me in a special book. It was a kindergarten book, but it was in English. So, I started progressing until I was in the same level as the other kids. In two months I had caught up. I could read some. I think the special kinder books helped me best because they taught the vowel sounds and everything. In math I was real good. At first I started real low because the teacher didn't think I'd be able to do it, but I ended up higher than the rest of the kids. In California we did a lot of math.

I played with the kids on the playground. I just didn't understand most of the things that they said. At the beginning, I wanted to be alone and didn't want to be with anybody. And then I got friends and started learning. I had a special friend, Jim, and he started playing with me. After about two months I could pretty much understand them.

After school, I mostly played, and then some days when it was raining I would write or read. Most of the books were from my "grandpa." He wasn't really our grandpa, but we would call him that because he lived next door, and he was very old. When we moved in, he welcomed us and invited us over, and he had a bunch of books. He was an English teacher, a high school teacher. He died a year ago in October. He had books to read, about five sets of encyclopedias, dictionaries, a lot of stories, good ones. He was real old, so he couldn't read any more, so I would just ask him if I could borrow a book.

At the end of fourth grade we moved to the city, my mama, my sisters and me. I have an older brother; he is twenty-four, but he lives in Mexico. He started school there and decided to stay there for the rest. He got his bachelor's degree, and now he's getting the other one. He's an architect in Guadalajara. My mom's parents and great-grandma are there, too. I only saw them about three times, but I write to them. I write, and then my mom writes her own letter, and we just send them together. We write in Spanish to them because they don't know English. I can write pretty good in Spanish and English. English is easier for me now, but before about fourth grade, Spanish was easier.

I visited Mexico for three years before kindergarten. In Mexico they have three stages of kinder. I had two years of kindergarten there and then one year in California in Spanish. So I started English after that. The Mexican kinder really did help because they helped you early with the alphabet and everything, writing words too. I remember the teacher had lots of stamps with pictures of frogs and things, and we had to write down words. That's when I was four.

I still write in Spanish; I never forgot. My sister, a year younger than me, knew a little bit of Spanish, but she had kinder in English, and learned to write English. She's the only one in the house who speaks only English. My mom, my little three-year-old sister, and I speak perfect Spanish, but not Lila, not a word of it. She never did catch it.

I knew how to write cursive before kinder because my mom taught me. She would just basically teach me the vowels and the alphabet, and words in Spanish. When I went to kinder, I would write in cursive; the teacher was real surprised. I would get in trouble because I never wrote my alphabet in printing.

We started teaching my littlest sister the alphabet right now, but she can't do them very good. I guess that we will keep teaching her. I don't read to her very much because she basically doesn't understand the big words. My mom is thinking of taking her to Mexico and starting her in that kinder over there, like I did, because they start reading and writing early. She could stay with my grandparents or my brother.

At home, when I was small, I pretty much wrote a lot, sentences and stories mostly. I remember I made a story about a frog jumping and those little kid kinds. My mom would read stories to me in Spanish because she didn't know English so well then. Now she reads in English very good. When I got older she wouldn't read to me because I could read for myself.

Now, here at middle school we have lots of homework, math mostly or sometimes literature where I'll have to write stories or do an essay sometimes or rewrite some stories for final copies. Really I don't have much time to read with all the homework and chores for my mom. And writing, I don't do very much at home now. I used to write for fun, but now I don't do so much.

I write for enjoyment I guess; I don't write for anyone else, just for myself. Just to get my mind off things. I like to write mysteries, usually in English, but I did two in Spanish, just to keep in practice. I write mysteries with clues, with ghosts and nuns that died. Reading helps my writing because I get a lot of ideas from reading. Like if I read a book that has real good detail, I would start learning to write like that, in detail.

I like to read the Hardy Boys mysteries or ghost stories, Edgar Allen Poe and "The Telltale Heart." I read that in the fifth grade. We have lots of magazines, *Time, The New Yorker,* and travel magazines. My mom's boss has subscriptions to them but mostly doesn't read them, and she tells my mom to take them. My favorite magazine is a cookbook really. I like cooking a lot, mostly desserts and pastries and pies, cakes. Mama taught me to cook a long time ago.

School writing is ok. We do have to write essays in composition and literature and social studies. They're all right, but whenever we're writing, like when we had to do an Earth Day essay, we had to look up some information. Then we take a little piece of information and make it into like three pages long. That's pretty easy because you basically say the same thing over and over again and make it long. The teacher makes it real clear, like real detail will give you an A if you just don't just slop through it. I think what really helps is when the teachers let you pick your own topic. In social studies we get to pick our topic. It seems more interesting than whenever he picks them. Things I'm not interested in I just can't write. I just stop.

Sometimes I wait to do my writing homework. If it's due the next day and I've barely started, I'll start worrying. I don't know why I leave it. Usually I'll stay up pretty late trying to finish or get up early. I like writing early in the morning because my mind is refreshed, and I'm real energetic. I write in my room mostly, where I get the most privacy. Whenever I have too much stress and I'm too nervous, I just can't write. Stress like when something is going to happen or like my cousins are coming or something, I just get all nervous and can't write.

I like a small school like Hastings was. Schoolwork is much easier because the teachers give you more attention. Here at this big school, the teachers can't help you out individually because there are so many kids. I like teachers to give individual help if you don't understand.

This summer I'm going to a special camp at the high school for good students which can help you with computers and sports. And my mom is thinking of going to college. I don't know what college, but she's trying. She will probably go to college before me. Maybe we will both go there to get degrees. I'd like to get a job with reading and writing. Yeah, that would be fun to do. Read and write books and have them published. Yeah.

JOEY

English? Well, it gets easy after a while. When you've been living in both countries, you start to make friends in both of them, make contact and learn both languages. My mom used to know English too, but she forgot it after spending too much time in Mexico. Before kinder I was living in Houston, and I knew English until I was five, and then we moved to Mexico for three years. Then in fourth grade I came back to the United States, and I only knew a little bit of English.

We moved three times that year, but finally I went to Madison School. It was pretty small, but it's, what do you call it—comfortable. You can have lots of friends. All the teachers were nice. The school is never lonely; there's always people in the hall, teachers or kids that get in trouble, or old people that help the little kids. Only two of my teachers spoke Spanish, my math teacher and my composition teacher. My teacher, Mr. Laken, he had this student from the high school come with me every day and study with me, behind the classroom. She would help me, like about the last two hours of school. I read for her, and she would tell me to write this and that in English, but she spoke Spanish, too. I was pretty comfortable with it. Mrs. Kramer, in reading lab, and this one I had for learning English, Miss Josie, helped me the most. With Miss Josie, I learned English a lot. Mrs. Kramer gave me tips on how to learn and how to study better.

My principal, well, he was pretty nice too; he knew Spanish and everything. And once in a while we used to talk, about school and stuff. He was pretty regular. And then the janitor, I had pretty much contact with him, too. He was a friend; we talked sometimes. And I had friends from my neighborhood. They made me comfortable, most of them. Some of the kids would get to me, and they got to my temper because they talked to me in English. They tried to tell me stuff; I did not know English then. And I wouldn't understand anything, so I would get mad. Sometimes I would get in fights. But, mostly it was a really good school.

Sometimes, my cousins and my sister help me with English. Sometimes when I talk with them, I say something wrong, and they tell me how to say it and when to use it. Some of my cousins know a little bit of Spanish, and some don't know any at all. Three know a lot of English and a little Spanish; seven cousins know Spanish and English. Me, well, I really speak equal now because when I'm at home I speak Spanish, and when I'm at school I speak English.

We usually, on Sundays, go fishing with my dad or go to the park or visit my grandma and grandpa in Alameda. So usually the whole family goes there, all the cousins. There is around twenty-six of us. I'll say it's a bunch! We all get together on holidays and most weekends. Grandma lives by a park, so we go there and play basketball or tag. We do stuff, play. It's good with all my cousins.

We go to Mexico, Juarez, each month or maybe two months; we skip sometimes. I have two aunts there and my mom's grandma. I like to visit my aunt or go shopping, buying candy. They have lots of different kinds of candy that I can't get here. My mom reads kind of a lot of—what do you call it—stories like novellas, in Spanish. She buys them in Juarez.

Mom feels pretty great because I can write English. Sometimes I translate letters to my mom. I can write letters for her in Spanish and English both. Like when my little brother has to take a note to school, she tells me in Spanish what to write, and I write it in English. I can help her this way. I make phone calls and all, to the landlord and for some other work, someone to fix something.

When I want to be absent from school, she makes me to do extra study instead of just be home. She makes me do extra, so when I go back to school, I have really learned a little bit. She wants me to be something that I like when I grow up, like a doctor or something. Well, I was thinking of working with my dad. He has his own land-scaping company. I was thinking of going with him because he said when I grow up, he might make me go in charge of it.

At my house we have a few joke books and novels and some magazines. We have *Sports Illustrated;* it comes to our house, and my dad takes mysteries. My dad used to read to me, fairy tales and novels. He reads Spanish and English. My big sister doesn't do too well with English, not really. She's kind of lazy. She could learn because my mom encouraged her to start learning. Mom hired her a tutor; her grades went up, but then she stopped at *C*'s.

Usually in the summers when there's no school and I want to go back to school, I'm bored and I just start writing. What I mostly do when I'm bored is draw cartoon characters. They speak English mostly because that's the only kind of cartoons I watch now. I write all kinds of stuff. Copying stuff out of books. On one book, I copied about the first twenty pages, last summer. That helps me to write better because there's a lot of words I haven't heard before, and I sort of get the hang of them, what they mean. When I feel like writing, I write pretty neat—good stuff!

This teacher, she asked me when I write if I think in English or in Spanish. That's kind of hard. Because sometimes when I write in English, I write in Spanish, and when I write in Spanish, I write some in English. I mess up a lot. I go back and forth. I'm thinking about something, and all of a sudden I'm thinking of it in Spanish and writing it in Spanish. In math I think of it in Spanish because it's easier for me to do math in Spanish. I learned my adds, minuses, division and times in Spanish, so therefore I do it in Spanish and write it in English. I didn't do geometry at all in Mexico, but since it has division and times, it's easier to do in Spanish.

I like writing in Spanish and English. It gets kind of fun and interesting because a lot of people know only one language. And when you get in a fight and they try to tell you stuff in another language that you understand, they can't say almost nothing to you, because you understand everything. English, it's got its advantages.

25

Owen

"THE MIND IS QUICKER THAN THE HANDS"

(Grade 6)

Contributed by Caroline Tripp

The third child of four in a bustling and verbal family, Owen moves at his own measured pace and makes his own sense of the world around him. It is easy to tell when Owen is "writing in his mind" as he describes it below. Whether on a playing field or in the midst of a shopping trip, he can be transfixed by a word overheard, a person observed or a thought half-formed. Owen's theories and memories about writing and reading were gathered in three hour-long discussions plus several shorter sessions. When he was composing or editing a piece for school, he often had a thought he wanted to add to our "ongoing conversation." Owen is introduced by his nine-year-old brother Zachary, who offered these remarks after the two had spent a rainy afternoon at the computer.

> My brother Owen is eleven. He's in sixth grade. Owen thinks he wants to be a writer. We're writing a book called "The Reef" together. I'm doing all the illustrations because I'm really into illustrators. That's what I want to be—a children's book illustrator—and I'm paying close attention to everything they do, every line and all the spaces and stuff. Owen got the idea for our book when Mom was reading us *The Cay*. Only he's slow. *I've* got six pictures completely done and *he's* only into Chapter 1. I keep telling him we have to get going, but he doesn't do it.

Mostly he's a pretty good writer but sometimes I have to say I'm not so crazy about what he writes. We have different styles. See, I like to jump right into the action and Owen takes one topic and stays a long time, then another one, and stays a long time. He's more realistic. I guess if you read his stories you'd believe they really could happen. If you read my stories you wouldn't believe they could happen at all.

Descriptive writing is really important to me. Zack doesn't always understand that. He wants to tell about what happens. When I'm writing I like to get ahead to the exciting parts, too, but I know that I shouldn't. I know I should try to make my writing good quality and add details. Actually, I *like* words. I like words that make really good pictures in your head.

I guess I get a lot of my words from books. I don't remember when I first started noticing words, but in fourth and third grade, I would misuse a word. I would have heard it, and I would really like the word, but I wouldn't always use it right because what I would think it meant wasn't quite right. I would say something off the top of my head, like I'd have a man eating a "gingerly pie," and then everybody would stare at me and say "Do you know what that means?" Then I'd say, "I think so," but I'd have to go and ask someone.

I have a composition book for writing and if you look at it, it's really funny. I like to doodle a lot. Sometimes a doodle gives me a really good idea. I'm the type of person who doesn't usually brainstorm, at least I don't write all my ideas down on paper. I know a lot of kids who do, but I don't like to. I daydream. I guess I daydream a lot. I love thinking about stories.

When I'm in the mood to write a story, I like to just think about it and lay the story all out in my head and then reverse some things, take out what I don't think will fit in, and add parts that will make it clearer. That's the fun part. Then you have to go to the drawing board, sort of, and write it all out. That's the yucky part. The easiest part is getting the ideas; the hard part is writing it all down. And the finished product, that's the glory.

We have Friday writing group. I have a whole backlog of Friday stories, but I'll never get to write them. I hate writing! I mean I love writing, but I hate writing it down. I wish I had a little computer in my brain that could print out everything I think. I hate writing it all out because I have this great idea and while I'm writing it down, I skip ahead and think about what I'm going to do. And I'm still writing, and then I skip sentences and words. That's what I hate. The mind is quicker than the hands.

I don't like to write true stuff usually. I like to write fiction. I like to use some of the good ideas of what I read. I like to take them and change them and use them with other things. But when I have to do an assignment, then I do write what's mostly true. I don't like to write a lot of "what happened when" pieces. Sometimes the teachers will give you these assignments like "write about the first time you went on an airplane," and I don't enjoy doing that. I really don't like to be forced to do a topic I don't want to write about, like why I say no to drugs. I hate opinion writing. No, that's not true. I liked the personal opinion piece when you had a wide, wide choice of what you could write about and I could write "In Defense of Lefties." I have to know what I want to say, though.

I just need to get seeded when I write. If I only have a little seed, I can't write very much, but if I have a big seed, I can write a lot, no problem. When I find the right thing to write about I know it's the right thing because I can keep going and going on it. If it's not the right thing then I'm brain dead.

Something I *do* like to do is to mix in some of my childhood stories, or things I've seen, with fantasy. One time at Fenway Park we saw a man crawl out on the rafters and onto the wires holding the net over home plate, and then he came down the net onto the field. Well, I used that. The man in my story went to England to try to see the queen, and he got through all these people astonishingly. When he got through he had a heart attack and died because of all the stress he'd gone through. It was kind of a weird story. But I took the basic idea of getting over people by crawling on the net. He used that to flip himself over the guards. Sometimes I take the present era—what's going on now like the Persian Gulf—and maybe I would write a story about something in the Persian Gulf. But it wouldn't be the real thing.

My writing can sometimes reflect my feelings. When I'm in a rambunctious mood, my story will be of courage and adventure. I love reading books about survival and adventure like *My Side of the Mountain* so I might try something like that if I were in that kind of mood. When I'm in a happy mood, my story will be all magic and happy endings. But you can tell when I'm in a hurry because then everything will be all short and dry.

When I think back, I can remember what I hated to do but it helped me. When I was in first grade and second grade we had this huge paper with the big lines and we had to draw a picture at the top and then you'd write "We went to the aquarium" and we'd draw a fish. And I *hated* that kind of writing. I hated writing about field trips and what we're studying, but I guess it helped. It got me to work out what I was doing and think about the sounds because the teacher would correct it. She would also give you points.

I was already writing stories in first and second grade. I would write a story sometimes and I would like it. I'd ask the teacher if I could publish it. You'd get to put a cover on it and a label, and that was a big honor, putting a cover on and all. I was always writing stories and never finishing them. I'd think them up, and then I'd actually write them, and the sentences would get all jumbled. As I said, writing was the hardest part.

We did have a lot of time for writing then, but I didn't know it. I didn't use it. We would have quiet time, time after lunch when you were supposed to rest, and then I could write in my head. Then I could think, but I didn't take advantage and write things down.

I don't remember a lot about third grade, except one of my third-grade teachers didn't know *anything* about writing. I say that because I found so many mistakes on my papers later. I thought she must not have cared about what we were doing but maybe that wasn't true. See, I like rereading my stuff, so I'd put it away and then later I'd read it again. Maybe I'd take the good ideas and do them differently. When I wrote about "Spider's Great Adventure," that was an example of going back to a story again. I started that in second grade, but I didn't finish it. So then I took the basic idea and did it again in fourth grade and liked it so much better.

I remember fourth grade; fourth grade is when I decided that I really liked writing and that I should get into it and that people liked my writing. I remember feeling so proud when Mrs. Garvey, this big high school English teacher, told me she really like my pieces about Tsao Chun. It was the fourth grade Chinese dinner, and everybody was sharing their stuff. She loved it, and I felt really good.

My fourth grade teacher, Miss Wells, really got me to like writing because she was a good all around teacher. We were similar type people. I could really understand her, and she disciplined me, and then I really got interested in writing. It's funny with her, she was really into proofreading, and I hate proofreading, but I know its important and you have to do it.

There are various techniques that I've seen people use to proofread for things such as spelling. Mrs. Tobias, our first third-grade teacher, told me to read each word backwards. That was good. For Mrs. Prior, because she's more of a construction type, we cut out a little square of paper with a little box in it. We called it a spelling checker. You put it over the sentence and looked at each word separately. And there was another not-quite-proofreading but changing-around-our-ideas technique Mrs. Prior taught us. I know people who still do this. What kids do is go through and look at the first word of every sentence. If you have a lot of "the's" and "they's," then you change some of them. Mrs. Prior would give us a whole list of other words we could use. We called it our first word list. But I didn't like it because I didn't really have much trouble with that problem, and it was only a waste of time. I like to use different words. I like to be descriptive. I guess maybe that helped other people, but it didn't help me. Also, I didn't like that because sometimes I'd forget to do it. Every paper we'd have to do a first word list. You were supposed to staple it on, and if you didn't have it on every piece, the work was late. Sometimes I wouldn't have my first word list on a story, and then I'd be late even if I had everything done and it was a good story.

One of the big things in fourth grade was learning all about computers. We would have to do *four* drafts on the computer, and we would have to label each one in the corner—first draft, second draft, etc. One time, on the third or fourth draft, Miss Wells taught us how to move a block of text. We all experimented with it. That helped me a lot because I would be typing things twice and then going down to delete what I didn't want, or I would see that sentences were all mixed up. You could move them around to see if you liked them better another way. For example, when I was doing my speech about "why I say no to drugs" the other night, and I saw that it was all choppy and didn't make sense, I could move the paragraphs around. That's one thing I remember from fourth grade.

We don't do lots of drafts anymore. I haven't done a second draft in years which is probably too bad. We only have "corrected first drafts" and final drafts in sixth grade now. Corrected first drafts can be messy but you're supposed to have fixed all the mistakes and they're not supposed to have any misspellings. Everybody who does a final draft doesn't really change anything anymore, just the spelling.

I don't even move things a lot because I don't really think about it. Usually you don't make something the way you *don't* want it. I know what I want to do, the way I want it to be. That might sound kind of weird but that's just me. Sometimes if an assignment is asking you something purposeful, I might do some moving. Say I was writing an article and the question was "Why do sixth graders use #2 pencils?" Say I was writing that, and then I added in some extra meat, some details that weren't just about sixth graders and #2 pencils exactly but might make it more interesting. If I go back, and if that meat was first, then I would separate it out because it's an article I'm writing. I answer the question first and then add the meat. If someone wants to know specifically why sixth graders use #2 pencils, they don't want to find all this meat at the start. So I let them read down. Once they get their answer, then they just might want to know more. Nobody told me that was how you were supposed to do it, but I've thought about that through the years.

Fifth grade wasn't a big writing year. My teacher was into science and physics and math, everything but writing. I can think of four pieces of writing that went into final draft form for her all year because she gave maybe one assignment to write a month, and she'd forget about it. She wasn't the writing kind of teacher. She would say write your own Greek myth and I did that. They were due in late February, and we didn't get to read them until late April. The only reason we did that was because we were cleaning out our desks, and we said "what shall we do with this?" I was disappointed because I liked my myth a lot, but I had other people read it. I like my friends to read my writing, and then I like to go to people who have a keen eye for proofreading and who write a lot, like Liz.

Liz and I were two of the biggest writers in the class in fifth grade. We would write things at lunch recess because we never got to write in class. We were friends, and we're still friends, but what made us the same was we really missed writing. We would stay in and write together, make these drafts, and pass them in to Mrs. Prior. And she would say "Great, that's good," and she *would* like it and everything, but she wouldn't realize that we really liked to write a lot.

I miss Liz. We don't have too many good writers in our class. Kevin hates writing. Almost all the kids my age hate writing. They like to listen to people's pieces. They like to read, but they don't like to write. Most of my friends are mathematicians. They have the left kind of mind, all precise and neat. They don't have the knack for writing.

Jenny is a big writer, but I find her boring. Her stories are kind of dry. She has great plots, great plots! I would use these plots if they were mine, but she doesn't carry them out very well. Say she wanted to talk about some cute little kitten coming in the door for Christmas, she'd write "the cute little kitten came in the door." She could have done something like "the tiny kitten straggled up to the door." Her writing is dry. Even when I don't like the assignment I try to be descriptive.

In fifth grade when I wrote about Dorothea I added more detail then I usually would, but I enjoyed thinking it all up. At the time that I was writing it down, it seemed like such a burden. I had my mom type the final copy while I dictated.

Dorothea Loses Her Money
by Owen

Dorothea walked briskly down the street. Her two dollars sweated in her chubby little palm. She was proud of her money, "Think of the things I could buy, candy, ribbons, Teddy Bears and even chocolate eclairs." She stuck her treasure in her dress pocket and skipped toward Ms. Prawn's house. As she skipped along, her dress pocket caught on Ms. Prawn's fake rosebush and tore. Dorothea hardly noticed the rip. Lightheartedly she rang Ms. Prawn's doorbell.

"Back so soon? Here's another quarter." When Dorothea dropped the quarter in her pocket she noticed nothing else was there!

Dorothea burst into tears. "Now, now child, what's the matter?" said Ms. Prawn trying to comfort Dorothea.

"I lost . . . my money," sobbed Dorothea.

Suddenly from outside a familiar voice said, "Someone left two dollars."

"That's mine," cried Dorothea. She ran out to meet Eddie who was bending over two damp dollar bills. "Those are mine," stated the happy little girl, who had been crying a moment ago.

"Here," said Eddie, sadly eying the riches he had salvaged from the damp earth.

"Thank you. I'll give you anything you want!" exclaimed Dorothea.

"Nothing for me, just give something to my cousin. She's been under a lot of stress lately." Having heard that, Dorothea ran down the lane towards the 5 and 10.

Meanwhile, Georgie was lying on her bed dreaming up ways how to fly, Ms. Prawn was thinking where she could plant a garden of fake daisies, Eddie was wondering what Dorothea would get Georgie, but mainly Eleanor was thinking of a way to scare Georgie out of trying to fly. Eleanor thought but it was to no avail. She heard a crash and ran out to stop Georgie from trying to be airborne again.

Dorothea was now in the 5 and 10 and looking at every item. "Hmm, let's see—a pair of bunny slippers? Too impractical. Bubble gum? Too cheap," muttered Dorothea fingering an assortment of queer thingamajigs. But then she saw an odd shaped package. It was titled "Whirlybird." Dorothea picked up the package and read further. It said,

"Blow up the balloon, attach it to the helicopter, and watch it spin off into the wild blue yonder. See who can make it fly the highest. You will hear it whistle too!"

"That would be perfect for a crazy kid like Georgie." Dorothea quickly paid for it and ran towards the Hall's house. When she got there she dropped the package on the doorstep, rang the doorbell, and ran away. Eleanor opened the door and looked about. No one was around her. She looked at the package. Scribbled on it were the words "for Georgie."

"Georgie, there's something here for you," shouted Eleanor. Georgie came down the stairs and looked at the package with wonder.

Georgie set up the whirlybird and let it go. it soared up in the air so high, then came down with a gentle thud. "Boy do I wish I could fly like that," remarked Georgie.

I imagined everybody would boo when I read my story the next day in school. On the contrary, they clapped when I was done. I love that feeling of having a final draft form of a story that I like so I can share that with other people. I just love that feeling. I wish I had a portfolio of everything I've written so I could look back, but I don't. That's another good thing about the computer—you have what you wrote. And you know, sometimes when I'm really bored on a day, I would just go back and look in that folder and see what I wanted to write.

Writing is a symbol of somebody's personality and a skill to discover with. A piece of writing is a treasure worth keeping. In future days when my children ask me for a bedtime story, I hope I'll be able to give them a homemade tale packed full with rich detail.

Note: This piece was in response to the teacher's request that the class write an episode which would fit into Jane Langton's novel *The Fledgling* (Harper, 1980.)

26

Matika

"I PICTURE MYSELF AS BEING THIS WOMAN"

(Grades 7 and 8)

Contributed by Beatrice Naff Cain & Eleanor Blair Hilty

Throughout the summer of 1990, as she had just finished seventh grade, Matika, a twelve-year-old black girl, participated in a weekly book club composed of ten mostly white, working class girls (ages 9–14) from her North Georgia, marble-mining community.

As researchers, we were interested in how the female book club members would respond to the multiple versions of femininity, a theme around which our discussions were focused and which was represented in the various texts. We wanted to know whether their conceptions of themselves would in any way be affected by our readings and discussions. By participating in each book club session and by interviewing Matika at the end of the summer book club and then about eight months later, we began to see that the book club enabled Matika to reflect on and even transform her way of seeing and being.

Before book club began, the young club members chose the books that they wanted to read from many passed around for their inspection. Matika championed the selection of *The Secret of Gumbo Grove* by Eleanora Tate (Bantam 1987) which was discussed in the seventh session. The following information appears on the back cover:

Raisin Stackhouse doesn't mind doing odd jobs for old Miss Effie Pfluggins, but when Miss Effie talks her into cleaning up the old church cemetery, she has no idea what trouble she might dig up. Mama says Miss Effie talks much too much, but Raisin loves hearing her remember the old days—especially when one of her stories puts Raisin smack in the middle of a real-life mystery.

When Raisin is grounded for sneaking a night out, she not only misses her chance to compete in the Miss Ebony Pageant, but her efforts to uncover the famous person buried in the cemetery are brought to a halt, too. Somehow Raisin's got to solve the big mystery no one in town wants to talk about. Will her discovery bring her glory, or is the past better off left buried?

What follows are Matika's transactions with *The Secret of Gumbo Grove* and her reflections on her changes since the book club experience.

On a late July afternoon, the ten book club members were seated in a circle around a red and white tablecloth full of munchies, drinks, and books. Several young women shared stories about their family history. Matika, who had already recorded her transaction with *The Secret of Gumbo Grove* in her journal entry below, made efforts throughout the book club session to refine and enlarge it:

The Secret of Gumbo Grove was a really, really special book for me. I thought some of the secret that nobody wanted to talk about should be brought back. I like books that talk about black folks back before my time and the things they did. I could see my self in the story taking notes and trying to write a book about the history. Raisin is the kind of girl that tries to prove the history teacher was wrong about there being no history of black folks. I like that in Raisin, being strong and trying to find out about things.

When I was in the fourth grade, we were supposed to do some history and stuff, and my grandma—kind of like Mrs. Pfluggins—had some history books, and I read them. And she liked what I was doing. Grandma says she can't tell us apart because she does what I do. She's tall, dark-skinned colored. She's got brown eyes and beautiful brown hair. I get to see her all the time since she lives near me. I like the way the family in the book talks because I've got some cousins that talk like that. I can relate to the way they talk because I've got family from all over the world—from South Carolina and in Dalton. A lot of them up there, they talk like they come from the south. And then, I've got some cousins from Ohio, and they talk like city people so I can relate to how they talk southern.

I also felt that Raisin's dad was too mean because he didn't like Raisin sticking her nose in other people's business. And I didn't like her history teacher saying that nobody around there had done anything worth talking about. Raisin didn't like that either because she knew about Sojourner Truth, and Raisin was determined to find out about the history of the people of her county.

When I got done reading this book, I started thinking that if we had a history book of everybody's history around here—about what people used to do—and somebody got that big old book and started reading about her people, and then there was an old grave with somebody's relatives in it, I bet somebody would want to go and dig it up and clean it up and show them that there is where their relatives are, right there. And then they would want to read about what those relatives did. I like reading about history.

Remember when Raisin and her dad were selling crabs on the back of their truck, and they went by that place, and Raisin said some man winked at her? I think she froze up right then because she thought that guy probably wanted to come after her because he was like smoking or something like that.

I thought the way that old man treated Raisin was stupid. When he told Jennifer and everybody else Raisin was dumb, I got pretty—no real upset. And Raisin wasn't going to hand him a crab when he said, "Not that one dummy!" Then, Jennifer told her mother about it and then the mother said [to Raisin] not to get upset about it because he calls everybody "dummy."

What I like about black history is hearing about black folks. I mean it's no offense or anything, but I like reading about black folks and what they did. If they had a history book of Sojourner Truth, I'd like to pick it up and sit for two hours and read it. I mean it's no offense or anything, but at school I just can't stand to read about white people, and when they start talking about white people, I just want to stomp out.

I want to write a black history book. That's what I want to do. I mean, I try to get started on it sometimes. We had to do a report on Sojourner Truth, and I still got my paper, and I made an A + on it. I mean I picture myself as being this woman. This is my hero right here! It's funny too. Her master didn't want her to see her family, and even if she did, they would beat her or something like that. And it was back in the 1800s, and she spoke out for slave women. And she tried an underground railroad, and she led these women to freedom. And I thought that was neat. And she led about two hundred. And if she were ever caught, they would of hung her, but she died as a hero— to me she did. I just liked Sojourner Truth. And she changed her name to "Sojourner" which means a woman with strength. I know about her family, her background, and what she did, and the places she'd been to.

I liked *The Secret of Gumbo Grove* mostly because I could compare it to myself. I'd like to picture myself in that book and what it was like, how it used to be back in those days, and how those people were treated. I also like the beauty pageant in *Secret* and imagining what it would have been like if Raisin had won first prize. I liked that banner they had at that pageant: "BE YOUNG. BE GIFTED. BE BLACK. BE FREE." I liked that.

Raisin would put her nose in everything. She wanted to prove that the history teachers were wrong about black folks in saying that they never did anything worthwhile. She was willing to find out, to prove, to prove that they were wrong about what happened. She wanted to turn the community around because everybody else wanted to keep this stuff about what happened a secret.

I'm still trying to get at my family history. I got some of it at my home. I'm trying to go down to the library to see if I can dig up some history and see what these old people are saying about black and white people back in those days. I've been looking at some of the pictures down at the library that they have had around for a long time.

END OF SUMMER BOOK CLUB

I liked the book club discussions because all we talked about was women. I mean that's the kind of subject I can get into. I couldn't sit there if they were just gonna talk about men. I liked it when we took some of the chapters out of the book and compared them with some of the people we knew. I liked the people in the club too. I know them all, and I'm friends with them. I liked coming to the meetings to have a talk about stuff. I just liked our theme. But, we need to get more books like *Secret of Gumbo Grove* because—I'm not particular or anything—because we need to get more books about black persons. We had all those books about white folks, and Susan (our adult book club leader) said it was kind of hard for me to follow all those books, but when I got into *Secret of Gumbo Grove* that got me. I liked the history in it and the names that they called people. We usually call people like that. But in book club, I just wanted to hear what everybody else was talking about, what their opinions were, and what they believed, and what they said about the people in the books.

I'm not an A student. I don't apply myself as much as I could. I make mostly Bs and Cs. I'm not a good student because I am not in the high class, but I usually do feel that I am an A student. I usually say that to myself. Like, if I make a C I say, I can do better than this. I could take that test again, and I could do better if I had more time on my hands; if I had a study hall every day, I could pass the test, and then they would have to move me up. I would like to move up. I mean, it's not that I'm particular or anything, but I'd just like to have experiences with the A students. I'd like to be in their classes and see how it is, how it feels to be in those classes instead of being in the regular classes. I felt like book club was kind of special like an A class because everybody in it was like smart. They were intelligent. They knew what they were talking about. I just felt proud of myself, just being in the club.

EIGHT MONTHS LATER

I've been reading and writing. I've been reading about Frederick Douglass, and I've seen a movie called "Glory," and I've been reading about B. B. King because he's my favorite jazz player.

Like B. B. King used to be a gospel singer. And, he had to work to pay for his guitar lessons. He had to shine shoes and he scrubbed floors and made about twenty-five cents an hour. But most of his money went to his family for support. He came from a big, southern family. Since book club, I've been working on my history book. In 4-H I'm doing a history project. I'm doing it on general recreation, but I'm going to talk about black jazz players.

I learn more in 4-H than in school because for like this project, I have to look up everything and really get to know the history. Like, now, I can get up in front of the class and say jazz probably came from the blues, and I can list people who were into jazz. But, like at school, in social studies they just have one paragraph on jazz in the textbook, and that was in the depression section. What I do for my project is I make a bunch of cards with notes on them, and I have a lot of pictures with jazz people. And I have a lot of jazz songs. I listen to the jazz station and hear who plays it. Then, I look up the musician and try to find out stuff about him. So, when I give my talk, it will be about forty-five minutes, so I'll share one of the songs and talk about it and give the history, and tell what I've learned.

I've been doing some reading on Louis Armstrong, too. What I like about him was that he was in a band, and it was made up of his family; his brother was in it. And, his band became bigger because he would meet people on the streets who were singing the blues. He heard B. B. King's music, and it inspired him.

I also read some books on Martin Luther King for my class project. It was a ten-page report. I used those books that you gave me. And, I used about five that I got from the middle school library. I learned that he was the founder of the Ebeneezer Baptist Church in Atlanta. I've been there, and I love it. I also found out about the civil rights march. King had to go help Rosa Parks because she got kicked off the bus for not giving up her seat. So King had to help his soldier. He called Rosa Parks his soldier. He had to help her because she was in trouble. Rosa Parks was a fine woman. She wouldn't give up her seat, and I wouldn't either. She had been working four or five hours, and her feet had been hurting. So, she got a seat on the bus, and this man asked what she was doing. She said she had just finished shopping. Then, he told her to get up out of her seat. But, she was really hurting, and she was tired and had taken off her shoes. And, so he said, "Let's cart her out." This made me mad. But, then I heard about Martin Luther King, what he did after that. He started a foundation in his church, a youth foundation, to help all the black people that want to do the same thing that he was doing. And I think they've still got it.

I got an A + on my project. I decided I could be an A student. So, after book club, I decided to bring up my grades and study harder. I'm even getting some A s in English sometimes. In the books we read in book club, there were some girls who were studying, and so I put them as myself so that's what I'm trying to do now, study more.

I've also been reading some poetry by black people. The one I really like is called "What Is a Black Woman?" [by Gwendolyn Brooks] I read it, and I copied it down. I gave it to the teacher to see what she thought of it. She said she liked it. It's hanging up in my locker at school. It's about a woman who is in distress. She had to get up at one or two o'clock every morning. She had to tend to her kids and then go down to the store and sell her food. She had to try to get enough money to give her kids to go to school because back then you had to pay to go to school. They didn't have free schools. And she also talks about her younger life. And her mother and her grandmother. It's about four or five paragraphs long. I just love it. And every time I open my locker, I read it, and I start smiling. And I think, what is a black woman? And, I say I AM a black woman. She was willing to sell her food to help other people. She helped other people in the community. She clothed people, bathed them. I liked that.

I showed our media person at school all the books that we read this summer, and she liked them. She didn't have any of the books we had read. I showed her *The Incident at Loring Grove* and *The Secret of Gumbo Grove*. She said that she was going to get some of those books for the library. She took some of them and read them and said she liked them. She said she might want to start a book club if she could get enough books. She's got *Izzy, Willy-Nilly* now in hardback after I told her about it. She told me to keep on doing what I'm doing because there's a big future in front of me.

Since I've been talking about book club, one of my teachers (not my language arts teacher) has been bringing in some of her books for me to read. She's been giving me funny stuff to read. Like she's been giving me *The Far Side* cartoons.

My language arts teacher, she like reads and reads and reads to us out loud. But, we never discuss the book. We take notes and take quizzes. It's not like book club. She's reading Anne Frank, and then we're going to do some Greek mythology. We're not reading books like in book club. We read like a chapter a day, and then we get tested on it. It's not fun. It's all right though as long as I'm reading.

Whenever I don't have nothing to do, I go to the library and check out books and read them. Then, I think about what I read. Book club has helped me a lot as a young woman. When I read books and poems now, I go home and look myself in the mirror and think that I could be like that. I could help other people out. I liked book club because I got to be with all of my friends and talk about books. It was free. I could say whatever I wanted to about the books without people saying you can't say this. I've given some of our books to my other friends. I've told my friends about the book club, and they ask if they can be in it.

I'd like to like start a book club with younger people. Let them read those little biddy books so they could say, "I've read this book. I know what this is about." If I were starting my own book club, which is what I want to do, I would first call up all of the people I know and see if I could get them to come. Then, I would invite them all to my house, and we would talk about the book club. We would look at a list of books and let them decide which ones they want. Then, when the books get in, I would have a meeting every Wednesday. We would discuss the books each week, and sometimes we would go to the places that were in the books. Like if it was the underground railroad, we would go visit the place where it started. It would be a mixture of whites and blacks, girls and boys. Boys need to learn to express their ideas too. They are having the same experiences that girls are. We would read some history, probably just a little romance, a few scary books, and all different kinds.

I would probably have to talk to the author to see if I could get some copies. Or, I could go to a bookstore where they sell books to see if I could get some there. Twenty dollars for each member would be too expensive. I would end up coming up with some money some way. I'd probably try to sell something like candy or clothes. Or, the book club members could all help raise money. They'd be willing to do it.

I know some girls that really like to read, but at home, they don't have anything to read. So, I tell them about book club and that we might have one this summer. I tell them if you give me your phone number, I'll call you about it. So, they're out there. But, if the librarian at our school starts up a book club, I could help her. I'd have each person be responsible for bringing refreshments one week. I'd bring them one week, then someone else. I want to start a book club bad. I even tried starting one in 4-H, but all they've got is books on how to raise horses and stuff like that. I want to read history.

Me and Jennie, we started this book club. We go and get the same book, and then we read it and discuss it. We read *This Place Has No Atmosphere*. They had that in the library, two copies of it, so we read that. I usually have some questions, and I run them off, and she has some, and so we switch them, and then we discuss them.

I am changing. My attitude has changed. My snobby personality has changed. People thought I was snobby. I changed a whole lot. I'm making some more friends now. I used to be one that never liked to talk. But, now, I can like talk about the books that I've read. If I see somebody in the hall and they have a book, I can say, "Hey, I've read that." Or, I can give people some interesting clues, and let them read some books I've read. I'm coming through to them. I'm not shy now. Before book club, I like never wanted to talk in front of people, but now I can get up in front of class, read a story to them, and have them discuss it with me. I've changed.

27

Matt and Kristy

"I LIKE CLAMMING MORE THAN BEING IN SCHOOL"

(Grades 7 and 8)

Contributed by Kim Hutchinson, prospective teacher & John Lofty, Kim's former middle-school teacher

Fitting in at school in a Maine island fishing community can be tough and harder still if your family has less money than your friends. When your older siblings were remembered for raising Cain, then even teachers can be wary of you. By fighting back, Kristy in grade eight reacted to adolescent taunts about her friends and family. Fiery red hair reflected her independent, volatile personality—not mean but unwilling to take any nonsense. In contrast, Matt, gentle, almost delicate, accepted with quiet dignity his hard times in grade seven. Usually smiling and laughing, he preferred to walk away from any trouble.

Unlike many of their friends, Matt and Kristy were encouraged to write at home. From an early age, they had discovered that by writing they could amuse themselves and delight their families. Many students, however, quickly left reading and writing behind when they returned home to such chores as babysitting, chopping wood, carrying water, and helping to prepare the evening meal. Schoolwork then often took second place to pressing domestic duties. After the work day was over, students sometimes would socialize or watch television, a popular time for doing homework. More often though, students turned to making wreaths, canning garden produce, or knitting lobster trap heads, activities that needed to be done for their own homes and to provide the extra income much needed by these young adults.

The young person who always had his or her face in a book was often seen both by peers and adults as lacking in the skills necessary

197

to produce practical items needed for use at home or on the boat. Consequently, many students came to view school as infringing on time that could be better used for fishing or earning extra money in the community. Islanders tended to see reading and writing as the pastimes of tourists or people from "away." On the island, people often measured success less by school-based learning than by the ability to provide for oneself and one's family. In this context, literacy appeared to have little pragmatic value, and many of Matt and Kristy's older friends were already quitting school to go clamming, lobster fishing, or to start their own families.

Staying in school until graduation, however, was very important to these two students. In 1984–86, Matt and Kristy participated with many of their friends in a kindergarten through grade twelve study of students' responses to the writing process, a new approach to writing instruction being introduced in their school district. Interviews took place in a corner of the library, at home, or by the clam flats while waiting for the tide to drop.

MATT (GRADE SEVEN) "IN SCHOOL THEY TALK TO YOU SO LONG"

When I was just a little kid, y' know, I never knew what I looked like because we had this house fire, and it burnt everything up. After the house fire, my mother took more pictures. I keep on thinking about that fire trying to think back as far as I can. The farthest I can get back is to when I was five years old. My mother used to sit me down and talk about the past, tell me stories about growing up and her problems.

I think my mother reads more than she writes. She buys romance and drama books when she goes down to the drug store. She'd buy two and read one in one night—maybe in about three hours. Then she'll read one another night. She'll just sit there reading while I'm watching TV or out doing something else. My dad just reads the newspapers.

My mother will also write. If she has a day off from the fish factory, and she ain't doin' nothing, she will sit down and write. She'll write half of something, set it down, go watch movies, then come back in and write some more. What she writes is suspensable stuff and happy stuff, like Abbott and Costello. She would take part from that, then she'd take part from another movie and put them together. Me and the whole family sees it when she writes it, and everybody just looks at it.

My sister likes writing jokes out. She writes horror stories and jokes, and we sit around at night watching channel TV with low flashlights and read them. It's a lot of fun. My two brothers don't write. They're off too much. They have the time, but what they do is sit around the house and watch TV. When I was in about third grade, I used to write all kinds of stories. I'd just write out bedtime stories and throw it underneath the bed.

Now in seventh grade, I'm writing about this guy who lived in a house, and his friends just kept on disappearing, and he called in the five best detectives in the world. They tried to figure it out, and they're sitting here searching all around, and one of them disappears. Then they try to find out who did it.

If the story is good, I might want to look how much I've improved over the years in writing. Then I get all of them out, and I keep on improving. Usually I just keep on throwing them away though when they're done. I'm not that interested in being able to look back and see the improvement over the years. I show it to my family, and then I throw it away because everybody knows what it's about. I will throw away a story 'cause I'm bored of it. When I clean my room, I just look at it and say, "Oh yes, I remember writing that," and then I throw it away because I've already read it.

Best story I ever wrote was that eight-page story about that house there. The way the sky looks and the silvery clouds, and I went across the bridge and got toward the other side. The bridge disintegrated, and there was all this crap around. I still got the story somewhere. I like to lead on [from reality] and make it better. Not the everyday thing. Make it better so it's interesting. Like realistic, but not realistic.

Like you are going through the woods, you add moss on the trees and the rocks and the dirt, what color it looks like. You going through that stuff, and it turns to swamp. You got your vine hanging off the trees and your green stuff. You search the woods and through a crack of light you see the house. You go to the house and all that stuff. And you take a long time to get there, and you see all this stuff on the way.

My character, he's driving through town, and his car breaks down. He's got to find help, and he gets lost on his way. Eerie stuff happens. You have to make it real good, like a movie. I always thought I could make a real good movie. I didn't have film and camera and stuff. I'm not so into writing no more. But I still think about it. I write short paragraphs about things that interest me.

Sometimes it's hard to start out, but once I get down the first couple of lines I have to write so fast 'cause I get so many ideas in my head. I have to write so fast it gets even sloppier, and then I can't remember what I've written 'cause it's so sloppy. I have this little stand, and it has a hard surface, so I just take it and throw it on the double bed and write on that. Last year when I had a girlfriend I had to call her up every night. But sometimes instead of calling her up, I'd just write to her.

I like clamming more than being in school. When I go clamming, I go to this good place, and I sort of get excited because there's all kinds of holes there. But when I come to a bad place, I look at it and there's nothing there. So I just sort of skip it. I've got a tide chart that shows how long the tide is going to be out and how long it's gonna be back in. If it's gonna be a short tide, I do everything faster. If it's gonna be long, I just go right slow. When the tide comes back in, I have to speed up a little bit. I keep movin' back with the tide.

When you're at home, it should be your time. They should have more study halls, so you can do your writing at school. When you are supposed to be at home, like on the weekend, that's supposed to be time off, not time to do stupid work. You are supposed to have fun at that time, but you don't if you have to do work. You shouldn't be thinking about school when you are at home and thinking about home when you are at school. One time I was out for a week, and then I had my homework at the house, and I did it all in about three hours. At school they talk to you for so long, you are left for only five minutes, and then you can't do your work.

KRISTY (GRADE EIGHT): "I WOULD LIKE TO BE READ TO STILL"

Sometimes I like getting up and starting a bright morning or something like that, y'know, going to school and writing everything out about it. I just love to write. Sometimes, like the other day, I was in the mood when I just wanted to write a lot. If I had a whole week, I'd probably try to split it up so I had plenty of time. The more time I have, the more I give and the better I do.

We never started writing until we were in the third grade. Then we didn't do much, but we did some. When teachers really started making us write stories and stuff, 'twas fourth grade when we really did a lot of writing. Every day, two or three times a day, it was reading time or writing time. We would be told, "It's time to write a story." And we'd sit there, and the boys would go, "Yuk," and then they would ask "Why?" I would be taking my free time and trying to get everything organized.

A lot of girls, when they get into reading, read mysteries and romance, and they know what they like. I don't think the boys take their time. I do see boys sometimes go up there and look at a book and say, "No, I won't take that one." They don't take half as long to choose as girls do. They just grab a book, and they don't really know what they're interested in. I think that they're more interested in drawing and stuff like that. Boys do draw more than girls. Boys just sit down at the table, and they'll be drawing a lobster boat or cars right there in class.

I really used to love doing plays. Me and Lisa used to do plays all the time when we were in fourth grade and show them to the class. I was keeping a lot of old stuff from fourth and fifth and sixth. Under my bed I had a lot of stored folders, and when I was cleanin' up, I just looked around at my books and old stories. I could see the differences in my writing now.

Before I'll write a story, I'll sit there and I'll say, "Well, what am I gonna write?" And I'll have this picture in my mind. I pictured right now that I'd like to write about maybe a runaway girl or something. And I'm picturing this girl fightin' with her mother. And she goes to her room. And she packs her suitcase. And she jumps out the window. Something like that. Y'know, how you picture it before you write it? And then I write it down as I go along. I may continue the story with the picture as long as I have it in my head.

Usually I do that with all my pieces of writing. I'll do my first draft and just put down my main ideas on what I really want in the story. Then I'll go over it with all my add-in stuff, cut out what I don't need. If the teacher has anything to say about it, then I have to write it all over again. About that time I sit down, and I look at it. And I read it all over and think what I want, need, and don't want. By that time it should be about done. Before I could get the whole story down and ready to put away, I'd sit outside and put it on paper. That was writing it down, getting the main story. It took me almost three days.

I think the more you tell it [an idea], the more interesting it gets, and the more you understand it. Some of the kids just didn't want to write it over. They figured they got it down. They got the main idea, and that's good enough. I don't know if they just didn't like it or if they were just lazy. I enjoy most of all English, but my enjoyment depends on what we are doing. Right now, I've been enjoying it for the last couple of days because we were doing stuff that I understand.

I remember one piece it must have took me two to three weeks to get it over with. What I wrote was like four or five pages long, and that was one story I really liked to write. Once I had got it all done, I had to go over it with the teacher. It took me almost a week to do it over again. It helped me to do it over because it gave me ideas, and it showed me stuff that I didn't need.

I used to have two pen pals in fifth grade from some place far away. I can't remember where. I think it began with an *A*. I don't write to people 'round here. Yea, I did. I take that back. I wrote to one of my friends when I didn't have her phone number during the summer. Or I'll write stories at home and not show them to anybody but my mother. I used to have a lot of my stories, but I lost them when we moved here. My mother says she didn't throw them away, and she thinks they're at my grandmother's where we've been keeping some of our stuff.

When I was little, my parents would come in to say goodnight and read me a story. They don't do it any more because they figure, well you know, "You are old enough. You've got a book, and you know how to read. You are a smart girl, and you can do it for yourself." But I would like to be read to still.

28

Chandra

"TO LIVE A LIFE OF NO SECRECY"

(Grade 8)

Contributed by Judith Wolinsky Steinbergh

Chandra is an eighth grader at the Edward Devotion School in Brookline, Massachusetts, a neighboring suburb of Boston. Devotion School has a very diverse population of about seven hundred students, grades K–8 whose families include many professional people, families visiting from other countries to study in the Boston area, recent immigrants including refugees from Asia, Russia, and Latin America, and a number of METCO students (Metropolitan Council for Educational Opportunity). METCO is a program that buses African-American and Hispanic children in grades one through twelve from the city of Boston to suburban schools in the greater Boston area. Since first grade, Chandra has been one of nine METCO students attending Devotion School from Dorchester, a section of Boston. Dorchester has quiet lovely sections and sections afflicted by poverty and random violence. Some families live there by choice, and some due to economic or racial considerations. As drug abuse and homicides have increased, many parents discourage their children from spending time outside.

I met Chandra in seventh grade when I visited her school in my capacity as Brookline's staff Writer-in-Residence. Several teachers brought her work to my attention; her reputation clearly had been established at the school. We were able to work together in her class for several months, and later she joined a group of my advanced writers from across town. I interviewed her during the fall of her eighth grade year during two afternoons at my home. This text is edited from her transcribed interviews. I also discussed with her as many of her poems and stories as possible.

Chandra began her writing career in second grade and between fifth and seventh completed five novels, and innumerable poems, short stories, and essays. She is currently at work on two novels, a long poem, and drawings to illustrate a children's book along with her normal load of eighth grade homework, her personal reading program, her extracurricular activities, two hours of commuting each day, and family and community commitments. She says she identifies with one of her characters who wants to "be a journalist and live a life of no secrecy."

Chandra is a powerful young woman who is confident about her talents and who is eager to discuss her writing life. Her eloquence about her process, thematic material, and growing repertoire of techniques is a testament to how integral writing is to her daily life.

Everyone in my family has a certain kind of talent. We give ourselves stereotypes: my brother, Derrick, the athlete; my brother Bobby, who loves to make jokes; me, the writer; my Mom, the speechwriter. She has a little Shriner's group, and they have to write a lot of speeches. I call her the next Dr. Martin Luther King. And my dad, well, he's been a great singer. He's great at speeches too; he has the ultimate boom voice. We call my dad, "the bookworm" 'cause he's reading all the time. There's a novel around the house everywhere. My dad reads novels about this big. He can be done with that novel in a week. That's where he probably learned how to speak so fluently. I think that's where I learned most of it from 'cause I've always been daddy's little girl. And from my mother's way of writing. I have to say that her writing is a lot like mine. I'm sure she's written poetry too. She has boxes and boxes of stuff upstairs. Mom's also been a nurse for a long time. And you've got to look past my family and go to our relatives; they do mostly reading and writing and music.

Since first grade, I've been getting up at five o'clock in the morning, taking my shower, getting something to eat. I'm on the METCO bus by 6:30. During the winter and the fall, there's no light really—I mean there are street lamps, but it's still dark outside. My bus is usually late. If my mother cannot sit outside with me in the car to warm up, then I have to stand outside in the cold. The buses are always late during the winter, usually half an hour late.

I do my homework on the bus coming home, then as soon as I get home, I lock myself up in my room for about two hours, then I've really done my homework. Homework does not take as long as people like to expect. After that is dinner time, about six. Then I've got the whole time to myself probably until twelve at night.

I'm supposed to be in bed by nine, but when I go into my room I've got everything I need in there. So I can stay up and read or write. If a story gets really interesting, I don't want to stop writing or I'll forget. There's only one or two people I like to talk to on the phone, but other than that, when people call me I'm like, "Hi, Eva, I'm busy," even if I just don't want to be bothered. I like to give myself social time. Social time is needed as much as my writing time because exercising one can give you an advantage for the other. And I love to go to malls; that's the only thing I love to do. I like to put them in my stories and give every detail if possible.

> "I'm going to tell mom you've been up late watching Dr. Ruth again," I said thinking she'd dig a hole and burrow herself back to her room.
> "You're not going to have time today."
> "Why not?!" I became curious.
> "Because."
> "Because what?!" Now, curiosity was turning to anger.
> "Because . . . mom wants you to take me to the mall today . . . with you."
> from : *If You Can't Understand Love, Don't Worry, No One Can!*

Now about whether living in Dorchester has influenced my life as a writer. I've got to say most of every event that I've really come to love has been in Brookline, so I can't really say that Dorchester has given me anything that I really needed. I only see it as a place to live, not as a place to gain things from. But I can use people from both societies because I live both lives.

Recently, I've been working on two major stories. One's called *What is the Meaning of Forever,* and that is about students at a high school who are going through a real tough time. They're sophomores, and the fact is that everybody's having a little bit of a problem, their own personal problems. And what I do is I write them in different chapters, different parts. Like for instance, my first chapter is called, "Kristen." And really it's about sophomores wondering if they're going to be friends as seniors . . . and when they go on in life, you know. At the beginning of Chapter One I say,

> Friendship is like putting a puzzle together. It definitely takes time and effort. Sometimes the edges need to be roughed out a little or sometimes it may not belong to the same puzzle. But no matter when or how, it will always find a way to come together. To most of us, this is what it's like from school to death. To Kristen, her friends were life.
> from: *What is the Meaning of Forever*

It's really about my own life with my friends. I've been friends with them for so long, since first grade up to eighth. We've had our arguments—boy, have we had our arguments. And we've had to cry a little because I lost a friend of mine who died in sixth grade from a brain tumor. I based one of my characters on her. Two other kids, Chris and Daniel, were best friends themselves and me and Ayesha.

We used to call ourselves the "forever kids" because we've been together as friends for a long time.

I asked them for permission, whether or not I can use their real names, should this ever get published, and they say, "Yeah, okay, I really want my name in a book." And no one really cares anymore whether or not I do it. Actually they're thinking more along the lines—if this ever got published, well she'll probably come to me and give me money.

I use my own experiences. I don't really like using my own name, saying this and this and this happened to me. I like to hide it a little bit, get another character to take in some of me, and mold it, mold it into a character which has a little bit of me and a little bit of everybody else that I know, instead of having to just say it's me.

There's a character like me in *What is the Meaning of Forever* named Kristen, also Alexandra. Alexandra is the one that's completely kind of spoiled. And I am spoiled by my parents, so I try to use that. Alexandra, she's not too beautiful. She's really, how do you say, rambunctious a little bit. She's energetic and everything. I mean she's overweight, she's confused about which direction she's going in. She's interested in music; I have a whole chapter for her. She's funny, and she makes a lot of wisecracks about people, but she's really dependable. Everybody in the group always comes to see her when they have problems. And that's just like me in school, and I love to use that too.

> First day of sophomore year and Kristen was as lively as ever. All her eight friends, who had known her since second grade had shown up. That was a good sign. As she stood now, leaning on the door of the high school as other students rushed past her, happy to be back from summer and move up a grade, she noticed jet black hair coming through a flock of heads of outrageous color. And from that, she knew just who it was.
>
> "Hey, Eric!" she called, laughing and giggling in her happiness.
>
> He saw her and came pushing and shoving toward her. They hugged, laughing as he kissed her again and again on her cheeks.
>
> "God, I've missed ya, babe!" he told her, still hugging her. He picked her up. She cried to let her down, still laughing as hard as before.
>
> "Boy, if you don't let me down right now, you won't have a Kristen for a friend anymore!"
>
> from: *What is the Meaning of Forever?*

There's a part of me basically in all of the characters in my book— except for the guys—maybe a little bit. Maybe my, how do I say, my female side appears a little bit with the guys in my book, because one of the characters, Eric, cries a lot, and he's a guy, and people have this problem with him because they think he's like, how do I want to say this? They think he's going in the direction, that he's turned homosexual. He cries a lot, if he doesn't get the right grade. If he can't get what he wants or something he'll cry—and I used to do that myself.

My characters are all different races. Let's see, Kristen is half-Black, she's half-White. And then Jason's White. I'm not really sure about Eric quite yet because I've only mentioned that he has black hair so far and a certain kind of eye color. The other kids are a mixture of Asian and Black and White. They live in an area where this kind of thing is very usual, where a lot of mixes are together. I like to do that a lot because I've never believed that there is one color to every person. I believe there's a varied amount of color. Everybody's mixed and as far as I'm concerned, nobody practically can say that they aren't. So I like working with that. That's one of the parts everybody likes about it, at my school anyway. "Like where's the Asian people?" "Where are the White people?" It's great, and I love having their feedback.

First, I like to find out my title. I usually start doing something like this. I start to write names. [Chandra is sketching this out with names in circles connected by events.] Let's say these are three brothers. Now I can move on to thinking what can I do with them. I think of these as dolls, basically. And in this story, let's see, three brothers living on their own, out in the wilderness. From there, I just make events, one to a number of them. Like, let's see. Guy gets hit over the head with frying pan, and then I usually end up to my end, and I write a conclusion. And all through this, in the middle I would write about their own personal views.

Sometimes I'm writing, and I can just see it. Sometimes my hand does all the work and my mind, they work in unison, and I won't even know it, and I'll be just sitting around, and the next thing I know I probably have a page. And then sometimes I don't know if it actually will turn into a novel. Sometimes if I'm writing a story, and I see that this looks a lot better as a poem, then I will change it over to that. Or if a poem begins to look better as a story, I'll change it to writing. [Chandra's equivalent of prose.] So sometimes the form that I start in will change. Sometimes I add both, but sometimes it doesn't really work out so hot, doing that. As I get older, I think I'll be able to try it more, and it might actually work.

Writing dialogue is the part I've always loved. I usually use Brookline kids because I'm really good friends with them. When I hang around with them, I listen to the dialect they speak. If they're Black I like to use "ethnic slick," but sometimes it depends on the character. If it's a female, [the kind of Black English she speaks] depends on where she's living, what kind of school, what kind of a place she's in. Because some Black people will not speak their own ethnic way of dialect, except at home. But at home, they'll speak it freely, and it will just come out of their mouths. But at school, that'll all be pushed down and then they'll bring out what I like to call—don't take offense at this—I like to call the "modern class white version." A lot of the kids at my school who are Black and Chinese and everything, they switch their voices so everybody sounds almost the same. It's more of a melting pot. Everybody starts to speak almost the same.

Dialect and certain words and certain ethnic views for a character usually just come sometimes by heart, and just sometimes by what I think they should be. Or by laying down what they look like, the descriptions. From there I can move on and say whether or not this person is Black, this person is living in an urban residence instead of a suburb, and so I think I'm going to let this person speak with their own ethnic dialect. And from there I just keep going, keep going, keep going. But all of this is being programmed into my head and not all the time do I write this on a piece of paper.

For instance, there's a girl named Eva who has certain sayings she likes to say. I have little girl characters that are, maybe, twelve or thirteen. I like to use Eva as the basis, her dialect. Like, "I can't believe my parents like did that to me, it's so unfair!"

I used to go over to Eva's house over the weekend. Eva has a mother and five sisters. I just wake up in the morning, and I like to listen to the house when people are going through their "Like, give me my brush." "No, no, no." And, it is really funny, how they say it too, and I like to use that a little bit. I laugh, and I joke about it, but when it comes to the writing process, if I'm sitting down at my desk and I think of Eva—I'm like, "That's great, I'll write that down. I can use it. It's perfect."

Chapter One, from the James Dean Project

"Let's face it! There is no life after David! From now on, I'll be a lonely zombie girl cursed to walk the earth without a man!" I said, pulling my hairs from their roots, walking back and forth in my room as my best friend Laura did her nails on my desk.

"You know what your problem is, kiddo?" she said turning to me. Her face was covered with a European mask, excuse me, a mud mask.

"I'm afraid to ask! Enlighten me, oh great one with your divine wisdom!"

"You exaggerate the situation, Beth."

"I don't think you understand me. David Ryans? Captain of basket ball, swim team, student body. Ring a bell?"

She hit her hand to her head. "Oh that David Ryans! In that case, you might as well go dig yourself a hole in the backyard and bury yourself six feet under."

I looked at her. "You know, Laura. Sometimes I question whether or not you're truly my best friend or my worst critic. David is going to never let up that I broke up with him because he wasn't my type. I mean, sure I'm looking for a popular successful, . . ."

" . . . and extremely gorgeous." she added.

"I was getting to that! But I want him to like the same things I do! I want him to go places with me! Talk to me about life!"

"You don't want a man, you want . . . God himself! Pass
the dryer."

I handed her the dryer and watched her blow dry her nails as
she hummed "Bad Medicine" by Bon Jovi.

from: *The James Dean Project*

I don't actually lean and listen a lot. But, if I'm just sitting around
where two people are having a conversation between themselves
and I'm in ear reach, I will listen to this conversation. Then the next
day, maybe even a week, two weeks later, if I'm writing a story and
I'm trying to figure out how my characters should be, I will think of
those two people having the conversation, and I will use it in the
book. The public places are the best, a place like a restaurant. Now
that's a good place to go. I have a notebook which I usually take.
There was actually a story that I wrote about a couple who were
always in an argument together. Oh, God they were always arguing
in public; they were yelling and screaming. One night my parents
went out to a public barbecue where they have different people come
in. I was just eating, doing my book. Two minutes later out came this
man and this woman, and they were screaming at each other, just
having a good old time, letting everything out into the open, and
people were just sitting around and saying, "This is very interesting."
And I'm just sitting there jotting down what they were saying 'cause
I thought it was too funny. And sometimes I also use my diary. So I
like to have a lot of things that I can get my hands on, and then reach,
whenever, wherever I am.

I keep three diaries. A personal diary, a journal which I can take
just about any place, and then my ultimate, ultimate private diary—
which nobody's ever seen—since third grade when I first found out
about diaries. With those other two, I do one each year. The journal
I take just about everywhere I go. The diary I like to leave home
because I don't really like people getting into it. But the journal, it's
more of a jot-down book like how beautiful the sky is today. And I'll
describe the sky, and I'll write that down and then a couple of days
later, maybe it will come back into my head again—I can't remember
how I described it. And I'll go to my journal, and then I'll copy it out
if I can use it in a book I'm working on.

I think writing for me probably began somewhere in second grade
because it was about then that I was hearing from older kids at the
school that there were things like writing and math and English and
all this interesting stuff I'd never heard before, and of course, I decided that when I get older, I'll need to find something. A while later,
in third grade, we started work on writing. Now at first, I kind of ap-
proached this thing, like "This is really boring. Who wants to sit down
and write? Just write—words." And then, after a while, I'd been
doing it for a few weeks, it got pretty interesting because our teacher
had started giving us subjects to work on. And we had fun reading it
in class, and I loved to get the applause I got whenever I read my
stories, and I started saying, "Oh this is great; seems like everybody

loves me, reading my stories." All my teachers from third to eighth grade knew that I had a certain gift with my writing.

In fifth grade I had a teacher who I'll always respect in the highest manner. Mr. Roth was really somebody who, if I wanted to do writing, he would say, "Here is the writing bench." There were four of my friends, Davis, Roman, and Andrew, and I think it might have been Norman. I was the only girl. And we'd sit in the back at this table, and we'd just write stuff that came out of our heads.

Then I met a boy named Michael. Michael is a very good writer. Michael was the one who got my stuff together. He used to help me do my sentences. If my sentences didn't sound quite clear to a lot of people, he would tell me. And then Mr. Roth used to sit me down, and we used to talk about the writing I did.

I think it was in the middle of fifth grade I wrote my first big novel. We had to make a little book or a little story about school. I called mine *The Devotion Blues*. On the very last day of school, we all sat in a circle—everybody in my class. We read our stories, and we got little awards for the year and everything. I put everyone in my book. The nerds, the geeks, I would call them "the nerd," "the geek," "the pops," "the weevil." It was lots of fun. People were always thinking that they liked each other, and I put that in there. And I also took pictures and put them in. People really did like it, and I loved it.

It was that fifth grade year that I also made my first play, called "Nobody's Perfect." It was about a girl and a boy. And the girl belongs to a group, the pop crowd, as I like to say it, and they like to stick together. A new boy comes to school. She starts to become really good friends with him. Then one day she has to tell him that she can't be friends with him anymore because her friends don't like him. And if she still continues to be friends with him, they're not going to talk to her or be with her anymore. So it comes to a conclusion where she says, "I really don't care what you people think. I really care about him, if you can't accept him for who he is, then I can't accept you for who you are."

We put it on for the whole fifth grade. It was great, and people were asking questions, how I came up with it and everything. And ever since then Miss Johnson's been asking kids if they wanted to make up their own plays.

In seventh grade, I finished *If You Can't Understand Love, Don't Worry, No One Can*. This is how it begins:

The mystery guy is coming over. I act shy. Innocent. Wait a minute! I am shy! He asks me to dance. I say yes. Next minute, we're waltzing. The moment engulfs us as we look into each other's eyes. We lean to kiss. I can feel the warm air from his lips on my own. So warm. So warm . . .

My alarm clock goes off and like every morning, I'm awakened in the midst of a good dream. Death to alarm clocks!

"Ya know, Kristen, perfect guys are figments of the woman of today's imagination. You shouldn't let those kind of dreams take

over you," said my little bratty sister, Eli, from my door. I
couldn't really hear her because I had the pillow over my head.
But I had the general idea.

from: *If You Can't Understand Love,*
Don't Worry, No One Can.

On the cover it says, "Drama Club 1990's New Release." "Drama
Club" is something I've made for every one of my books. I also have
my own copyright and my own personal codes. And I have little
dedication pages. And on the back of this story is: "My Other Stories
by Chandra Edwards:" *The Empty House, Long Sleep Will Kill a
Dragon, A Strange Kind of Love, Teri's Dream Book, The James
Dean Project, The Virgin Club, How to Get Experience During Your
Sixteenth Birthday: The Virgin Club, Part Two.* And I have my little
order forms for my friends—they suggested that I copy my books, a
couple each time and give them away to my friends to read. This year
I decided since most of the people could not read it in my cursive, I
changed it to regular handwriting so it not only looks better, but it
sounds better. I cut out a few pages, and I added more.

Poetry takes a lot more time for me. If I have a subject that a
teacher has given me, for instance, it'll be a lot faster for me. But if
I am working on my own kind of a poem, from my own heart, then
it will take more time than a poem I would be doing for my teacher
or for writing prose; it might take me about two days sometimes, from
my heart, to do a poem. Where from a teacher, it takes me just a few
minutes.

It's probably because there's a certain part of you that's for school,
and there's one at home. The one at school knows just how to bring
things into the mind quickly. It can be creative, just like the one at
home, but the one at school does a lot of things faster because it
doesn't really have a lot of time. So if I'm working on something it will
come out of my pen really fast, and I won't even stop to see what's
happening. But I can have fun with it, too, so that's why I like to do
things in school.

But the one at home, I think I like a lot better. My parents are
usually in their room and I only see them a little bit, and my brothers
can't bother me when I'm in my room. I have a little upstairs study
now, a little attic. And I just sit there. I just sit down, and I write, sometimes I put music on, soft little classical music or kind of new wave
music. Sometimes I even write about the music.

I don't really like where I live, and there's not a lot of people I like
to hang around with where I live, but I like to just sit in my house—I
can't help it, I'm an indoors person. It's a lot of fun to be in my house
because I also know it's my house. I can do whatever I want. I can
scream. I can cry. I can laugh in my own room, in my own house.
And I don't have to feel bad about it or hide it like in school. I really
have fun if I'm at home. At school, the teachers give you five minutes
to finish up—what can you do? You don't know where to end it or

anything. Then you have to share it in class. I have to say, I really like home a lot better than school.

When you're at home I think the thing about it is that you don't have to be censored, there aren't certain things that you can't write. At school the teacher might ask you to write about little lambs crossing the road or something. I'm not going to write about that; I am going to write about life, and I am going to write about death. And the things that go on between life and death. Or life in itself, and death in itself. I am not going to write about a little lamb crossing the meadow because a little lamb crossing the meadow is not common. So, I'm not going to do just everything my teacher tells me to do. Unless it's for like a grade, and that's the only time it counts.

There Is No Secret

There is no secret to my name,
No myth that I should hide,
There is no password or code,
It's not as solid as ice.

It doesn't drift upon the wind
Or float the sea with ease,
There is not rhyme or reason,
no melody to sing.

It does not give me special power,
Nor does it weaken me,
It does not label or have much meaning,
It's really not a thing.

My name is here like a shadow,
To give me a blanket of existence
Shelter me,
Feed me,
Clothe me,

I do not complain
Boo or hiss like the rain,
But smile like steel
To show the me inside the beast
Proud I'll be of my name.

CHANDRA EDWARDS, 7TH GRADE

Poetry actually takes a lot more time than average writing because poetry you want to make so it's in a poem [form], so there'll be rhythm to it. Or, there'll be growing. A poem is really telling a story—but in a quick, easy manner. In writing, it takes more time to explain why you said something than in a poem. In a story you've got characters. And you have places, and you have to describe these places. In a poem, you can leave it off. [In a story about] Little Red

Riding Hood, you can say "Little Red Riding Hood had a beautiful, beautiful bountiful, bountiful orchard in her backyard." That would be writing [prose]. But if I was writing a poem about her, I'd say, "In her orchard, bounty fair."

Poetry is a fine activity, and it can get you in tune with yourself, more than a book might. A book, you're writing it basically for somebody. With poetry you're writing what comes from the soul and is meant for yourself—unless you want to share it. And, I think that in poetry you can let out all that anger because all you have to really do is make up some words, a brain storm. How you feel. It releases tension. That's great. That's what I love about poetry. And how beautiful I hear poetry when I read it. I love the style the person uses. But if anyone ever asked me what do I prefer, I really might want to say, "writing stories."

In poetry, I've read Emily Dickinson, I've read a bit of Maya Angelou. I just finished reading a new poetry book which is called, *Raining Marshmallow Clouds* by Nikki Giovanni. My mother bought it for me at Savannah Books [a bookstore in Cambridge specializing in books by authors of color]. And something from Andrea Lee. But I think my favorite person who does poetry is Maya Angelou. And she was my mother's favorite; she's been my father's favorite for years. So, I just got kind of hooked on her myself, like a drug.

When I was in second grade, my parents bought me a book. I think it was *An Invitation to the Butterfly Ball*. I read that, and I thought, "Oh, it's so cute." I loved it, and my parents would get me more books because I asked for more. I became a bookworm. I was the ultimate bookworm! Kids saw me with a book, they'd be like, "Look, there goes the bookworm." And it didn't make me feel bad 'cause I felt really good that I was reading. And I was really successful in my reading classes because I liked to read.

Maybe about in third grade I was reading *Harriet the Spy*. In the fourth grade I think we did *The Friends*. We tried it a little bit. It didn't work out so hot, probably because we were fourth graders; we really didn't understand anything we were doing. But, that was a good book for me by Rosa Guy; I read a lot of her books in fourth grade. She came to our school and I talked to her. That was great. From there I just read books on the sly that I found in my father's study, big books, that are really for grown-ups. My father has Stephen King books and *Flowers for Algernon*. That was in fifth grade, that was fun. We had them at home. Also I would read "Sweet Valley High" books when I was in the fifth grade—and that's only because it was a girl's thing.

Sixth grade now, we started to move up to books like *The Eyes of the Dragon* by Stephen King—I think I will never forget that book. Then I just started picking books out from random. Also, I have my own series that I read, *Robotech* by Jack McKinney.

When I began writing more of my own books, I did begin to look at the novels I was reading for how the author did things. To exercise one skill, you have to exercise another. I looked at a lot of Rosa Guy's books, maybe because my parents made me read her more. I would read her, then about a week later, something would come into my mind about it. I would see the way she wrote from views of different characters. I learned from her, by reading her books.

I learned from Stephen King how he could put together a story so it would actually drop off the audience and then pick them up real quick, in a snap, and really make them look again, and be really surprised and shocked.

Right now I'm reading *The White Romance* by Virginia Hamilton. And *Beloved*. And I'm reading other books on the sly. I like to read books in portions because maybe I find something that sounds almost the same in a few books. And when I find that, it usually means that this has worked for a few authors, why can't it work for me? I can use my own creativeness, my own uniqueness is the way I like to put it, and change it around a little bit.

I started working on *Teri's Dream Book* probably a week ago. I've got thirty-one pages so far. The inside blurb of *Teri's Dream Book* says:

> "Sometimes you have to look a little more to see the truth." Teri, for starters, is no average girl. She lives in a broken home with a father who would rather have her in his bed than in hers, a brother who's a druggie and is in a color gang. She's an 18 year old, trying desparately to get out of a poor neighborhood. She wants to be a journalist and live a life of no secrecy. And her key to that is in Donovan Myers, a rich, white boy who goes to her school. When the two meet, it's love at first sight. Donovan and Teri try hard to get Teri out of her home and into college, but what can you do when no one will help you but yourself?
>
> from *Teri's Dream Book*

This one's not really fiction because I know two different people who've had this kind of a problem before. I'm taking both of their life-stories and putting them together and making a plot out of that. I kind of see this character like me. She wants to be a journalist, and live a life of no secrecy.

> Coming home from school for Teri was not always a good idea. If her father was home from the construction site, after probably stopping at the store to get whiskey, then it definitely was not a good idea. He'd probably try to get her in bed again, and if she resisted, she'd get hurt like the last time. The best thing to do was to go to her best friend's house, Leslie Monet.
>
> Leslie was a white girl who lived between the rich white and the middle class black. She and her parents were white and middle class. . . . they had been arch rivals for a while, until an incident, the death of Teri's mother, brought them together. Since then the girls were never apart.

As Teri walked briskly through the fall's brown leaves, down the street of Leslie's home, she looked at the pretty nice homes and compared each one to the little apartment she lived in. It made her cry sometimes . . .

from: *Teri's Dream Book*

My friends read a couple of pages of it and they usually say, "I don't think I can read on, because . . ." or they just sort of stop and say, "Well, that's a nice story." I never ask them why they've done that. Maybe they think the issue is just a little too hard.

I've done teen pregnancy, AIDS, and a couple of other things, and my family doesn't . . . they just want me to be a successful person, have a good life. They want the best for me. So if they think that I need to do that, they'll let me do it. Anyway they would know, even if they put guidelines for me—what to write, what not to write—I'm going to write it anyway. Oh sometimes they'd give me like a look. It's like, I went, "Mom, Dad, I'm writing a story about teen pregnancy." They'll be like, "Right. What do you know about this?" And I'll go, "Like only what I've heard."

But, I know people who've gone through this kind of thing, so it's not like I'm writing the statistics. I'm writing from the heart, from the real people, the experiences that I've heard from my friends. In this case, I was sworn to secrecy. One of the girls did call people. She told a "Hotline." And then another friend of mine just decided to keep it to herself. She didn't want the problems. See, she had a mother who knew about it. So, she just decided to keep it to herself. And, there you go. I had told her what my opinions were. I decided that well, if she wants to do it, I should not butt in; it's really none of my business. But, I'll help her through it as much as I can. It's really her decision whether or not she wants to tell.

I think books are really supposed to do a certain thing for people. In writing books of this nature, it helps people—as much as they don't want to admit it. If this book was sitting on a shelf in a bookstore, and somebody happened to pick it up and take it home and start reading and say, "Oh my God. This is so much like my own life," and put the book down, eventually they will want to pick it up and see what the ending's going to be like because they want to change their life as bad as the person in a book.

29

Noriko and Kirsten

"I COULD HAVE BEEN ANOTHER TENNESSEE WILLIAMS"

(Grade 8)

Contributed by M. A. Syverson

In a spacious home in a suburb of a large midwestern city, two mothers discuss reading and writing with their daughters, who are in the eighth grade. Both girls are high-achieving students in a progressive public junior high school that feeds into one of the top high schools in the nation.

Noriko is the daughter of an American mother and a Japanese father who was raised in Tokyo. She has lived in Tokyo, New York, and Chicago, but the majority of her schooling was in international schools in Japan. About three years ago her family returned to the United States, and her parents divorced. Her mother, Nora, is currently enrolled in a graduate program in social work. Kirsten, too, has lived abroad, in Japan, when she was five, and also in Pakistan, for the fourth grade. Her mother, Leslie, is a librarian. The mothers are neighbors, and the daughters are close friends, so the discussion is casual and digressive. In general the mothers shared the task of interviewing the two girls using a set of open-ended questions as a guide. This profile is based on the conversation between the two girls to keep the focus on children's voices, but the following bit of dialogue will suggest the rich complexity of the four-way conversation:

KIRSTEN: Oooh, I remember my first book. "Good Night, Moon." Of course, that wasn't really a book, it was like a picture book.

LESLIE: So, we're talking about bedtime stories. Did anybody in your family read you bedtime stories, Noriko?

NORIKO: No, not really.

LESLIE: Nobody read you bedtime stories? Wait a minute; reality check.

NORA: I never read to any of my children.

LESLIE: Aaaaggghhh! Are you kidding? You never read to any of your kids?

NORA: No, I was too busy reading to myself.

NORIKO: That's how I got so interested in reading; right? Because I wanted to find out what was so interesting.

NORA: They were so curious about what I was reading, they all read like maniacs as soon as they got the chance, which puts to lie that whole theory. I think it's wonderful if people are patient and read to their children, but I'm not, and I don't. I never did. I bought a lot of children's books, and I left them lying around, but I never read them. I had no patience.

LESLIE: Wow. I'm loaded with patience. I went the other way.

KIRSTEN: Mom used to read to me *all* the time. She used to read out of the Sesame Street library a lot; those are a good set of books, and what else did you read? I don't remember.

LESLIE: Oh, we had lots of stuff.

NORA: I don't think I ever read one book to kids.

LESLIE: Well, the thing is that John [Kirsten's brother] turned out to be absolutely a non-reader. And all that John ever liked to read was encyclopedias, The Hardy Boys, Encyclopedia Brown, and train schedules, and sports, and to this day, he's not a reader of fiction. He's just not a reader.

NORA: All three of my kids are voracious readers which is astounding to me since I did everything I could to avoid the whole question.

As the conversation continues, the two girls chat more directly with each other, with occasional queries from one of the mothers, and eventually they start to share with each other and explain to their mothers the writing and reading they are currently engaged in, beginning with their writing assignments for school.

KIRSTEN: We do various writing assignments. For English class, it depends on what we're doing. We do a lot of poems, rhyming and not. We had to do a character sketch a couple of days ago. We are assigned a romance story now which I'm just stumped about because all the romance stories I can think of have depressing endings. For math, we had to write an essay on cooperative problem solving.

NORIKO: I remember when we had to write something for math . . .

KIRSTEN: In reading, we have all sorts of essay tests to do, and we have to write countless things on the themes of the books we read like: what is the theme of Jack London's "To Build a Fire?" She had stated the exact theme in class, and basically you just had to write it over again. She always used to read mine out in class, which I just hated because she would read them out so often, my various assignments, that whenever she said, "I'm going to read something," the whole class would say, "Oh, is it Kirsten's?" and she'd say "Yes," and they'd say, "Oh my God, that's so annoying!" So I just didn't like that very much.

For social studies, we had to write various essays. Before the war started, we had to write a letter like if we were someone in Saudi Arabia who had just been sent over there, and we had to write a letter back to the parents telling where we were and everything. And the teacher liked mine very much, and so he read it to all the classes as if was a real letter, and everyone believed him. So the next time I went to social studies class, they all applauded. It was kind of annoying.

Outside of school, I write in my diary sometimes and if I get inspirations, like I have little fragments of poems and stories on little pieces of paper all over my desk, and I pick up one and "Oh, I started this two years ago," and I write another paragraph and then I put it away. Once in my diary, I had started this story, and it was going to be really long and cool, about this girl in Colorado, and she sat on a rock and it turned out that the rock was the home of this little elfin kingdom and she ate this piece of mushroom and she turned small and went into the elfin kingdom, and I had all these great ideas for how the adventures and details and descriptions could be in the story. I got half way through it and I lost the notebook it was in, so I never got the energy to start it. Basically, I just write stuff, if I ever get inspirations.

NORIKO: What about letters? Do you write letters?

KIRSTEN: I have a lot of people I write letters to. One in Woodbury, Connecticut, and sometimes I write to people in Pakistan, but not often any more because I haven't got any letters back.

NORIKO: I just finished my research paper, which is required to pass eighth grade, and it was a pain.

KIRSTEN: So, were you happy with it when you were finished? Did you like how it came out? It was okay?

NORIKO: It was okay.

KIRSTEN: Where did you get the idea for it?

NORIKO: Well, see, I wanted to do the bombing of Hiroshima, but it turned out that my brother did that also when he was in eighth grade, and since he had the same teacher, I didn't think that she would appreciate that. You know, it's just by chance that we both chose the same exact topic. So, I thought maybe I shouldn't do it because it would be kind of suspicious, so I changed my topic, and I did the Titanic because it seemed interesting, and I didn't know that much about the Titanic.

KIRSTEN: So, you got the topic from the teacher.

NORIKO: No. Well, yeah. She gave us a packet of topics. We also have a journal that we write in a lot. Actually, it's a team journal that you bring to every academic class, and the teacher might make you write a story or write an essay or something, you know, to just bring along with you.

KIRSTEN: Why is it called a team journal? Is more than one person writing it?

NORIKO: No, it's because it's for your team of teachers you have. [The academic journal is part of the interdisciplinary writing students do. It is reviewed periodically by the language arts teacher, and assignments for the journal are developed collaboratively by the team of teachers for each group of students.]

KIRSTEN: So, you have the research paper and a team journal, and what else do you have to write?

NORIKO: See, in LA [language arts] reading, we do a lot of writing from the books we read in class. Right now we're reading *Fahrenheit 451,* and we have to do a lot of essay questions on it and stuff.

KIRSTEN: Remember *Light in the Forest* last year?

NORIKO: Yeah, then in social studies we write in our team journal our opinions on issues. We have to write whether we're for or against abortion, and things like this, that, and the other thing. And then, in science, we do a *whole bunch* of lab reports. And you have to do a lot of answering questions and conclusion questions. In algebra we write numbers and we also wrote an essay about what we liked and didn't like about our class. And then she ended up using the essays to write a whole bunch of rules. And I tried to write music.

KIRSTEN: You tried to write music? Cool! What happened?

NORIKO: I've been trying to write songs for the longest time. I'll be humming something to myself, and I'll say, "That's a cool song, now let me try to find it on the piano. "So I'm playing these notes. "No, that's not it," and then I'll like one note and then I'll write it down. Or I'll be fiddling around on the piano, and I'll find something there I like, and then I'll write it down. The writing down takes so long that I give up on it. And then I don't know how to end the song. It's fun. And then, I write poems. Lots of times I'll be thinking of something, and I don't feel like writing in my diary, so I write a poem, and then I say "well, . . ."

KIRSTEN: What do you do with the poems?

NORIKO: Whatever I want to. Sometimes if I don't like them, I recycle them. I do a lot of drawing. I draw caricatures.

KIRSTEN: Good ones, too.

NORIKO: And then sometimes, I write Japanese, you know, like I have to write letters to Obachan, my Japanese grandmother. When she was sick, I wrote a letter to her. And thank you letters, and sometimes I write just to make sure I still remember it all.

KIRSTEN: The Japanese?

NORIKO: Yeah. I've lost all the Kanji—the Chinese characters that I learned . . .

KIRSTEN: Chinese?

NORIKO: Yes. Well, in Japanese, you use Chinese characters. Some of Japanese is phonetic, and some of it is ideographic, characters that don't have a sound attached to them. They have a meaning attached to them. So I knew some characters, like *book, tree,* and *flea,* the first Kanji you learn in school. I know *person,* I know the numbers, I know my name.

KIRSTEN: What about when you read Japanese comics? Can you read them?

NORIKO: Yeah, I can read; I can understand and read. I can take input and understand it—usually. But output is not quite so good.

KIRSTEN: Do you think that's because you don't have enough practice?

NORIKO: Well, yeah, if I continue taking Japanese classes like I was, in the International School . . .

KIRSTEN: You could take it in high school.

NORIKO: But, that's going to be really basic, you know.

KIRSTEN: But I heard the teacher gives you stuff at your own level.

NORIKO: If I can get into it, though. My brother only got in because he is a friend of Kochi, and Kochi is like, friends with the teacher.

KIRSTEN: Why wouldn't they let a student take the class?

NORIKO: I've already lived in Japan and stuff. They probably won't let me take it.

KIRSTEN: It sounds like you're concerned about forgetting Japanese.

NORIKO: Yeah, I don't want to forget it. Now, let's see what else do I write? Oh, I write stories sometimes. And I write lots of notes. Notes to you and notes to Carol.

KIRSTEN: Yeah, we all have made-up names.

NORIKO: Yeah, like I'm Tyrannosaurus Rex, or Rex or whatever.

KIRSTEN: So, let's talk about how you do a writing project, from the beginning to the end.

NORIKO: Okay. Well, first, usually I do a little bit of background reading, then I do a rough outline, and I take a *whole* bunch of notes. And then I write a rough draft, well usually, and then I edit it you know, change it, and I edit again, and then I revise it, then all these other things. Editing is when you check spelling, right? I *revise* it twice or three times, and *then* I edit it, and then I print it and do the end notes and the bibliography.

KIRSTEN: Where do you like to write?

NORIKO: I like to write on the computer because I'm faster at typing than I am at writing, and it's less tiring, and if I'm not at the computer, well it doesn't matter. I also like writing on the typewriter; it's fun.

KIRSTEN: I like to write on the computer, too. Like you say, it's a lot less tiring, and it's easier to move paragraphs around. You don't have to erase and scratch out and write the whole thing over again.

NORIKO: What have you been writing recently?

KIRSTEN: We're just starting the research paper. I'm feeling very pathetic. But I had to write a story for a contest a couple weeks ago. Actually, I was quite p.o.'d because it was a *very* good story, I thought, and it didn't get chosen.

NORIKO: Which one?

KIRSTEN: "Chardin's." Did you ever read it? It was really cool. My English teacher wanted me to read it in class, but we never got around to reading it.

NORIKO: So what happened to the story?

KIRSTEN: Oh, well, my friend Carol and I were both assigned to write something for this contest 'cause the English teacher thought we were some of the better writers in her class. And we both extended ourselves artistically, turned out these wonderful stories (because we must say so ourselves, these were *very* good stories). So Carol and I had written—the limit was ten pages, that's what we were told—we wrote like seven or eight page stories. Then the teacher said that she only had one vote and she thought that our stories were a lot better written than the ones that won, like Jason's, but the judges just weren't looking for that. Apparently this contest was looking for short-short stories and long poems that rhyme, things that aren't terribly deep. So, Carol and I just exchanged stories, we read them, and we oooh-ed and aaah-ed over them and said how wonderful the other person's was. Dad liked my story so much, he sent a copy to Grandma and Grandpa.

NORIKO: Who was running the contest?

KIRSTEN: I really don't know. I don't know what it was for. All I know is if your thing was chosen, you had to do this ninety-minute impromptu writing where you get these sheets of paper and they say something, I don't know what. They could probably say, "Light bulbs burn out quickly" and then you have to write ninety minutes on that.

NORIKO: Oh, I see. So it really *was* a writing contest. What about having the stories published somewhere else? Like *Highlights* or something?

KIRSTEN: Well, I don't know. That'd be cool, to send it . . .

NORIKO: I mean, if you like them really well.

KIRSTEN: I think it's an awesome story. I don't know what those judges were thinking. You have to read it.

NORIKO: I will. But you should submit it somewhere else. Those judges are probably out of their minds.

KIRSTEN: Yes, they probably are.

NORIKO: They were bribed, probably. Anyway, you were really happy with the story?

KIRSTEN: Yes, I was very pleased with it. To get an idea for the story, that's my main problem, I'm terrible with plots. I just can never come up with inspirations. I just sort of sit up in my room, and I just sort of look around, and usually, I think of a character or a situation, and I say, "Well, what would happen in this situation, like in this setting?" And then I think of a main event, and I spin little things out around that, and so I type the whole thing out, and usually, I just have to type anything that's like really bad, any kind of trash so I know what the plot is, so I don't forget it. Then I go back and I change it until everything is nice and I add details, and then I revise it again and I slim it down and try to take all the extraneous words out, and then I check the spelling and then what I do is I print it out and then I like to put it away. Then I come back and I see if I can read it as if I were reading it in a magazine or something. And my first reaction is, like, "Oh, that was something really stupid," or something like that or "That guy never would have said that." And I try to look at it from someone else's point of view.

NORIKO: So, you like to get your idea down before you forget it.

KIRSTEN: Yes, because there have been too many times when like I'm sitting downstairs and have this blinding flash of inspiration, and I go, "*Yes!* Immortal short story!" And I go running to the computer, and while it's warming up I forget it, and I go "Oooohhhhhhhh, I could have been another Tennessee Williams!" Sometimes I get a screwy, a weird idea, like I decided to spoof the soliloquy from *Hamlet,* and I got this cool idea: "To teach or not to teach." I just typed it out. And sometimes like for no reason, I say "Oh, that'd be cool" when I'm writing and I show it to the teacher and get extra credit sometimes.

KIRSTEN: Do other people ever help you when you're writing?

NORIKO: Well, my brother Masato is very critical, so I can bring my paper to him, and he'll say, "No, no, this is no good at all! You have to do this!" And he'll tell me something else to do. And that kind of helps. And then my sister Naomi doesn't help me at all. And then I can go to my mom for words, 'cause she was an English teacher at one point, and then finally, I just sometimes go to different people and just say, "What do you think of this story?" And they'll say, "Well this part is kind of strange, but this part is good." And I get an idea of what they think of it, and I can change it or leave it. What about you?

KIRSTEN: Well, sometimes I get little ideas for what I'm going to write from little things people do, or say, or I've seen them do on TV. Like there's one story I wrote that's strangely like this TV show. And then I write them and then I print it out and I give it to Dad, but he ooohs and aaahs over whatever I do, and then I have to go to Mom. And Mom pounces on it. She tries to pull out all the adjectives because she doesn't like them. But I say, "No, I want to keep these adjectives," and so she goes over it with me. But, I very rarely come to her. The most recent time was when I was writing the "Chardin's" story thing. And I've no doubt that it would not have been as good as it was if I had not come to Mom. But Dad only goes, "Oh, wow, this is cool!" Which is wonderful if you've written something and you don't think it's very good. Anyway, for other things like reports and stuff, I usually just give them to whoever and they read it, and I don't ask them to give me specific details, just little general things, and then I go fix it myself because I have this phobia that someone's going to be writing it for me and I want it to be my own.

NORIKO: My mom never has time. I just say, "Oh mom, what's another word for 'run?' " And she'll say "jog," and then I'll go, "Oh gee, thanks."

KIRSTEN: Do other people ever get in your way when you are writing?

NORIKO: Masato gets in my way because he comes into my room, and he starts bugging me. "Noriko, Noriko, do you want to play the computer? Let me play you this new song I have." And then it's kind of hard to write when he's blasting Led Zeppelin in my ear! Then Naomi gets in my way when she tries to get me to do things with her: "Will you keep me company while I clean my room, Noriko?" "Well, no thanks." Kind of hard to get her off my back anyway. And the dog even gets in my way. For some reason, she always knows when I'm writing, and she comes in and starts nosing me. My mom doesn't bother me too much except when she says it's dinner time, so I have to stop. Then there are teachers who say, "You can't do this and you can't do that . . ."

KIRSTEN: "Don't use first pronouns . . ."

NORIKO: You can't say "I" or "you" in your story because otherwise that ruins it all. And then it becomes second person or first person, and then sometimes you don't have enough time because you have all this homework from all your other teachers. What about you? Do other people get in your way when you're writing?

KIRSTEN: Well, I really don't like people to read what I've written until I've finished it because like I said before, I just put down any kind of garbage I can about the plot so I don't forget it. And so when people come over and read it, and think that's how I really write, I think "No! no!" because my drafts are infinitely better, see. Sometimes Mom and Dad come ambling along and just happen to casually glance over their shoulder at my computer screen, and I'm like, "NO!" and I cover it up! And sometimes, they come over and offer suggestions and I'm like, "Don't give me any suggestions." Sometimes, my brother comes over, and says, "I want to play John Madden Football on the computer," and I'm like, "Excuse me, my creative juices are flowing; I want to write." He's like, "I want to play John Madden Football!"

NORIKO: So you kind of have a struggle—a tug of war—over the computer.

KIRSTEN: And, like you said, the teachers give you so much work, they scroosh your creative . . . My desk is right near the window, and without fail, whenever I start writing, these people are having a shouting match next door or across the street, and I try to hear what they're saying and I forget about my writing. It's that just noises, you know, like Led Zeppelin blasting in your ear, can get kind of annoying. And then just people coming in and out, because I cannot write when there's people around. Don't you think it's different writing at home and writing at school?

NORIKO: Well, at school, you're forced to do it. You know, you can't do this, and you can't do that. You have to have it done by a certain date and it has to be a certain amount of pages long, and so it's very restraining. But, at home, you can finish it whenever you want to, but sometimes in some ways that's worse because then you never finish. But they're the same because you're writing. At home, it's harder to find out what other people think of your writing; at school, they grade it and say, "Now this is wrong with your writing and this is wrong with your writing, and this is good and this is bad."

KIRSTEN: I go along with that. You know, when you're writing something for school, it's assigned, it's a specific topic to write about. You have to write about how Hitler could have been dealt with differently, and you have to write expository writing about how to make your bed, or you have to do this, due exactly on this date. I was absent on the day our character sketch was assigned, so I wasn't quite sure what it was. And so I wrote this little thing about my aunt Kirsten. Then my English teacher read it and she said, "Well, this is a really nice piece of work, but it isn't what the assignment was," so I got a *B* + on it. It didn't quite bother me, but I was a little miffed about that—it didn't matter what good writing it was; it wasn't the assignment, so you didn't get an *A*. So, that kind of bothers me. And you know that you *have* to do writing for school, like you said, and you don't feel relaxed and you can't do it whenever you want. Sometimes you find little things you learned in class creeping into your writing, sometimes to your horror! It's like, "Oh my God, I'm not using any first person pronouns! School has slipped into my writing—aaargh!" Sometimes you get ideas on what to write at home, in school.

KIRSTEN: Well, what would you tell a teacher about how she should teach writing?

NORIKO: I wouldn't, she'd get pretty pissed! What kind of English class are you talking about?

KIRSTEN: Any class where they're teaching you writing.

NORIKO: Well, I suppose I'd have it be like, you have regular writing, you know like a story due a month or a week or whatever, and then you could do peer editing, and then the teacher could look at it, 'cause then you would see what was wrong with your writing and what was right about it and then it wouldn't be graded or anything, so it wouldn't be like you're *frantic* about writing it, but then you could also do it regularly and you would get better at it. What would you tell teachers?

KIRSTEN: I would tell them, of course it's my opinion, that they shouldn't combine creative writing with grammar. They should have a separate class for grammar because you get really bored with grammar and then you associate writing with grammar and then you start to hate writing because you hate grammar.

NORIKO: You know, the British never teach grammar at all. In the International School in Japan, they thought it was appalling that Americans teach grammar, absolutely appalling. They thought that buying grammar books and teaching grammar was absolutely the most horrendous idea they ever heard in their lives.

KIRSTEN: How do the British do it?

NORIKO: Well, you read great literature, and you write about it. In other words, you know it's right because it sounds right. You just keep writing. It's not that they never correct grammar; it's that they never do grammar as a separate thing. They never teach grammar like we do with grammar drills and grammar classes and all that.

KIRSTEN: Well, we have this really neat journal in LA writing classes. We have these really weird questions like, "Which is taller, Monday or Friday? Write a couple things on which one you think is taller." And sometimes like, "What would the taste of a marshmallow sound like?" Or "What does the sound of lightning look like?" Interesting things like that, you know. And, I really think you should stress the creativity, let people become really creative.

NORIKO: Suppose you knew somebody—an eighth grader—who was bad at writing, and they said, "Why don't you teach me how to write?" What would you do?

KIRSTEN: I'd take a look at some of their past writing things, and I'd ask them what they thought of it, if they truly liked it, or if they just wrote it because it was assigned. And if they just wrote it because it was assigned, then that's their answer; they look upon it as *work,* okay? And anything you do as work is not nearly as good as something you do because it's fun. And then you gradually move them on to—well, gee, I don't know. The main thing is you'd have to get them to like to write, which is kind of tough.

NORIKO: I think first of all, you should just have really easy due dates and things like that so you don't feel forced, and then find what they really *like.* Somehow people don't think of writing poems as *writing,* or they don't think of writing stories for fun as really writing, so . . .

KIRSTEN: Try to get them to do an assignment that would be fun for them.

NORIKO: Something that's—well, no matter *what* you assign them, they're not going to go "Yippy, skippy, we get to write something." You know?

KIRSTEN: It's also attitude. Because if you have to do something, you might as well live with it and try to make the best of it. Some people just refuse to do anything to enjoy themselves.

NORIKO: So, do you think there are some people who are just hopeless; they're never going to like writing?

KIRSTEN: Well, we might not say they'll never like writing, they might just not like it in school. For example, Dad was telling me about one of his college roommates who just absolutely hated English, and he never read anything that he didn't have to read, okay? But, when he hit like thirty or something, he picked up some book, I think it was something by one of the American writers like John Steinbeck or someone like that, and he read one book by him and he said, "Hey, this is kind of neat!" And then he just read everything he could get his hands on; he'd been deprived all those years. I think it's something that you're going to get around to it when you feel like it. It really isn't good to force it on someone because they're really not going to like it.

NORIKO: Well, you can expose them to the good things and hope they like it, but you can't just say, "You'll like it!!!"

KIRSTEN: But maybe you could talk to them about what writing means to you.

NORIKO: To me it means like ventilation, or kind of like when you wake up in the morning and you stretch. Writing is kind of like that because you know you have all these wonderful thoughts in your head and you can write them down. *Or*, sometimes it's like the waking up part of the morning instead of the stretching part, you know? And then it's like, "Oh do I have to do this?" Usually, it's more like that for school.

KIRSTEN: I think that writing is sometimes like a relief.

NORIKO: It's a relief? Why?

KIRSTEN: Well, say you get an idea and you want to be another Tennessee Williams, and then you have these great thoughts, and then if you don't write it down, then it's inside you and, you're like, waiting for the moment when you can write it down. "Have to write it down! Have to write it down!" And then, when you finally can write it down, it's such a relief that you got to write it down. "Now, I can be a Tennessee Williams!"

NORIKO: It's kind of like going to the bathroom.

KIRSTEN: Yes!

NORIKO: Then, it's like something is stopped up inside you and you release it.

KIRSTEN: Like you take this wonderful drink and then you have to go to the bathroom and then finally you get to go to the bathroom and you're like, "Aaaaah."

NORIKO: I guess you wouldn't want to flush the toilet, though.

KIRSTEN: I think the cool thing about writing is that there is something for everybody. I mean, everyone likes some kind of writing. I mean, some people don't consider something like . . .

NORIKO: —*Car and Driver*—

KIRSTEN: —great but it is, and there's a kind of writing for everybody, and it's just sort of like the people's thing. And there's such a wide array of things that you can write about. There are no limits when you write, except that you have to use words. And that's very unlimiting, too. And you can just do whatever you want. There are no boundaries; there's just this great theory of freedom.

NORIKO: It's like flying.

KIRSTEN: Yes! Yes! There we go! I mean, we know there's a limit up there somewhere. I mean, you go up into space, you get asphyxiated, you know. But I think it's just really good 'cause there are no limits and there are people who can't do anything else, but they're good writers, and when you have good writing, it's just such a joy to read because—it's good writing. And it's fun to write because you can put down all your ideas, and you can give vent to the other side of your personality that you can't actually act out because most people will think you're weird. So you can do all the other things that you've always wanted to do except you aren't doing them, you're just doing them in a story. You can do anything when you write.

NORIKO: You know when something you write is good. When you read it, and then you finish reading it, it's like when you're really thirsty and then you drink a whole bunch of lemonade. It's really satisfying to read certain things, and other things—it's like drinking sand. And you're like, "Oh that didn't help very much." There are some books that you just pick up and you just can't put them down again. And even when you get to the end, you could read it over again in the same sitting. It's good writing if you feel like, "Oh, that's the sort of thing I can read a hundred times." Like *Illusions,* I could read that a hundred thousand *billion* times and still want to read it again. When I'm finished, I just think (sighhhhhh) and it makes me think. When it makes you *think,* that's good.

KIRSTEN: Well, there isn't any list of characteristics of good writing because it's just something that you *know* when you read something that's good. It's like when you hear music. There's a *big* difference between good music and bad music, and everyone can tell, but they can't give you a list of things of what's good music and what's not. Everything's just perfect, I mean, it just flows smoothly, it just reads easy, but it still makes you think. A book like *The Babysitter's Club* isn't terribly exciting because it's not good writing because it doesn't make you think, it's just this garbage stuff. Good writing adds more to your life, you know, it's just more exciting. You can get into it and it just says something, and it just makes you feel like you want to read it, that you want more of it.

30

Page and Dave

"WRITING'S SNARLS AND CONTRADICTIONS"

(Grades 3, 6, and 8)

Contributed by Mara Casey

Page and Dave are now in tenth grade. Since 1984, I have followed them, and fifteen of their classmates, through a suburban school system in Massachusetts, interviewing these upper middle class white children in groups of three or four in January of third grade, September and June of sixth grade, and May of eighth grade. The interviews occurred wherever I could find space in their school: in the elementary school library, a storage room, the counselor's office, the junior high's conference room, and on the back steps. I have also collected writing samples since third grade and interviewed all of their elementary teachers, as well as the principal, resource room specialist, language arts coordinator, and their junior high English teachers and department head.

I first met these children when I, an independent writing consultant, worked as a volunteer for six months in their classroom, helping their third grade teacher, a former student of mine, develop an experimental writing program. The kids chose their own subjects, met twice a week in small writing groups, as well as for whole-class brainstorming and sharing sessions, and revised extensively, publishing after six months a class book for the school library and every family. When I left their classroom, all of the children thought of themselves as writers.

Page's and Dave's experience with writing after third grade has not been as happy. In third grade, Page likened writing to combing her long snarly blonde hair. It was hard, but she knew she could do it, if she kept at it long enough. For Dave, writing involved practice and making mistakes, like learning to be good enough to get on the Bruins. But by the end of elementary school, both children were like alienated factory workers who knew their writing was not as good as it had been in third grade.

This profile, shaped from two separate profiles based on audio-taped group interviews, shows that children will not continue to be enthusiastic and able writers without time and support for writing, access to listeners, and teachers with high expectations who, as Page says, know all of the field of writing, "not just punctuation." In the profile I alternate the voices of the two children at four levels: third, beginning of sixth, end of sixth, and eighth grades.

MID-THIRD GRADE

PAGE

I can do writing good, but, you know, sometimes I feel like it's boring, like combing your hair. I have really snarly hair, and, you know, I hate combing it. And then I keep on combing it, and that's like revising it more and more times. And then, once I'm done combing my hair, or once I'm done writing my story, it's fun. Then I feel proud of myself, and I get a lot of compliments.

It's the same in reading. If you don't like reading, but you want to accomplish reading at least one book in your life, when you're starting it, you're like, "I don't really wanna do this, but I want to get it over with, to at least read one book." You kinda don't feel like doing it, but once you keep on reading and reading, and writing and writing, you feel like you're getting better at it, and you'll try again.

I like being in my writing group because you get more attention on your story. If the class was all together, instead of in small groups, the teacher would be rushing around trying to help everybody, and one person wouldn't get attention or the other person wouldn't. And then they'd have really hard trouble in doing it. There'd be too many questions. You'd be confused.

DAVE

We spent a lot more time on writing this year than we did in second grade. It's become a major event in our class. At first it was boring, and then it started getting fun. Even though it's kinda hard, it's worth the time.

Reading stories after people do a lot of hard work on them is fun, too. At first most of the kids were really shy about reading their writing to their group. But now they like to express those feelings that they have. And now we've published a class book for the library. It was hard for most of us, especially me, but we managed to do it. I sat right down and read the whole thing as soon as it was finished. I was really impressed at what the kids wrote.

It'd stink if we just wrote something and put it away in our writing folder without reading it to the other kids. You kind of felt better when your group gave you compliments. But in a way it didn't help you because if I got so many compliments, it feels like I don't need to write any more, and I'm done. But in a way it does kind of help because it's saying when you do more drafts—as you do more—you get better.

Like if you have a lot of trouble on your story, and you don't know what to write about, once you get started, it's easier than before because you know more of what you're doing. You could do it. Like Page said, you keep combing and combing until you get your knots out, and it stops hurting. You have to practice. Just like in hockey, when you're littler, you fall down, and you wipe out, and can't dribble the puck. But when you get on the Bruins, you're really good.

I had to do three or four drafts before I made my final draft and finished my story about the owl in the corner of the dollar bill in my pocket. My first draft was not really my main story. This was kinda like telling about my dollar bill. But when you do tell about it, it kinda helps you learn about what writing is because that's only the beginning. But then, as you write more, it becomes harder and harder, but it seems the same because you're getting better, at the same time everything's getting harder. Just like in school, you get older, and you know more, but the work gets harder.

EARLY SIXTH GRADE
PAGE

I love writing. Since third grade I really just like to sit down with everything quiet and just think of different things to write. I don't like to be assigned. That's pretty boring. Sometimes I like to write about monsters and silly things, but not outrageous animals with three necks and stuff. I like to write mostly about natural things with trees in it and colors and a lot of describing words.

Different authors all have their different ways of writing. There's no right way to write any kind of story, except if you want to get it published. But if you want to grow up to be a good writer, you have to keep writing, and you can't just stop. And sometimes you have to brainstorm and let yourself fly. You have to just let your imagination go wild.

In fourth grade we didn't have writing groups, but we had writing time. We had a big project on autobiography. Well, I liked it, but I didn't really like it because she assigned you what you had to write. It really didn't let kids think about what they wanted to write about and give them the chance to do it by theirselves. It made my writing feel dull. It would have been more exciting if she was more interested in what we had to write by ourselves.

Fifth grade wasn't really a year to learn how to write. We had different assignments that had writing in it, but not a lot of free composition writing. We didn't get composition books, but I asked her if I could have some, 'cause since like third grade on, I been so interested in writing that I've wanted to write at home. So I got a couple, and I wrote pretty much actually.

When I write by myself at home, I do it much different than we have to do it in school. I don't always have to have everybody throwing ideas at the blackboard the way we used to brainstorm with the whole class in third grade. I can do it by myself usually now. If I sit on my bed for about five minutes, and I can't find a story, I just put down ideas, anything I see like "wood" or "nail" or something. And then I come up with like either a fairy tale or fiction.

It doesn't take that much energy to write. You can just let your mind go free. Sometimes when you're writing and you feel "this isn't really good," it's really good. And it's just like when you see modern art. A kid could just go up to a piece of paper and draw something so simple. And it could be beautiful, and somebody could hang it in their house. And it could get sold for millions of dollars.

DAVE

If you don't want to write, you can't write. You get to be a good writer by writing. You have to think, and you need a lot of different skills. You have to be able to read your story. You have to be able to spell the words. You have to do punctuation. Speech sorta also helps with spelling because if you know how to say something, sometimes you can learn to spell.

I start out like blank. You think, "This is going to be hard; I'm doomed." But then all of a sudden everything just comes to me. You think of one word, and then you know the whole story. But it sort of scares you when you have to pass in the piece. You always think it's either too long or too short.

In third grade I got my ideas just by looking at things and hearing things. I did more than ten drafts. Everybody was helping everybody, and the stories got better. You wouldn't go, "Oh, I think your story stinks and mine's good." They said, "Oh, you have a great story."

What we did in third grade really showed us how to write, like by instinct. After awhile it just came to you. It became like a habit to put in periods. You didn't really have to think about what you were going to write and how you were going to do it.

In fourth grade writing seemed much more fun. They showed us how to do things, like a little bit higher. They didn't use the third grade method as much because we already knew how to do that. We knew how to shorten it. Say we did ten drafts in third grade. In fourth grade we learned how to put five in each one, so we only had to do two. You could start off, maybe halfway through, and then you could go halfway to the end. Really your first draft in fourth grade is like the fifth draft in third grade. You just like skip six, seven, eight, and nine because you know what to add.

In fifth grade, writing was work. We each had to write a story every week about something that had happened to us. You didn't have that much time. And then we'd get in a group at the table, and the teacher sat at the end. There's not like the highest group or anything because everybody was the same in writing. So people would raise their hand and comment on each others' stories. The kids' comments helped. You don't go, "That's dumb. That part was so stupid." You go like this: "You might be able to change that into that. And then it might sound better."

The teacher would make unhelpful comments. She tried to make good comments, but she never did. She said one thing to you, and then she said the other the next day. She pretended like she knew what she was doing, but sometimes she didn't.

LATE SIXTH GRADE
PAGE

Writing kind of reminds me of a factory production line 'cause it goes through so many steps. Like thinking and jotting things down. First draft. Go through it to see if that's the way you like your writing to be. Second draft, third draft. Proofread it.

I did better writing in third grade than I do now because of all the revising we did. It made you think about what you were writing. We went over our drafts about sixteen times. It made the story good at the end. Like you could publish this now.

At home I do as many drafts as I need, but in sixth grade we write two. Drafts and drafts and drafts aren't required. You don't have time, and the subjects are boring. We do like five writing assignments at a time, so you kind of rush it. When we revise, you read it over, and correct run-on sentences or bad English. My writing group doesn't make any suggestions, and my teacher always writes like good comments on my stories.

But if you really want to do good writing, you have to concentrate and think about it. You have to work on one subject for a long time. The teacher has to keep the idea going that you should do drafts and drafts and drafts. She should assign drafts and drafts and drafts, even if the kids don't like the drafts and drafts and drafts.

In school you have to write an outline. If I hadn't heard about outlines in school, I wouldn't be using them now. I've written a lot of stories that have turned out pretty good without an outline. An outline doesn't change how good your story is. It just helps you remember the ideas. You don't have to use it in the future. In school you just use it.

We can't write freely. They don't let you write any fiction. They say, "Well, you can write fiction anytime." I'm losing all my ability to write in fiction. Most of the writing subjects this year have been pretty dull and boring, but I think that's just to teach us that eventually we might have to do these in work.

We were assigned to write this essay on Africa. Mine was so dull. This was the sixth, seventh, or eighth "Something-You-Feel-Strongly-About" story we've written this year. I didn't like any of them. So when it came time to hand one in, I just turned this one in. I wasn't happy about the paper, but I wasn't all that sad either. I was so bored of doing it.

We're not supposed to research it. Well, she didn't tell us to research it. Maybe I should have. She told me to expand it more, but I couldn't. I would have written about ten more pages if I had known more about the subject. The only real information that I wrote is— and I don't even know if this is true—that "people are starving in Africa. Some go for weeks without food, some months. Many die, and others turn very sick." This is all from what I see on TV. I've never looked at a book about Africa and starving people.

DAVE

Writing is kind of a pain. You know, writing and writing and writing. You've got to think of an idea first of what kind of story you want to write—a true story, science fiction, fiction, whatever. And then you have to think of the story itself.

It depends on what you're writing. I like science fiction the most. That's probably the easiest 'cause you can make up things as you go along. You can usually just write anything you really want. Fiction isn't too tough either, if you know a lot about the thing already. Like I know a lot about skateboarding, so I could write a story without doing any research. But say you are going to think of a story about the Air Force. Maybe you would do research first to know the different kinds of planes they have.

I like thinking up stories, but I hate writing it down. My mind goes faster than my hand does. If I could just tell it into a tape recorder and then have it typed, it'd be great.

And then you have to think of something the people would be interested in. You have to think of a snappy beginning. And you have to have some kind of way to end it. And a lot of good body in it. And it can't be too short. And not too long because no one's going to want to read something that's twelve hundred pages. And no one's going to read something that's half a page. So you really got to think about what you're writing and how you're writing it.

If I want to write something that I like to write, and I want to be creative, I need a teacher who gives me space to write the way I want, someone who understands my stories and how I think about them. Like they'll look at it and say, "Well, this has good content," or, "This has bad content." They don't say, "You can't write about these certain things," or "Oh, that's a stupid story." Someone, like an English teacher, who really knows what they're talking about and can tell me if this is something that someone would like to read.

One of the things I like about going to the junior high next year is they have different teachers who have different qualities. Normally, if they're someone who knows about writing, they usually like to write themselves.

LATE EIGHTH GRADE
PAGE

I don't know how to say what kind of writing I'd want to have done this year, or still do this year, but I know I haven't done it. Everything's so lined up, kinda like a checkerboard. He gives you an assignment, and you hand it in, and you get it back. No one ever talks about it. Reading groups that give constructive criticism would help. If you talk about it more, then you understand what you can do to make it more what you want it to be.

And he doesn't write any comments. Well, spelling and punctuation and grammar. He has a lot of grammar. I can't stand grammar.

I remember in elementary school, I cannot remember what grade, we sat in the corner, and we had to do drafts and drafts and drafts until it was perfect. Good writers do that. I don't know if a lot of other people enjoyed doing all those drafts and stuff, but I always had a good time. Writing groups were awesome.

I liked elementary school much better than the junior high because it was more hands-on. You got to know your teachers so much. I know nothing about any of my teachers here.

All the teachers have different styles of how they want to have you write. I liked the stuff Mrs. Robbins did last year in seventh grade—hands-on stuff. You got to do activities and stuff, besides just sit down and write things. You could vary the assignments and make it the way you want it to be, instead of having exact guidelines to follow.

Mrs. Robbins always had a really good attitude about things. I liked the way she taught. I can't explain it, though. She got more involved with us and the writing and all that. And not as much into just grading and telling people what's right and wrong. She'd listen to you. If she said something, and you didn't agree, you knew you wouldn't feel bad saying something. Another teacher would give you no leeway or anything.

I wish other teachers would make you feel as if you could talk to them, and you didn't have to just do the assignment and just hope you got a good grade on it. You could talk to them and ask them for help and stuff. Just so they would be open with the student.

This year Mr. Brody doesn't make us do drafts and drafts and drafts, but I do it at home on my own. We have mostly assigned topics. He works the writing into what the unit is, like poetry. When he gives you the assignment for the weekly writing, he gives you a checksheet with the requirements of what you have to have in it. Like how many words. If you write too many, he gets mad. You have to go down the checksheet and do each poem the way it was assigned.

The way he grades it is you exchange with somebody else in the class. On the board he gives you a set of specific guidelines to go by, depending on what the unit is. If you're working with similes and metaphors, you have to make sure they have the requirements. If they have all the words, you give them ten points. When I do it, I don't really read it. I just kinda glance over it and give them a good grade. I don't think kids really take it seriously.

I don't like English just because of the teacher and the stuff we do. I used to really like it, having journals and being able to write in them. I don't like writing any more.

DAVE

Writing is not lined, but teachers think it's very structured, like math. It seems like they don't want us to write anymore. They want us to do so many superficial things that really don't matter in your writing. They just want us to do things their way, and it's not writing. It's writing, I mean physically, but you're not writing what should be written. Like the five-paragraph essay. The first and last paragraphs are just kind of wasteoid.

Elementary school was way better than this dump. If you choose your own subject, it's a lot better. When we used to do creative writing, like in sixth grade, it was fun. She said, "Just write something." And then we used to get in a group and read it to the whole class. And that was fun because it was like your own. And no one ever made fun of anybody.

I hate writing now because they make it so boring. Ninety percent of the time we're doing bad stuff. They grade you on grammar, not your writing. If you write a poem, it has to be about a certain subject. If you write a story, it has to be about "If people couldn't talk in 1991," or "If pictures could come to life," or, "Imagine if you were invisible for a day" and all these stupid things. And then they tell us, "And be creative."

And it's like "I didn't imagine this. *You* did. And you're making us write about it." I look at the list, and I'm like, "Which one of these will be the easiest?" It's not worth doing something really hard because it's not interesting anymore.

The teachers here don't just say, "Write a story or write a poem" because they're lame. They can't teach. And they don't think we can handle choosing our own subjects. They feel we're immature, and we'll just sit there and talk with our friends. People have your stereotype of teenagers as being party animals—irresponsible—who don't care about anything. And they don't like anybody, and they use people. They make us look real bad, like in movies and stuff. And it's like, "Gee thanks, guys."

We don't have anything like writing groups, and we don't have conferences with our teacher. Only one draft is required. The teacher writes the story for us practically. You just fill in the "but's," "then's," and "a's." We just hand it in and get it corrected according to a checklist. "How many words do you have?" That's thirty points. "Spelling? Grammar? Use of figurative language?" And then ten points for creativity on this assignment that said "creative writing." It just kills me. I wanted to bring it up and go, "Why did you call it creative writing? You should have called it grammar writing." It's like the biggest contradiction I've ever seen.

APPENDIX: CONSTRUCTING PROFILES FROM INTERVIEW DATA

"Cultures do not hold still for their portraits" (Clifford 1986, 10). Neither do children. When we make them do so, we must simplify, exclude, select, and in other ways narrow the picture of who they are. Of course, all research reports filter data—both qualitative and quantitative—through researchers' eyes. Observed and/or collected data are used to support perceived patterns and categories or findings and implications. In *all* such reports, data is selected and shaped by the questions asked and the presentation format.

In this book, however, data have been shaped not to support findings, but to present the actual words of children as they discuss reading, writing, literacy, and schooling. As a result, those who have shaped the data intrude very little in the final presentation, while readers are invited to participate far more than in most research. We provide the kaleidoscopic camera, the juxtaposition of voices; readers contribute their own decisions about what these voices may mean. Thus in some ways, contributors to this volume "shape" their data less than usual. But it is nonetheless important to understand how this type of data has been shaped. In this appendix, we explain both how most of the interviews were conducted as well as how profiles were shaped from collected interview transcripts.

Most selections included in this book come primarily from phenomenological and other forms of in-depth interviewing (see Seidman 1986, 1991; Schutz 1967; Schuman 1982). This approach "assumes that the experience that students have with writing [and reading] affects the way they go about it" (Cleary 1991). We therefore asked children to talk about their perceptions of literacy and their experiences in reading, writing, and schooling. We wanted to stay out of the way as much as possible and get to the meanings that children hold. (See Erickson 1986, for discussion of interpretive research aimed at accessing the actors' point of view.)

The editors provided the following information in the form of handouts for potential contributors to use in collecting data and/or editing previously collected data into profile format. We hope these guidelines will be useful to others who might want to construct profiles for their own purposes.

COLLECTING DATA FOR PROFILE BUILDING

I. E. Seidman and his colleagues at the University of Massachusetts at Amherst, have developed a process for in-depth phenomenological interviewing and presenting the data in profile formats. (See Seidman 1985, 1991.) The basic assumption of this method is that the meaning we make of any experience affects the way we carry it out. The technique has been used in qualitative research since the 1970's.

Seidman's interviewing process is usually based on three distinct and separate interviews with a research participant. Ideally each hour-long interview is held on a separate day to allow for accumulative reflection. Although Seidman prefers an hour and thirty minutes with adults, Cleary (1991) found that hour-long interviews work well with high school students. We have found that younger children fare better with shorter interviews. It is important to find a mutually agreed upon time and place that is not subject to interruption. During the interview, the researcher takes detailed notes which capture the words of the participant and tape records the session if the participant agrees. Extensive practice in notetaking allows the researcher eventually to capture almost verbatim the stories and experiences that the participant relates. Seidman finds that using only one open-ended question at the beginning of each interview works well with adults. Other researchers work out certain areas they want to cover with further, open-ended sub-questions. Frequently, the sub-questions are not necessary because in talking about the preliminary questions participants naturally cover the sub-questions. Following is an interview structure which might be used.

STRUCTURE AND TOPICS FOR A
THREE-INTERVIEW SEQUENCE
INTERVIEW 1—HISTORICAL
"Describe, in as much detail as possible, your past experience with reading and writing."
Stories and details about family, schooling, reading, neighborhood, and friends are important. Usually the interviewer has to ask few questions in this interview, but pertinent questions may include:

- What was writing/reading like for you in elementary school? Junior High/Middle School?
- How did you learn to write/read?
- Do your parent(s), siblings, peers, or other adults help you with writing/reading? How was that helpful?
- What kind of writing/reading did you or do you see your parents doing? Siblings?
- Can you tell a story about a time when writing/reading was really good/bad for you?

INTERVIEW 2—CONTEMPORARY

"Describe what writing/reading is like for you in the present, giving as much detail as possible about what you do when writing/reading and what it is like to write/read."

The questions of when, where, how, for what, for whom are all important to elicit the concrete details of experience. Again ask as few questions as possible, but if your participant runs out of things to say, you might ask the following questions:

- What are all the kinds of writing/reading you do inside and outside of school?
- Could you try to give as detailed a picture as you can of what writing/reading you might do during a given day?
- How do you go about a writing project or paper from beginning to end? same for reading a book.
- How do other people help or hinder your writing/reading processes?
- When is writing/reading uncomfortable for you?
- Describe the audiences for whom you currently write. What part do those audiences play in your writing?

INTERVIEW 3—REFLECTION

"What meaning do you make of your experience with writing/reading?"

This is the most challenging of the interviews because it asks the participant to reflect on experience and understand it. Asking the same question in different ways is useful in this meaning-making process. Variations on the primary question include:

- Thinking about your past life, your life now, and your writing now, what sense do you make of writing/reading?
- Explore the nature of your experience with writing/reading. What things are important to you in your life, and how does writing/reading connect with those things?
- Are you realizing anything through these interviews?
- What is there that is important that we haven't covered?

You may want to follow up on questions that you still have about your participant's writing/reading experience.

INTERVIEW TIPS

Although there may seem to be limited structure to these interviews, researchers and participants alike will be surprised by how much there is to say about each facet of the main interview question. Feel free to ask further open-ended questions when you:

- do not understand, "Can you explain that further?"
- want more information or detail, "Can you tell me more about that?" or "Was there another time when that kind of thing happened?"

In this way, you focus attention on what is of interest to the participant. In the first two interviews, ask for stories and concrete details so that the reconstruction of experience provides a strong foundation for the reflection that occurs in the final interview.

Once interviews were taped and detailed notes taken, tapes were transcribed and notes fully fleshed out. (Notes supplement taped voices by reminding the interviewer of nonverbal behaviors as well as relevant aspects of the interview setting.) Then the job of shaping or constructing the profiles began. We also provided a written description to all contributors explaining how profiles are built. It follows here.

BUILDING A PROFILE FROM PREVIOUSLY COLLECTED DATA

The purpose of building profiles from transcripts and/or notes of in-depth interviews, group interviews, classroom observations, composing aloud sessions, or case studies is to let readers be exposed to participants' perceptions about a certain subject. The profile is focused so that the reader gets an essential part of the total of what the participant had to say about writing and reading. The profile builder's task is to select portions of the interview material and to *weave* those portions to present the experience of the participant primarily in his or her own words. General principles for constructing profiles are:

- Use the first person as if the participant is actually speaking to the reader. By presenting the profile in the words of the participant, you reduce as much as possible the reinterpretation of the experience of the participant by the interviewer.
- Start by underlining the sections of transcriptions or notes that seem important or by transcribing sections of the audiotaped interviews that seem important.
- Cut whole segments of transcribed material if they do not seem relevant or important.
- Try to leave sections intact as often as possible.

- Group sections and sentences that relate to the same subject and weave these sentences into paragraphs with logical meaning and progression; original order of sentences may be rearranged.
- For syntactic and transitional purposes, and in a discriminating fashion, add words in brackets and change verb tenses to make meanings more clear. [Brackets were later removed for readability except to add explanations.]
- Strive to present a cohesive picture of at least a part of the participant's experience with writing and reading.
- Assure the anonymity of the participant [if participant wishes]; leave out any material that may give clues to the identity of the participant and change the names of friends, teachers, places, etc.

The composition of the profile is a creative process. By selectively weaving and thus making connections among sections, you highlight the sense that the participant has made of the writing experience and your own understanding of it. In doing so, you must create a profile that preserves the dignity of the participant and is fair to the interview material.

Studs Terkel describes this process as editing out the interviewer's voice to present a profile that is "like a soliloquy" (1972, pp. 35–36). By selecting comments on similar themes from across interviews, by meshing a child's comments into coherent talk, by making decisions about punctuation, paragraphing, and order, the contributors to this collection consciously shaped the data throughout the process of constructing a profile. We have skillfully, we hope, shaped useful artifacts for your examination.

REFERENCES

Cleary, L. M. 1991. *From the other side of the desk: Students speak out about writing.* Portsmouth, NH: Boynton/Cook.

Clifford, J., & G. E. Marcus, eds. 1986. *Writing culture: The poetics and politics of ethnography.* Berkeley, CA: University of California Press.

Erickson, F. 1986. Qualitative methods in research on teaching. In *Handbook of research on teaching, 3rd edition,* ed. M. C. Wittrock, 119–161.

Schuman, D. 1982. *Policy analysis, education, and everyday life: An evaluation of higher education.* Lexington, MA: Heath.

Schutz, A. 1967. *The phenomenology of the social world.* Evanston, IL: Northwestern University Press.

Seidman, I. E. 1985. *In the words of the faculty.* San Francisco: Josey-Bass.

———. 1991. *Interviewing as qualitative research.* New York: Teachers College Press.

Terkel, S. 1972. *Working: People talk about what they do all day and how they feel about what they do.* New York: Random House.

CONTRIBUTORS' NOTES

SALLY HUDSON-ROSS (LACEY, CHAPTER 1; NICOLE, CHAPTER 8; MARY ELIZABETH [WITH SUSAN ALLCORN], CHAPTER 17)

For my dissertation in 1983–84, I sought out twenty avid young writers. All of the participants in grades one through five wrote extensively in home and school settings, but Nicole, who I decided not to include in the study, was unique in that writing almost consumed her life at this stage. She was happy to talk freely about her extensive writing but did not like to categorize her products as I asked the others to do.

The other children collected their writing for four months and categorized each product for six contextual factors: ownership, setting, audience, purpose, genre, and degree of involvement. Aspects of that research are published in *Research in the Teaching of English* [Hudson, S.A. (1986). Context and children's writing. *20*, 294–316.] and *The Social Construction of Written Communication* [Hudson, S. A. (1988). Children's perceptions of classroom writing: Ownership within a continuum of control. In B. A. Rafoth & D. L. Rubin (Eds.), (pp. 37–69). Norwood, NJ: Ablex Publishing.] I replicated this study in 1989–90, and the children presented here by Hoffman and Jones were in that group.

Nicole continues to be an avid writer—although middle and high school have opened up new vistas for her. Lacey and Mary Elizabeth, my other two profiles, are my nieces who live in Pennsylvania. My co-author, Susan Allcorn, is their mother. I interviewed them both in 1990 specifically for this book. I am an associate professor of English Education at The University of Georgia where I teach and conduct research in composition and teacher education.

BEVERLY E. COX AND LEAH JONES
(MARTIN, JERALYNN, AND MARK, CHAPTER 2)

Martin, Jeralynn, and Mark's contributions come from a larger study in 1988–89, when we were exploring what four and five year olds know about making continuous text (oral for a dialogue partner and written [dictated] for a reader). Leah was particularly interested in examining young children's planning and control over their written text and so, we looked at the dialogue surrounding their dictations hoping to find indications of their knowledge of story and their perceptions of authorship and writing in the world of readers and writers. We think we did.

Leah has since graduated from Purdue with her Master's degree and moved first to Georgia, and then to Arizona. After adding a third daughter to her young family, she now hopes to continue her graduate studies in Arizona, planning to pursue her Ph.D. in language and literacy development with young children.

As an assistant professor of Language and Literacy in the School of Education at Purdue University, I am teaching courses in literacy development and continuing my research with preschoolers as well as older learners. Earlier work addressing evidence of planning in dialogue and monologue by kindergartners was published by B. E. Cox & E. Sulzby. (1982. "Evidence of Planning in Dialogue and Monologue by Five-Year-Old Emergent Readers." In *Thirty-first yearbook of the National Reading Conference,* edited by J. A. Niles and L. A. Harris, 124–130. Rochester, NY: National Reading Conference.)

The research reported here was funded in part by an XL Summer Faculty Grant from Purdue University and has been continued through a Spencer Foundation Grant.

JANET B. TAYLOR AND N. AMANDA BRANSCOMBE
(SCOOTER AND CHANELL, CHAPTER 3)

Since 1986, we have collaborated on a number of research projects that focus on how children learn to write. A part of that collaborative effort is published in " 'I wanna write jes like in dat book!': Talk and its role in the shared journal experience" (Branscombe, N.A. & J. Taylor. 1988. in *The word for teaching is learning: Essays for James Britton,* edited by N. Martin & M. Lightfoot, 107–134. London: Heinemann), and in the 1992 publication *Students teaching, teachers learning: Reclaiming the classroom, Volume 2* (edited by N. A. Branscombe, D. Goswami, & J. Schwartz, Portsmouth, NH: Heinemann).

Taylor is an associate professor of early Childhood Education at Auburn University, and Branscombe is an assistant professor of Early Childhood Education at West Georgia College in Carrollton, Georgia.

HEIDI MILLS (KAREEM, TONY, AND AMANDA, CHAPTER 4)

Kareem, Tony, and Amanda are three of eighteen children in Timothy O'Keefe's whole language classroom. They are featured in this segment simply because they were part of the conversations that naturally emerged as the children reflected on reading and writing while being videotaped on a typical day in April, 1990. David Whitin and I were in the midst of a three-year collaborative research project with Timothy O'Keefe and his children. We were exploring how children learn language and mathematics and ways to develop curricular experiences that are consistent with the learning process. Data from this research project formed the foundation for *Living and Learning Mathematics: Stories and Strategies for Supporting Mathematical Literacy* (Whitin, Mills, O'Keefe, Heinemann 1990); *Looking Closely: Exploring the Role of Phonics in One Whole Language Classroom* (Mills, O'Keefe, and Stephens, NCTE, forthcoming), and "A Day with Dinosaurs" in *Portraits of Whole Language Classrooms: Learning for All Ages* (Mills and Clyde, Heinemann 1990). While our primary data sources included videotapes, field notes, photographs, and written artifacts, these vignettes were transcribed directly from videotape.

These three children, their young colleagues, and their artful classroom teacher have taught me a great deal. I have attempted to share their insights with graduate and undergraduate students at the University of South Carolina where I am an assistant professor.

RONALD D. KIEFFER (JUSTIN AND DYLAN, CHAPTER 5)

Currently, I am an assistant professor in the Department of Language Education, The University of Georgia. As a former elementary teacher, my research interests are in oral and written language development, emergent literacy, and children's literature. I am particularly interested in ways that literature can be used in classroom settings to advance the learning of reading and writing.

Justin, age six, and Dylan, age eight, the students who appear in this profile, completed their collaborative writing project between March and June, 1990. The profiles of Justin and Dylan were constructed from data gathered for my dissertation research, an eight-month case study in a literature-based computer magnet school. The purpose of the study was to explore ways that students worked together as co-authors within the social context of a first-grade classroom. For a more detailed description of Justin and Dylan's work along with the authorship experiences of other students from the study, the unpublished doctoral dissertation is available through Dissertation Abstracts, volume 52, issue 08A, publication number 92-01689.

BETTY SHOCKLEY, JOBETH ALLEN (SHANNON, CHAPTER 6) AND BARBARA MICHALOVE (REGGIE [WITH JOBETH ALLEN], CHAPTER 9)

We have been observing, listening to, and writing about these children as part of a longitudinal study of how the children teachers worry about the most develop as literacy learners. We set out to study the effects of a stable school environment, with meaningful and predictable opportunities for literacy learning. We began studying Shannon in Betty's first grade, and continued as she moved directly to third, skipping second because of Betty's concern over two previous retentions. We began studying Reggie in Barbara's second grade; the next year he joined Shannon in a whole language third grade. However, the third-grade teacher had to resign due to illness; a succession of ten substitutes gave us insights on the effects of instability on literacy learning.

These portraits are drawn from quarterly interviews with the children on how they are learning to read and write. We asked the same questions each time, questions adapted from Jane Hansen and Don Graves' evaluation study: What are you learning to do as a reader [writer]? How are you learning that? What would you like to learn next year as a reader? How do you think you'll learn that? What do you think you'll read when you are a grown up?

Betty and Barbara teach and conduct research in their whole language classrooms; JoBeth in their co-researcher, and teaches at The University of Georgia. Other reports of the research are available elsewhere, including *The Reading Teacher* (March, 1991) and *Engaging Children* (in press, Heinemann).

BONNIE CRAMOND (EMILY, CHAPTER 7)

The series of interviews that I conducted with my daughter in order to compose this chapter took place in the winter and spring of 1991 when Emily was seven. However, the research that contributes the background for the piece began before she was born. My husband and I both have training and research interests in creativity, and have been professionally concerned with fostering creative development in all individuals. When our daughter came along, it was natural that we would encourage and note her own creative achievements. At times, this creativity has caused us all more grief than joy, and we have jokingly chided our mentor, Dr. E. Paul Torrance, creator of the *Torrance Tests of Creative Thinking* and author of numerous books and articles on the development of creativity, for training us too well.

I am presently an assistant professor in Educational Psychology at The University of Georgia and Coordinator of the Gifted/Creative Education Program.

LINDA MILLER CLEARY (KATHERINE, CHAPTER 10; HOBBES, CHAPTER 18)

My two contributions to this book are profiles of children who have spent many hours in the "resource room." I was interested in knowing what meaning these children made of their experience of leaving their classrooms for substantial parts of the school day. After the children picked their own pseudonyms, I used in-depth phenomenological interviewing (as described by Seidman 1991). With fifth-grader Hobbes, it was relatively easy to get good material in this three interview sequence, but third-grader Katherine was quite shy at first, and I interviewed her in seven twenty-minute sessions after we baked and ate cookies together. If you are interested in how this interviewing method is used in a larger study, along with classroom observation and written protocols (analysis done by analytic inducation), see reports I have done of a study of the experience of eleventh grade writers: *From the Other Side of the Desk: Students Speak Out About Writing* (Boynton/Cook 1991) and "Affect and Cognition in the Writing Processes of Eleventh Graders: A Study of Concentration and Motivation" (*Written Communication*, October, 1991). I am currently an associate professor of English education at The University of Minnesota, Duluth.

BARBARA BIEGNER HOFFMAN AND FRANKEY JONES (ASHLEY, NATHAN, MATTHEW, AND KRISTIN, CHAPTER 11)

Barbara Biegner Hoffman and Frankey Jones collected data and wrote this piece as graduate students at the University of Georgia. Frankey was a research assistant for this 1989–90 study, funded by a grant from the Research Foundation of the National Council of Teachers of English and designed and conducted by Sally Hudson-Ross of the University of Georgia. The study focused on children's and their teachers' perceptions of the contexts of children's writing. Frankey carried out interviews with these and other children, all avid writers, and observed extensively, especially in Ms. Sara Ann Mason's third grade classroom. Barbara shaped the interview transcripts into profile format and worked with Frankey to edit it.

Frankey currently teaches talented and gifted children in the elementary grades and continues work on her Ed.D. in Language Education. Barbara has completed her master's degree and is now a high school English teacher.

RASHIDAH JAAMI' MUHAMMAD (MARIO, CHAPTER 12)

I had been trying for a few days to re-establish contact with the co-ordinator of my summer research program at the Black Child and Family Institute, to find a third grader to talk about literacy, when my son Abdul-Jaleel came home from school with Mario, and announced: "Mom, we have a half-day at school, can Mario stay here till his Mom gets home?" So after missed phone messages thwarted my efforts to locate a participant, my son hand-delivered a willing third-grader. After approvals from Mario and his mom, we settled down to discuss his ideas about reading and writing.

Most of the interviews were conducted in his den, with the exception of the first interview at my house and parts of the fourth at bookstores and in the car between bookstores.

For the past three summers, I have examined the impact of American African literature on third through eighth grade students at Lansing's Black Child and Family Institute. I hope Mario joins my summer session at the Institute. His presence would not only enrich his own personal Afrocentric perspective, but would generate enthusiastic class participation from the other students.

During the regular school year (September to June), most of the summer enrichment students as well as Mario attend predominantly white middle class and working class schools. Evidence indicates that the curriculums of these schools are not often enriched with American African history. So, Mario's lack of historical perspective concerning Martin Luther King, Jr., is not surprising. In fact, when I asked a group of fourth graders at the Black Child and Family Institute: "Who was Martin Luther King, Jr.?" One student replied: "He was the one that freed the slaves."

Mario was always eager to share his stories. He has made me more curious to examine just how much the popular culture (i.e., books and movies) does or does not validate one's life experiences. After I complete my master's degree in English Education, Fall 1991, I will enroll in the Ph.D. program, at Michigan State University, and continue my study of children's experiences with literature written by, for, or about American Africans.

BOBBIE A. SOLLEY (REGINA, CHAPTER 13)

In 1990 and 1991, I conducted correlational studies in order to examine the relationship between writing performance, anxiety, and attitude of fourth graders. Children in two fourth-grade classrooms in East Texas participated in the study. I found a significant negative correlation between anxiety and performance, so as they wrote stories, children were trained in self-awareness and self-instruction techniques in an attempt to alleviate anxiety. Ten children, selected at random, were interviewed in order to further understand their perceptions about writing and stories. Regina was one of the ten children I interviewed.

While collecting these data, I was an assistant professor at the University of Texas at Tyler. I am now an assistant professor at Middle Tennessee State University where I teach Language Arts and Reading. I conduct research in children's writing and teacher education.

DAVID P. SHEA (ASUKA, CHAPTER 14)

I first met Asuka when she was a student in the third grade at the Japanese Saturday School in Atlanta. I wanted to interview Asuka because of her outgoing personality and also because she has lived her entire life in the U.S. The series of interviews, which I tape recorded, totalled a little over six hours in all. They were conducted at the dining room table in Asuka's home. Her mother was with us for each interview, and while her comments don't appear in the profile, she was very cooperative and helpful.

Currently, I am in the Doctoral Program in the Department of Language Education at the University of Georgia, where I am writing a dissertation on the sociocultural dimensions of language use. I am particularly interested in Japanese who are living in the U.S. and the dynamics of conversation between native and non-native speakers of English.

MARA CASEY (BEN, CHAPTER 15; JOSÉ [WITH JULIANNE ELLIOTT], CHAPTER 19; PAGE AND DAVE, CHAPTER 30)

Although I began audiotaping seventeen Massachusetts children on a whim, Page and Dave (pseudonyms chosen by them) got me hooked on talking with students about writing. After moving from Massachusetts to California, I showed the transcript of these conversations to Bob Land and John Hollowell in the English Department at the University of California-Irvine where I was working. They, and members of Cathy D'Aoust's research group at the UC Irvine Writing Project, encouraged me to follow the children through high school and to apply to graduate school to learn how to do classroom research. I took their advice on both counts and am currently writing my dissertation at UC, Riverside, on the meaning of collaborative writing in a college composition classroom.

The three interviews with Ben were conducted in the spring of 1990. Before beginning the second and third interviews, Ben and I listened to the tapes of our previous session. He enjoyed hearing what he had said, but did not seem to feel a need to comment on it nor did he seem at all concerned about the way I would present him; however, he did read and approve the completed profile. The profile of Ben, unlike my interviews with Page and Dave, was written specifically for this book.

WILLIAM MCGINLEY AND GEORGE KAMBERELIS (LISA, ROSA, AND PAUL, CHAPTER 16)

The three children, whose published writing and spoken voices served as the basis for this chapter, were part of a collaborative teacher-researcher project in a fourth-grade classroom in an inner-city elementary school which explored the personal and social functions associated with the writing children did about their communities and their lives. In particular we sought preliminary answers to several questions: How would students respond to the invitation to write about their own experience and the communities in which they live? In what way might such writing help children to make sense of their everyday experiences? How might children use writing while attempting to construct and reconstruct their personal identities? Finally, how might literacy be used by children to participate in the process of envisioning, exploring, and shaping new forms of community life?

As part of their membership in the classroom, these children were initially invited by their teacher, Victoria Rybicki, to write about themselves, their families, and their neighborhoods by first planning and then video taping a "neighborhood tour." Subsequently, the children in the class wrote and shared writing on a wide range of personal and community-related topics, some of which they selected for publication in a small student anthology. These children were interviewed throughout the school year about their writing. In each of the interviews, we focused on the functions that writing served in the life of each child. Throughout the year, we came to know the children well, and as we read their work and listened to them talk during numerous interviews, we came to better understand those aspects of their communities and their lives that they sought to affirm and embrace as well as those aspects they wished to change or transform. All of the children's written products and interview responses were analyzed using both quantitative and qualitative techniques. Some of the results of these analyses were reported at both the 1990 and the 1991 National Reading Conferences. These papers are available from the authors.

Bill McGinley is in The School of Education at The University of Colorado. George Kamberelis is at The University of Illinois, Champaign–Urbana.

JULIANNE ELLIOTT (JOSÉ [WITH MARA CASEY], CHAPTER 19)

I sought José out in July and August 1990, after his fourth grade year. On several occasions, he happily hung around my summer school classroom after the other kids left, answering my questions as I tape recorded his comments for later transcription. He was very helpful when it came to elaborating on an idea. All I had to do was indicate that I needed more information or some clarification, and José was able to provide me with the data after a moment of thought.

I am especially interested in José because of his bilingual background. Approximately ninety-seven percent of the students at his elementary school (and his school district) are Hispanic; many of these students are bilingual and biliterate. I was fascinated to find out about José's parents' efforts to learn English and to encourage their children to learn to speak, read, and write in English. I was also intrigued by José's large extended family, some of whom share his house with him and his nuclear family.

I am now teaching sixth grade in Linden, California.

JAMIE MYERS (BUTCH, JANE, AND BOBBY, CHAPTER 20)

I met Butch, Jane, and Bobby through their teacher, Mr. Allen, who thought they would be interesting students to talk with about reading because of their different reading levels. When we met in 1986, reading educators were emphasizing the importance of a purpose for reading—how reading strategies were dependent upon reading purposes. It seemed appropriate to learn just what some young readers believed about their purposes for reading, perhaps even to explore just what made up a reading purpose.

Butch, Jane, and Bobby are part of a larger study that involved four students' and two teachers' reasons for reading, which is published in ERIC as "Purpose—need—task: A case study of six respondents' beliefs about why they read," 1991. Two patterns about reading purposes emerged from this study: reading to fulfill an internal need, and reading to meet external task requirements. A sense of ownership, or lack of it, was fundamental in each reading experience. As Assistant Professor in Language and Literacy Education at The Pennsylvania State University, I currently argue that these students' stories about their purposes for reading reveal how literacy provides a sense of personal identity and social membership in the various home, academic, economic, sporting, and local communities to which the reader wants to belong.

PENNY OLDFATHER (NICKI, ANDY, ABIGAIL, AND PAUL, CHAPTER 21)

The four students whose profiles are presented were among thirty-one co-researchers in a fifth/sixth-grade classroom with whom I conducted a series of indepth interviews over eight months as part of my dissertation research in 1989–90. The unpublished dissertation is entitled, *Students' Reasons/Purposes for Being or Not Being Involved in Learning Activities: A Qualitative Study of Student Motivation* (The Claremont Graduate School, Claremont, CA: 1991).

Several of the co-researchers have participated with me in sharing the results of the research in scholarly meetings, as well as for in-service teachers, and the Claremont, California, school board. I am now an assistant professor of elementary education at The University of Georgia. My areas of interest are student motivation, qualitative research methodology, and constructivism.

JUDY STOREYGARD (ADAM, CHAPTER 22)

As a researcher for TERC (Technical Education Research Centers, Cambridge, Massachusetts), I became interested in how children write during my work on a project about technology integration. I interviewed students and teachers about the writing process and observed writing classes. After talking with others about their writing, I became curious to explore the writing process with my own child.

Adam presents a unique picture because of the challenges presented by Tourette's Syndrome and because of his special talents.

My involvement with Adam's writing, mainly through dictation, helped me to elicit his reflections during our interviews. In preparation for my questions, he spent time reviewing the writing he did in elementary school. After he read the transcribed interviews, Adam played the major role in the shaping and editing of this profile.

KATHY KNIGHT (BECKY, CHAPTER 23)

I'm a second year elementary teacher with a combination class of fourth and fifth grades. I decided to work with my daughter Becky for this profile because she and I knew each other and could communicate easily.

Becky put in many long hours in front of the tape recorder. Being able to talk freely with my subject really helped the interviews go well. I'm convinced from all the interviews I've conducted with Becky and my own students that taking a personal interest in a student helps to improve their performance and increase their interest in school. I learned many things from my daughter and my students, but the main thing is that they want to have a lot of interaction with their teachers and peers. With an interested audience, they flower and do well.

THELMA A. KIBLER (ROBERT AND JOEY, CHAPTER 24)

In the past five years here in the Southwest as an assistant professor of Language Arts/English Education at New Mexico State University, I have become fascinated by the way children function in a world of two languages. My interest has grown during the time that [Dr.] Dan Doorn and I, with substantial help from local ESL teachers, have planned and implemented a twenty-four credit ESL endorsement program. It was through one of these teachers that I met Robert and Joey, and at their school we found a semi-quiet nook in which to tape our conversations. After four sessions with each boy, we culminated our joint endeavor to teach me about second language acquisition by a day-long visit to the university. We lunched in the student union, visited sports facilities, the bookstore, classrooms, and offices. The boys met deans and faculty, including some fine Hispanic role models. We did just a bit of early recruiting.

CAROLINE TRIPP (OWEN, CHAPTER 25)

I am currently Assistant Superintendent in the Shrewsbury, Massachusetts, Public Schools. Although this profile was prepared with my "mother's hat" on, the majority of my professional life has involved working with students and teachers and administrators on writing and the teaching of writing. Almost every young writer I've known has relished talking about his/her work, or process, or the miseries associated with having none of the above under control. That kind of one-to-one careful listening and attention is so rare. For Owen, and for me, the time we spent talking about this profile was special and valuable. He thoroughly enjoyed perusing the drafts and making suggestions about how to clean up or clarify some of his points. I wished that at other points during my life as a high school English teacher, curriculum specialist, consultant or central office type, I'd taken time out for more talk of that kind.

BEA NAFF CAIN AND ELEANOR BLAIR HILTY (MATIKA, CHAPTER 26)

During the summer of 1990, Matika was one of eleven girls who participated in a summer book club that we developed for research purposes. Although many of the participants had rich transactions and personal transformations as a result of the book club experience, we chose Matika's story as one that best represented the kinds of influences such a club could have in the life of a minority girl from a working class community. Book clubs have typically been for white, educated adults with leisure time. We wanted to see if they could be beneficial with young girls from working class communities.

Aspects of our initial research are published in Cain, B. N. & E. B. Hilty. 1991. Book clubs: A rich educational alternative. *Reaching through teaching.* Vol. 5:1, 6–8. Our work was funded, in part, by the Assembly on Literature for Adolescents within the National Council of Teachers of English (ALAN) and by the A. L. Burruss Institute of Research and Public Service.

Beatrice Cain is an associate professor of English education at Clemson University where she conducts research on creative educational design and book clubs for youth. Eleanor Hilty is an assistant professor of curriculum and instruction at Kennesaw State College where she conducts research on the moonlighting of teachers and women's voices.

KIM S. HUTCHINSON AND JOHN S. LOFTY (MATT AND KRISTY, CHAPTER 27)

Kim Hutchinson, herself one of the students in John Lofty's dissertation study during her junior and senior years, has recently completed a Baccalaureate in English and Psychology at Johnson State College in Vermont. She is now writing about her own experiences of growing up on the island and considering a career as a teacher.

John Lofty is an assistant professor of English education at The University of New Hampshire, Durham. A conference paper based on aspects of the doctoral study of island students' responses to literacy is published in *The Right to Literacy,* (1990, pp. 39–49). Eds. Andrea A. Lunsford, Helene Moglen, and James Slevin. New York: Modern Language Association. The study itself is presented in *Time to Write: The Influence of Time and Culture on Learning to Write* (1992). Albany: The State University of New York Press.

JUDITH WOLINSKY STEINBERGH
(CHANDRA, CHAPTER 28)

Since 1986, I have been staff Writer-in-Residence in the Brookline, Massachusetts, Public Schools teaching poetry three days a week in grades K–12. In addition, I have taught poetry in numerous other Massachusetts schools since 1971. This experience has allowed me to observe children grow in their writing over the years, to see how culture and family background affect children's writing style and subject matter, and to follow a number of very talented writers as they mature. (Some of these observations were published in the *Harvard Educational Review,* February 1991, Symposium: Arts As Education.) Chandra's intense commitment to "the writing life" caught my interest. I wanted to learn more about what led to her prodigious output of prose and poetry, what her process of writing involves, some of the obstacles she faces, and what supports allow her to grow as a writer.

In addition to my work in Brookline, I have trained teachers throughout New England, served as adjunct faculty for Lesley College, and developed curriculum relating poetry to many aspects of student learning. I co-authored *Beyond Words, Writing Poems with Children,* with Elizabeth McKim, and my latest of four poetry books is *A Living Anytime* (Talking Stone Press, 1988). I perform, lead workshops, and produce tapes for children with Victor Cockburn of Troubadour. Victor and I collected songs and poems from around the world and have just released *Where I Come From! Songs and Poems from Many Cultures* for children in grades K–5. We also write and produce songs and poems for literacy programs published by a number of national educational publishers.

M. A. SYVERSON (NORIKO AND KIRSTEN, CHAPTER 29)

This profile is a decidedly collaborative effort. Mara Casey provided the original framework as well as the impetus for the study. Nora Ishibashi and Leslie Trainer deftly handled the actual interview process, and of course Noriko and Kirsten provided the data on which the profile is grounded. The selection of details, final editing, and shaping is very much a cooperative effort for which I provided the overall direction and final polish. I am currently a doctoral student in composition studies at The University of California, San Diego, where I teach in the Third College Writing Program. I have done case study research of collaborative writing groups in a college classroom, and collaborated with Mara Casey on several ethnographic studies of collaborative composing. Results of these studies were presented at both fall and spring NCTE conferences in 1991. I have also served as a consultant to the State of California Direct Writing Assessment for eighth and twelfth graders. My research interests include the role of writing in making knowledge and the relationship between the cultural and the individual in composing.

REFERENCES

Atwell, N. 1987. *In the middle: Writing, reading, and learning with adolescents.* Portsmouth, NH: Boynton/Cook.

Casey, M. 1986. If you become a researcher, by your students you'll be taught. *English Journal* 75 (8): 64–67.

Cleary, L. M. 1991. *From the other side of the desk: Students speak out about writing.* Portsmouth, NH: Boynton/Cook.

Cleary, L. M., & I. E. Seidman. 1990. In-depth interviewing in the preparation of writing teachers. *College Composition and Communication* 41 (4): 465–71.

Clifford, J. 1986. On ethnographic allegory. In *Writing culture: The poetics and politics of ethnography,* ed. J. Clifford & G. E. Marcus, 98–121. Berkeley, CA: University of California Press.

Hudson-Ross, S. In press. Demystify the written word: Make writing a lifelong adventure. In *Parents, Teachers, and Literacy,* ed. T. Rasinski. Portsmouth, NH: Heinemann.

Rosenblatt, L. 1978. *The reader, the text, the poem: The transactional theory of poetry.* Carbondale, IL: Southern Illinois University Press.

Seidman, I. E. 1991. *Interviewing as qualitative research.* New York: Teachers College Press.

Smith, F. 1988. *Joining the literacy club.* Portsmouth, NH: Heinemann.

Terkel, S. 1984. *Division Street: America.* New York: Pantheon Books.

———. 1967. *The good war.* New York: Pantheon Books.

———. 1972. *Working: People talk about what they do all day and how they feel about what they do.* New York: Random House.

Vygotsky, L. 1978. *Mind in society: The development of higher psychological processes.* Edited by M. Cole, V. John Steiner, S. Scribner, & E. Souberman. Cambridge: Harvard University Press.

BOOK REFERENCES

Adams, D. 1979. *The Hitchhiker's Guide to the Galaxy.* New York: Pocket Books.

———. 1982. *The Restaurant at the End of the Universe.* New York: Crown.

———. 1988. *So Long and Thanks for All the Fish.* New York: Pocket Books.

Alexander, L. 1964. *The Book of Three.* New York: Dell Publishing Company.

Bach, R. 1981. *Illusions: The Adventures of a Reluctant Messiah.* New York: Dell.

Ballad, L. 1982. *A New True Book of Reptiles.* Chicago: Childrens Press.

Bargar, S. and L. Johnson. 1986. *The Snake Discovery Library.* Vera Beach, FL: Rourke Enterprises.

Bloom, Judy. 1981. *Superfudge.* New York: Dell.

Bradbury, R. 1967. *Fahrenheit 451.* New York: Simon and Schuster.

Broekel, R. 1982. *A New True Book of Snakes.* Chicago: Childrens Press.

Burnett, Frances Hodgson. 1912. *The Secret Garden.* New York: Penguin.

Byars, Betsy C. 1969. *Trouble River.* New York: Viking Penguin.

City Spaces. 1987. Glenville, IL: Scott Foresman.

Cleary, Beverly. 1983. *Ralph S. Mouse.* New York: Dell.

———. 1983. *Dear Mr. Henshaw.* New York: William Morrow.

———. 1990. *Otis Spofford.* New York: Avon.

Colville, Bruce. 1989. *My Teacher is an Alien.* New York: Pocket Books.

Dahl, Roald. 1983. *George's Marvelous Medicine.* New York: Knopf.

Danziger, Paula. 1986. *This Place Has No Atmosphere.* New York: Dell/Laurel Leaf.

DeClements, Barthe. 1981. *Nothing's Fair in the Fifth Grade.* New York: Viking Penguin.

Dickens, Charles. 1985. *A Christmas Carol.* Nashville, TN: Ideals.

Dixon, Franklin. (Various dates). *Hardy Boys Series.* (Various publishers including Minstrel Books).

Epstein, Sam & Epstein, Beryl. 1975. *Willie Mays: Baseball Superstar.* Garrard Sports Library.

Farley, W. 1941. *The Black Stallion.* New York: Random House.

Faucher, Elizabeth. 1989. *Honey I Shrunk the Kids.* New York: Scholastic.

Fitzhugh, Louise. 1964. *Harriet the Spy*. New York: Harper Collins.

Folktales of Japan. 1991. *Manga Nippon Mukashi Banashi*. Tokyo: Mainichi Hoso Television. Japanese television program.

Fox, Paula. 1984. *One-eyed Cat*. New York: Bradbury Press.

Gaeddart, Louann. 1985. *Your Former Friend Matthew*. New York: Bantam.

George, J. 1975. *My Side of the Mountain*. New York: E.P. Dutton.

Giff, P. R. 1984. *The Dinosaur's Paw*. New York: Bantam Doubleday.

Giovanni, Nikki. *Raining Marshmallow Clouds*.

Guy, Rosa. 1983. *The Friends*. New York: Bantam Books.

Hamilton, Virginia. 1987. *A White Romance*. New York: Philomel Books.

Hawking, Stephen. 1988. *A Brief History of Time: From the Big Bang, to Black Holes*. New York: Bantam Books.

Houghton Mifflin Basal Reading Series. 1986. *Trumpets, Carousels, Parades, and Adventures*. Boston: Houghton Mifflin Company.

Hutchins, Pat. 1986. *The Doorbell Rang*. New York: Greenwillow.

Jeschke, Susan. 1980. *Perfect the Pig*. New York: Scholastic.

Keene, Carolyn. 1941. *Nancy Drew: Mystery in Magnolia Mansion*. New York: Gosset and Dunlap.

———. 1990. *The Nancy Drew Files: Case 43, False Impressions*. New York: Simon and Schuster.

Keyes, Daniel. 1988. *Flowers for Algernon*. Mankato, MN: Creative Education.

King, Stephen. 1987. *The Eyes of the Dragon*. New York: Viking Press.

Lee, Andrea. 1984. *Sarah Phillips*. New York: Random House.

L'Engle, Madeleine. 1976. *A Wrinkle in Time*. New York: Dell.

Levitin, Sonia. 1988. *Incident at Loring Groves*. New York: Fawcett Juniper.

Lewis, C. S. 1970. *The Chronicles of Narnia*. New York: Collier Books.

McKinney, Jack. 1987. *Robotech Genesis* (Robotech Series, nos. 1–12.) New York: Ballantine.

Michaels, W. 1989. "The Unusual Pet Store." In *A Soft Pillow for an Armadillo*, edited by Donna Alvermann et al. Lexington, MA: Heath.

Morrison, Toni. 1987. *Beloved*. New York: Knopf.

Murray, Andrew. 1982. *How to be Perfect*. Springdale, PA: Whitaker House.

Park, Barbara. 1983. *Operation Dump the Chump*. New York: Avon.

Pascal, Francine. *Sweet Valley High* (over 68 in series). New York: Bantam. (For example: *Brokenhearted*, #58, 1989.)

Petty, K. 1984. *Snakes*. New York: Aladdin Books.

Posell, E. 1983. *A New True Book of Cats*. Chicago: Childrens Press.

Quin-Harkin, Janet. 1982. *Ten Boy Summer*. New York: Bantam.

Richards, Curtis. 1981. *Halloween*. New York: Bantam.

Roberts, Willo Davis. 1980. *The Girl with the Silver Eyes*. New York: Atheneum.

Ruckman, Ivy. 1984. *The Night of the Twister.* New York: Thomas Crowell.

Sachar, Louis. 1978. *Sideways Stores from Wayside School.* Chicago: Follet.

San Sonci, Daniel (Illus.) 1985. *A Bedtime Book: A Collection of Fairy Tales.* New York: S&S Trade.

Silverstein, Shel. 1974. *Where the Sidewalk Ends: Poems and Drawings.* Harper Junior Books.

Smith, Robert K. 1978. *Chocolate Fever.* New York: Dell.

Sobal, Donald J. *Encyclopedia Brown,* a series available from Bantam or Scholastic.

Spier, Peter. 1961. *The Fox Went Out on a Chilly Night.* New York: Doubleday.

Tate, Eleanora. 1988. *The Secret of Gumbo Grove.* New York: Bantam.

Taylor, T. 1969. *The Cay.* Garden City, New York: Doubleday.

Uchida, Y. 1985. *Journal to Topaz.* Berkeley, CA: Creative Arts Book Company.

Voigt, Cynthia. 1986. *Izzy, Willy-Nilly.* New York: Fawcett Juniper.

Wallace, Barbara Brooks. 1980. *Peppermints in the Parlor.* New York: Atheneum.

Wallace, Bill. 1980. *A Dog Called Kitty.* New York: Holiday House.

Warner, Gertrude. 1990. *(The Boxcar Children Series.)* Niles, IL: A. Whitman.

White, E. B. 1952. *Charlotte's Web.* New York: Harper & Row.

Wilder, Laura I. 1973. *Little House in the Big Woods.* (Trophy Book Series.) New York: Harper Junior Books.

Wilkie, Katherine Elliot. 1969. *Helen Keller.* Indianapolis, IN: Bobbs-Merrill.

Williams, Margery. 1990. *The Velveteen Rabbit.* New York: McKay/Random House.

Yolen, Jane. 1983. *An Invitation to the Butterfly Ball: A Counting Rhyme.* New York: Philomel.

———. 1988. *The Devil's Arithmetic.* New York: Viking.

York, Carol B. 1989. *Good Day Mice.* New York: Bantam.

ZooBooks. (Published periodically). San Diego, CA: Wildlife Education Ltd.

Index